D1237738

VOLUME 593 MAY 2004

THE ANNALS

of The American Academy of Political and Social Science

ROBERT W. PEARSON, *Executive Editor*
LAWRENCE W. SHERMAN, *Editor*

To Better Serve and Protect: Improving Police Practices

Special Editor of this Volume

WESLEY G. SKOGAN
Northwestern University

SAGE Publications • Thousand Oaks • London • New Delhi

The American Academy of Political and Social Science

3814 Walnut Street, Fels Institute of Government, University of Pennsylvania,
Philadelphia, PA 19104-6197; (215) 746-6500; (215) 898-1202 (fax); www.aapss.org

---

Origin and Purpose. The Academy was organized December 14, 1889, to promote the progress of political and social science, especially through publications and meetings. The Academy does not take sides in controverted questions, but seeks to gather and present reliable information to assist the public in forming an intelligent and accurate judgment.

Meetings. The Academy occasionally holds a meeting in the spring extending over two days.

Publications. THE ANNALS of The American Academy of Political and Social Science is the bimonthly publication of the Academy. Each issue contains articles on some prominent social or political problem, written at the invitation of the editors. Also, monographs are published from time to time, numbers of which are distributed to pertinent professional organizations. These volumes constitute important reference works on the topics with which they deal, and they are extensively cited by authorities throughout the United States and abroad. The papers presented at the meetings of the Academy are included in THE ANNALS.

Membership. Each member of the Academy receives THE ANNALS and may attend the meetings of the Academy. Membership is open only to individuals. Annual dues: $75.00 for the regular paperbound edition (clothbound, $113.00). For members outside the U.S.A., add $24.00 for shipping of your subscription. Members may also purchase single issues of THE ANNALS for $23.00 each (clothbound, $31.00). Student memberships are available for $49.00.

Subscriptions. THE ANNALS of The American Academy of Political and Social Science (ISSN 0002-7162) (J295) is published six times annually—in January, March, May, July, September, and November— by Sage Publications, 2455 Teller Road, Thousand Oaks, CA 91320. Telephone: (800) 818-SAGE (7243) and (805) 499-9774; FAX/Order line: (805) 499-0871; E-mail: journals@sagepub.com.

Institutions may subscribe to THE ANNALS at the annual rate: $490.00 (clothbound, $554.00). Add $24.00 per year for subscriptions outside the U.S.A. Institutional rates for single issues: $95.00 each (clothbound, $106.00).

Periodicals postage paid at Thousand Oaks, California, and at additional mailing offices.

Single issues of THE ANNALS may be obtained by individuals who are not members of the Academy for $33.00 each (clothbound, $46.00). Single issues of THE ANNALS have proven to be excellent supplementary texts for classroom use. Direct inquiries regarding adoptions to THE ANNALS c/o Sage Publications (address below).

All correspondence concerning membership in the Academy, dues renewals, inquiries about membership status, and/or purchase of single issues of THE ANNALS should be sent to THE ANNALS c/o Sage Publications, 2455 Teller Road, Thousand Oaks, CA 91320. Telephone: (800) 818-SAGE (7243) and (805) 499-9774; FAX/Order line: (805) 499-0871. E-mail: journals@sagepub.com. *Please note that orders under $30 must be prepaid.* Sage affiliates in London and India will assist institutional subscribers abroad with regard to orders, claims, and inquiries for both subscriptions and single issues.

Printed on recycled, acid-free paper

THE ANNALS

Editorial Office: 3814 Walnut Street, Fels Institute for Government, University of Pennsylvania, Philadelphia, PA 19104-6197.

For information about membership* (individuals only) and subscriptions (institutions), address:

Sage Publications
2455 Teller Road
Thousand Oaks, CA 91320

Sage Production Staff: Joseph Riser and Paul Doebler

From India and South Asia, write to:
SAGE PUBLICATIONS INDIA Pvt Ltd
B-42 Panchsheel Enclave, P.O. Box 4109
New Delhi 110 017
INDIA

From Europe, the Middle East, and Africa, write to:
SAGE PUBLICATIONS LTD
1 Oliver's Yard, 55 City Road
London EC1Y 1SP
UNITED KINGDOM

*Please note that members of the Academy receive THE ANNALS with their membership.

International Standard Serial Number ISSN 0002-7162
International Standard Book Number ISBN 1-4129-0938-4 (Vol. 593, 2004 paper)
International Standard Book Number ISBN 1-4129-0937-6 (Vol. 593, 2004 cloth)
Manufactured in the United States of America. First printing, May 2004.

The articles appearing in *The Annals* are abstracted or indexed in Academic Abstracts, Academic Search, America: History and Life, Asia Pacific Database, Book Review Index, CAB Abstracts Database, Central Asia: Abstracts & Index, Communication Abstracts, Corporate ResourceNET, Criminal Justice Abstracts, Current Citations Express, Current Contents: Social & Behavioral Sciences, Documentation in Public Administration, e-JEL, EconLit, Expanded Academic Index, Guide to Social Science & Religion in Periodical Literature, Health Business FullTEXT, HealthSTAR FullTEXT, Historical Abstracts, International Bibliography of the Social Sciences, International Political Science Abstracts, ISI Basic Social Sciences Index, Journal of Economic Literature on CD, LEXIS-NEXIS, MasterFILE FullTEXT, Middle East: Abstracts & Index, North Africa: Abstracts & Index, PAIS International, Periodical Abstracts, Political Science Abstracts, Psychological Abstracts, PsycINFO, Sage Public Administration Abstracts, Social Science Source, Social Sciences Citation Index, Social Sciences Index Full Text, Social Services Abstracts, Social Work Abstracts, Sociological Abstracts, Southeast Asia: Abstracts & Index, Standard Periodical Directory (SPD), TOPICsearch, Wilson OmniFile V, and Wilson Social Sciences Index/Abstracts, and are available on microfilm from ProQuest, Ann Arbor, Michigan.

Information about membership rates, institutional subscriptions, and back issue prices may be found on the facing page.

Advertising. Current rates and specifications may be obtained by writing to *The Annals* Advertising and Promotion Manager at the Thousand Oaks office (address above).

Claims. Claims for undelivered copies must be made no later than six months following month of publication. The publisher will supply missing copies when losses have been sustained in transit and when the reserve stock will permit.

Change of Address. Six weeks' advance notice must be given when notifying of change of address to ensure proper identification. Please specify name of journal. POSTMASTER: Send address changes to: *The Annals* of The American Academy of Political and Social Science, c/o Sage Publications, 2455 Teller Road, Thousand Oaks, CA 91320.

THE ANNALS
OF THE AMERICAN ACADEMY OF POLITICAL AND SOCIAL SCIENCE

Volume 593 May 2004

IN THIS ISSUE:

To Better Serve and Protect: Improving Police Practices

Special Editor: WESLEY G. SKOGAN

FORTHCOMING

Race and Community Development in the Urban United States

Special Editors: JAMES JENNINGS and MICHAEL BONDS

Volume 594, July 2004

Being Here and Being There: Fieldwork Encounters and Ethnographic Discoveries

Special Editors: ELIJAH ANDERSON, SCOTT BROOKS, RAYMOND GUNN, and NIKKI JONES

Volume 595, September 2004

Mommies and Daddies on the Fast Track: Success of Parents in Demanding Professions

Special Editors: JANICE FANNING MADDEN and JERRY A. JACOBS

Volume 596, November 2004

Preface

By
WESLEY G. SKOGAN

This edition of the *Annals* is devoted to research on the policies and practices of American police departments. Modern police research began in the 1950s, pioneered in the United States by the American Bar Foundation's exploration of how the criminal justice system actually worked. They "discovered" discretion (although the practitioners always knew it was there), and research on the system forever abandoned its blind emphasis on formal description and legal exegesis. The report of the President's Commission on Law Enforcement and the Administration of Justice, *The Challenge of Crime in a Free Society* (1967), moved this work closer to center stage among social scientists and policy makers alike. The commission's resources made possible large-scale field studies and sophisticated analyses of archival data that highlighted inequalities in crime and the outcomes of the criminal justice process, two topics that inspired more empirical research. Later, the

Wesley G. Skogan has been a faculty member at Northwestern University since 1971 and holds joint appointments with the political science department and the Institute for Policy Research. His research focuses on the interface between the public and the legal system. Much of this research has examined public encounters with institutions of justice, in the form of crime prevention projects and community-oriented policing. His most recent books on policing are On the Beat: Police and Community Problem Solving *(Westview, 1999) and* Community Policing, Chicago Style *(Oxford University Press, 1997). They are both empirical studies of Chicago's community policing initiative. His 1990 book* Disorder and Decline *examined public involvement in these programs, their efficacy, and the issues involved in police-citizen cooperation in order maintenance. This book won a prize from the American Sociological Association. He is also the author of two lengthy reports in the Home Office Research Series examining citizen contact and satisfaction with policing in Britain. Other articles on police-citizen issues include "The Impact of Community Policing on Neighborhood Residents: A Cross-Site Analysis" in Rosenbaum's* The Challenge of Community Policing. *He chaired the National Research Council's Committee to Review Research on Police Policies and Practices.*

DOI: 10.1177/0002716204264097

National Institute of Justice, the Office of Community Oriented Policing Services, and their forerunner agencies funded large and methodologically sophisticated studies that breathed new life into the study of the crime-control effectiveness of the police. More recently, problem solving and community policing emerged as the latest manifestations of the dynamism of American policing, and research on them has gotten underway. The National Research Council's report *Fairness and Effectiveness in Policing: The Evidence* (Committee to Review Research 2003) provides a summary of this four-decade tradition of research, with an eye toward its policy significance.

Most of the authors appearing in this volume were also involved in the work of the committee that drafted the report. Their contributions touch on themes that can be found in the report, but they take them further, and in different directions, than the format of a formal report allows. Of course, the views presented here are not those of the National Research Council, and they should not be taken as a summary of what is presented in the report.

Edward Maguire and William King open this volume by depicting with broad brush the large-scale, macro-level trends taking place in American policing. They note that the public police are losing market share to the rapidly expanding private security industry and that, throughout the world, a variety of nongovernmental organizations are increasingly performing policing functions. To a certain extent, police are restructuring themselves and taking on new investigatory and coordinating functions, as a result of demands that (at least) appear to be responsive to the events of September 11. They are frequently forming multiagency task forces to deal with problems that transcend agency jurisdictions. Longer term, the number of agencies with paramilitary units has increased, and police are beginning to rely on a host of nonlethal military technologies to augment their communication and surveillance capacities. They are also much more affected by federal criminal law, policies and programs, and—during the Clinton years—a massive infusion of federal hiring and technology money.

While these trends seem to portend an increasing militarization of local policing, Maguire and King argue that two parallel trends—the emergence of community policing and problem-solving policing—also represent significant transformations in the goals, activities, and responsiveness of the policing industry. Many officers are assigned to these duties, and many kinds of new programs have been widely adopted. The no-longer-so-thin blue line is also more diverse in racial and gender terms, and new roles are being found for civilians in technical and even managerial roles. Police are also excited about management reform, as witnessed by the widespread adoption of New York City "CompStat"-style accountability systems. The popularity of new communication and crime analysis technologies rounds out the list of trends that they see as transforming the policing landscape.

Current debates about policing focus on their crime-control effectiveness. Controversies over the effectiveness of tough "zero-tolerance" crackdowns, the wisdom of "quality-of-life" policing, the impact of "adding 100,000 new cops" via the Violent Crime Control and Law Enforcement Act of 1994, and whether Police Commissioner William Bratton (or perhaps it was Mayor Rudy Giuliani) worked a managerial miracle in bringing down crime in New York City are played out in the newspapers as well as academic retreats. Learning whether the police have been successful in reducing crime is important both politically and scientifically, but other equally important criteria play into our judgments about the police: their fairness and restraint. Concern about these issues arises because the police are authorized to use force as well as their authority in carrying out their mission, and all of us—including those who are subjected to it—have a right to question whether they are acting fairly and justly. These twin expectations of the police—to control crime while rendering justice—constitute their dual mandate.

The dual mandate of the police is nicely illustrated by several contributions to this volume. David Weisburd and John Eck review what is known about the effectiveness of the police in responding to crime, disorder, and fear. Wesley G. Skogan and Tracey Meares review the evidence concerning police lawfulness; Tom Tyler focuses on the roots of police legitimacy.

Weisburd and Eck challenge what is commonly known as “the standard model of policing.” The standard model features random “preventive” patrol, rapid response to calls for service, and follow-up investigations by detectives. Too many departments follow a “one-size-fits-all” strategy for implementing these efforts, basically applying the same tactics all over town, in cookie-cutter fashion. When pressed to be more effective, they call for hiring additional officers to do yet more of the same. The evidence is that more focused and locally tailored responses to specific situations are more likely to be effective. The kit bag of tools available to police is now much larger than “drive fast, and ask for just the facts, ma’am.” For example, research on police effectiveness in attacking chronic concentrations of crime, widely known as “hot spots,” has found that well-managed investigations and short, virtually random crackdowns can suppress crime, deter its future reappearance, and avoid simply displacing a similar number of crimes elsewhere. The effectiveness of these policing efforts has been facilitated by the widespread adoption of new computer mapping and crime analysis technologies by the police.

But as they respond to crime, police are bound at the same time to comply with the U.S. Constitution, state laws, and the policies and standards of their own organizations. These justify their claim to be a rule-bound institution that is engaged in the pursuit of justice and the protection of individual liberty, as well as the battle against crime. The question is, do they follow them? Wesley G. Skogan and Tracey Meares review research on “how the police get into trouble” and what we know about “how they can get out of trouble,” when the lawfulness of police actions is in question. A pattern and practice of violent and racist interrogations, for example, got the police the four famous Miranda warnings they have to issue. An unrestrained search of Dolree Mapp’s home got the exclusionary rule—which essentially knocks any evidence seized out of court—applied to their activities. Shooting a fifteen-year-old who fled when they approached earned police a more restrictive rule regarding the use of potential fatal force.

Social scientists nosing around after the fact, however, have come away less than convinced that big changes resulted from these new rules. Police use the rules surrounding interrogations and searches strategically, and they seem to have little practical effect on the outcomes of their investigations. The evidence on shootings by police is that departments vary widely in the rate at which they shoot at, injure, and kill suspects. Leadership and management follow-through plays a large role in this; having top executives who really mean that the rules are to be followed has a big effect on the rate at which citizens are killed by the police. Skogan and Meares also address research on police corruption and racial profiling, which come to the same conclusion. To be sure, there are externally imposed solutions to these problems. Many cities have some form of external review of police misconduct. There is the possibility that prosecutors will bring cases against offending officers, and aggrieved individuals can always have their day in civil court. Skogan and Meares argue, however, that the surest path to police reform is an internal, managerial one. It involves reinvigorating training, supervision, internal inspections, performance measurement, and policy making.

Learning whether the police have been successful in reducing crime is important, . . . but other equally important criteria play into our judgments about the police: their fairness and restraint.

Tom Tyler emphasizes what research tells us about what might be called "process-oriented policing." He notes research indicating that police need the support and cooperation of the public to be effective. His own work documents how voluntary support is linked to people's judgments about the legitimacy of the police: the public cooperates because the police are entitled to be obeyed. But where does this legitimacy come from? In part, it stems from people's assessments of the manner in which the police exercise their authority. These judgments about the "procedural justice" rendered by the police are central to public evaluations of them. Research on procedural justice in turn suggests a list of practical things that police can do that will help ensure public support and compliance with their mission.

For example, people are more satisfied when they are allowed to participate in an encounter by explaining their situation and communicating their views about it. People think that decisions are being made fairly when the police appear to be evenhanded and objective, rather than just acting on the basis of their own predispositions. Belief that there should be a "level playing field" is so important that people search for evidence that the decision-making procedures by which outcomes are arrived at are biased or unbiased. Of course, people also value being treated with dignity and respect and having their rights acknowledged. The quality of interpersonal treatment is consistently found to be a distinct element of fairness, separate from the substance of the decisions themselves. Research also documents that the "bedside manner" of the police is important too. When people believe that the police care about their well-being and are considering their needs and concerns, they view the police as fairer. If police are viewed as having acted out of a sincere and benevolent concern for those involved, people infer that the police actions were fair. Authorities can encourage people to view them as trustworthy by explaining their decisions and justifying and accounting for their conduct in ways that make clear their concern about giving attention to people's needs.

If this seems like common sense, there is still a considerable distance between these principles and routine police practice. As early as the 1970s, research on how police dealt with victims indicated that they violated most of the principles on a regular basis. A recent survey conducted by the federal government also found frequent complaints about the fairness of police actions among African Americans (Langan, Greenfield, Smith, Durose, and Levin 2001). But the principles appear to be sound. In a 1990s study of police-public encounters, McCluskey (2003) documented how practicing the principles of procedural justice—in this instance, the police were observed in action—was linked to peaceable and compliant outcomes in encounters with suspects.

Two other articles in this volume focus on the important issue of controlling the police. An important feature of policing is that it is mostly conducted by pairs of officers out alone in the dark. What they do there is largely monitored through the paperwork that they choose to file describing the events they think headquarters should know about. In most organizations, blue-collar line workers perform routinized tasks under the watchful eye of their supervisors; in policing, we ask them to obey the law while using their best judgment to resolve whatever unexpected problems come their way and to not use their guns unless they have to. The lawyer's response is to impose new rules and reporting requirements on departments, but—ironically—trends are moving in the opposite direction. The problem-solving policing and community policing initiatives described by Maguire and King recognize that problems vary tremendously from place to place and that their causes and solutions are highly contextual. Those initiatives recognize and celebrate officer initiative and autonomy. Decentralizing, reducing hierarchy, granting officers more independence, and trusting in their professionalism are the organizational reforms of choice today, not tightening up the management screws to further constrain officer discretion. These trends heighten interest in how police organizations can "control" officer behavior without "constraining" it, a challenge to traditional management strategies in policing.

Stephen Mastrofski concludes, however, that existing research provides few useful insights into how street-level police discretion can be effectively managed. It is not that managers are not trying but that researchers have paid little attention to the important processes by which police organizations manage themselves. Traditionally, police managed by publishing a book of rules, watching over the rank and file until they broke them, and then cracking down. Later, recruitment strategies began to change with an eye toward enhancing the professionalism—and trustworthiness—of officers. Psychological testing is used to weed out obvious misfits. Education requirements have been imposed by many departments to up the sophistication of the patrol force. As Mastrofski points out, however, there is no credible evidence concerning the benefits, or liabilities, of higher education for police officers. Previously, massive financial support for officer education was available from the federal government, but now that has gone away. Training is another virtually unexamined mechanism for capturing control of officer discretion. Whenever we ask police do something new, be it problem solving or doing

If police are viewed as having acted out of a sincere and benevolent concern for those involved, people infer that the police actions were fair.

their own computerized analysis, they have to be trained. If we want them to stop doing something, like being unnecessarily rude to the citizens they encounter, that calls for training too. But the most effective means of conducting police training (which is, after all, just a special branch of the adult education industry), and whether it works with regard to the things that are most important to us (including crime control effectiveness and ensuring justice), remain unknown. Controlling discretion by restructuring officer's daily tasks is another management strategy needing investigation. Community policing can be considered an officer-control strategy, in that it anticipates that police will do something different with their time when they are assigned (and trained) to pick up and act upon the priorities expressed by neighborhood residents. However, at best, the research literature tells us that the exercise of officer discretion is "very situational," highly dependent on the events and circumstances encompassing blocks of their time and their encounters with citizens.

This conclusion is true to the research literature but not very useful from a police perspective. The most important policy issues in many agendas for policing have to do with the exercise of officer discretion. Do we want police to make an arrest in every domestic violence incident? Do we want them to be aggressive about identifying and pulling over possible drunken drivers? Do we want them to exercise more restraint in the use of lethal force? Do we want them to really ensure that suspects understand and exercise their rights? Do we want them to engage in the process-oriented policing described by Tyler? Discretion lies at the heart of policing and at the heart of police reform, and we clearly need to know more about it via studies that emphasize the organizational levers in the hands of police managers.

David Klinger addresses larger questions concerning the role that organizational and environmental factors play in determining how officers behave. He is not so much concerned about understanding how to control individual officer behavior as he is in the impact of factors such as the size, bureaucratization, and policies of police organizations and of the political and social milieu in which they operate on such macro features of behavior as the rate at which officers issue warnings rather than make arrests, hand out speeding tickets, and choose to use force to resolve situations. What we know about these issues is scattered at best. For example, research on police organizations has examined the impact of the extent to which they are bureaucratized and professionalized on these kinds of aggregate activity and outcome measures. Organization size seems to be very influential. American police departments range enormously in size. Over half of them are very small, yet a majority of officers work in larger agencies. Smaller agencies seem to be more effective at putting officers on the street because they have fewer specialized and administrative units. Larger places tend to make arrests and use force against their citizens more frequently than do the small ones, while the smaller ones provide more services and assistance for residents. (In fact, in surveys, small agencies often give as the reason why they have not adopted community policing that they "have always done it.")

Research on shootings by police give some insight to the importance of organization-level factors in shaping officer behavior. Time-series data indicates that restrictive shooting policies can drive fatality rates downward and that the number of shootings nationwide has declined greatly due to these policies. Studies of domestic violence and evaluations of violence-reduction programs indicate that encouraging or mandating that officers arrest perpetrators can have the desired effect on their behavior. The *effects* of arrest policies on victims and offenders are another matter, and it is far from clear exactly what the desirable policing policy is in these cases.

One of the "environments" in which police operate is the larger criminal justice system. As Klinger points out, however, very little recent research has focused on the relationship between police and prosecutors, or with judges. Recent studies indicate that police also operate relatively independently of the local political system, evidencing a substantial ability to resist efforts of elected leaders to change their practices. On the other hand, the practices of officers on patrol seem highly contingent on the context in which they take place. For example, police are more likely to stop suspicious people in racially heterogeneous neighborhoods; the odds of arrest are higher for suspects in neighborhoods of lower socioeconomic status; and the odds that officers will take a crime report decrease as neighborhood crime rates increase. This reinforces the image of police work as highly contingent and situational, a view that is close to the research but distant from offering policy makers much useful advice.

The final two articles discuss the organization and politics of the police research enterprise. The National Research Council report estimates there are 300 to 400 American scholars involved in police research. Most are professional researchers working at colleges and universities or for independent for-profit and nonprofit think tanks and research consultancies. With a few notable exceptions, funding for their work comes from government agencies. The principal agency funding this research has been the National Institute of Justice, part of the U.S. Department of Justice; other federal agencies come and go with respect to supporting police

---

The most important policy issues in many agendas for policing have to do with the exercise of officer discretion.

---

research. State government research grants, contracts from municipal governments, and even research contracts from police departments themselves constitute most of the remaining support. The National Research Council report estimates that the federal government spent about $8 million on police research in 1996 and about that much per year for the previous twenty years. While this is not a large amount of money, it is far in excess of the support available for police research anywhere else in the world. There was a short-lived explosion of funding for police research shortly thereafter, due to the largess of another federal agency, but that revenue stream has since dried up.

In his article, Samuel Walker examines the political underpinnings of this research. He argues that the driving force behind much of it has been politics. Police researchers might imagine a world in which research questions are driven by deductive theories, measures are conceptualized in light of those theories, hypotheses are tested without fear of favor regarding the findings, and conclusions are described at a level of abstraction sufficient to transcend geographical and temporal boundaries—they all went to graduate school, after all. But in practice, the police and what they do touch raw nerves in American politics: race and racism, violence, and corruption are but a few of the obvious. One need look no further than racial profiling to see a topic that was politically identified (no one believes the police just started doing it), socially resonant (every paper in the country picked up on it quickly), and deeply divisive (plenty of seasoned observers were willing to defend it, though they were painted into an uncomfortable corner by a label that was successfully attached to the phenomenon). Walker argues that racial profiling is the latest of an unending stream of issues that have been thrown up from the street and ended up on the police research platter. He also notes influences that run on the other direction. Research findings have shaped the public discourse about policing and the direction of public policy; one need look no further than the discretion genie escaping from the bottle, thanks to the American Bar Foundation. And it is a good thing, too, says Walker. He argues that the influence of politics on research has greatly enriched research on the police, and vice versa.

Finally, Lawrence W. Sherman presents a bold new proposal for organizing federally supported police research. Sherman reports that National Institute of Justice funding for police research has been all but eliminated in the 2003-2004 federal budget, as part of a massive cut in funds for all social science research at the National Institute of Justice. Noting that the entire Department of Justice must be reauthorized by Congress next year, he proposes to restructure that National Institute of Justice in a way that ties it more directly to the local and state organizations that are the primary consumers, and coproducers, of evaluation research. By creating "Centers for Crime Prevention" in every large city, and in every state, for the cost of one dollar per year per U.S. citizen, Sherman suggests that police research could be stabilized in long-term partnerships with universities and research organizations.

Whether such an idea would ever be enacted by Congress is hard to say. It is clear, however, that some plan for the future of police research in the United States is necessary. Otherwise, the material in this volume will address only the history of police research rather than its future.

References

Committee to Review Research on Police Policy and Practices. 2003. *Fairness and effectiveness in policing: The evidence*. Washington, DC: National Academies Press.

Langan, Patrick A., Lawrence A. Greenfield, Steven K. Smith, Matthew R. Durose, and David J. Levin. 2001. *Contacts between police and the public: Findings from the 1999 national survey*. Washington, DC: Bureau of Jústice Statistics.

McCluskey, John D. 2003. *Police requests for compliance: Coercive and procedurally just tactics*. New York: LFB Scholarly Publishing.

Trends in the Policing Industry

By
EDWARD R. MAGUIRE
and
WILLIAM R. KING

Fairness and Effectiveness in Policing: The Evidence does a terrific job of discussing the limited research on trends in the policing industry, but what it does not include is perhaps as informative. Large gaps in the body of research limit our ability to make definitive inferences about how the policing industry is changing. These gaps result in part from a lack of systematic, standardized, longitudinal data collection and analysis on the nature and outputs of police organizations in the United States. As a result, we know little about basic descriptive features of policing and how these features are changing over time. Lacking the ability to track even the most basic descriptive trends, the police research industry is at even more of a loss in developing careful empirical explanations of these trends. This article discusses some of these trends, summarizes what we know and what we do not know about them, and provides some recommendations for how the police research industry can do a better job of describing and explaining trends in the police industry.

Keywords: police; transformation; longitudinal research; organizational change

The invitation to contribute an article on trends in the policing industry for this special issue of *The Annals* presented a challenge. No matter how hard we try to capture the major trends in the policing industry, we are bound to

Edward R. Maguire is an associate professor of administration of justice at George Mason University. He has held previous academic and research positions at the United Nations, the U.S. Department of Justice, and the University of Nebraska. The majority of his research examines police from an organizational perspective. His recent policing research has explored a diversity of topics, including formal organizational structure, case resolution patterns, civil suits, community policing implementation, staffing levels, and public opinion. He is the author of Organizational Structure in American Police Agencies: Context, Complexity, and Control *(SUNY Press, 2002). He served as a consultant to the Committee to Review Research on Police Policy and Practices, National Academy of Sciences.*

William R. King is an associate professor of criminal justice at Bowling Green State University in Ohio. He received his Ph.D. in criminal justice from the University of Cincinnati in 1998. His research areas include empiri-

DOI: 10.1177/0002716204262960

miss candidates for inclusion on the list. In his poem "La Luna," Jorge Luis Borges wrote of a fictional writer who attempts to capture the entire universe in a single work. When the writer is finished, he looks up and realizes he has forgotten to include the moon. On reflection, we will doubtless come to a similar realization. We have chosen not to employ any rigorous scientific method to select the trends we discuss below. There are precedents for doing so within the policing field. For instance, Mark Moore and his colleagues at Harvard University explored three methods to come up with a list of the most important innovations in policing: interviews of experts, surveys of practitioners, and content analyses of professional journals (Moore, Sparrow, and Spelman 1996; Moore, Spelman, and Young 1992). Although such systematic methods can be very useful, they would demand more resources than were available for preparing this article.

Our interest here is in broad-ranging, large-scale, macro- or meta-level trends in policing that are likely to contribute to a *transformation* in the "landscape of policing in the United States," to use a phrase from *Fairness and Effectiveness in Policing: The Evidence* (Committee to Review Research 2003, p. 47). Thus, we are not interested in whether police now carry 9 mm instead of revolvers, though we are very interested in whether they use more force or are more militarized than before. Similarly, we are not interested in whether some agencies have a peripheral special unit for some new and emerging social problem, but we are interested in more generic organizational transformations such as an increase in structural complexity or internal accountability mechanisms.

Not all trends constitute transformations. We follow the lead of organizational theorist Howard Aldrich, who defines a transformation as "a major change occurring along three possible dimensions: changes in goals, boundaries, and activities" (Aldrich 1999, 163). A transformation entails change on at least one of these dimensions, not necessarily all three. Furthermore, an organizational transformation need not be consciously enacted by the organization or its members. It is possible for organizations to change accidentally, to drift into change, or to suffer profound shocks that jar the organization so dramatically as to transform it unwittingly. Finally, transformations must be substantial. Changes are small alterations; transformations are substantial (Aldrich 1999).

As *Fairness and Effectiveness* (hereafter referred to as the "committee's report") points out, it is difficult to speak of the American policing industry as a monolith. Nested within it are thousands of separate police organizations of various sizes and types (and nested within them are hundreds of thousands of employees). Policing in the United States occurs within an organizational context. When transformations occur within the policing industry, they must diffuse throughout the population of police organizations. Sometimes, transformations start at the

cal examinations of police agencies and applying organizational theories to police organizations. He has written on structural inertia in policing, police civilianization, police innovation, organizational hierarchy, the disbanding of police agencies, and police-officer homicide. His current interests focus on describing and predicting long-term trends of change and continuity with large police agencies.

organization level and bubble up to the industry level. Other times, they are diffused down to the organization level from policy elites or government (Maguire and Mastrofski 2000). Any look at transformations in the American policing industry, therefore, should take into account transformations in police organizations.

Two questions arise when considering the extent to which some policy or practice has influenced or reshaped the policing industry: how deeply has the policy or practice been entrenched within individual police organizations, and how much has it spread across the landscape of these organizations? This distinction is not just academic—it is crucial. Some practices—like community policing, in our opinion—are implemented across the landscape of policing but so weakly, or in such a scattershot fashion, so as not to constitute a significant transformation at the industry level (we recognize that some readers will disagree with this controversial example). Others are implemented in earnest in some organizations, so they may constitute transformations of these individual organizations. But since they are not diffused across the landscape of police organizations, they cannot be considered transformations at the industry level. Finally, although many of the transformations we discuss are applicable to police around the world, this article focuses on trends in the American policing industry.

We begin by defining briefly the three dimensions of transformation—in goals, in boundaries, and in activity systems. We then examine the evidence for transformation in American policing within each of these dimensions. We close with some reflections on the committee's report. The report mirrors the research body on which it is based. Gaps in the report are not the result of blindness on the part of its authors; the gaps represent missing pieces in the body of research evidence. We assess the ability of the police research industry to adequately detect, measure, and monitor important trends in the police industry. As we point out, these reflections lend themselves to some clear policy implications for those agencies and organizations that conduct and fund police research. We make a series of recommendations that we believe will help make the police research industry more relevant to, and more knowledgeable about, the American police industry.

Three Dimensions of Transformation

Goals

The goals of complex organizations are often vague, particularly in those kinds of organizations, like police, in which the relationships between means and ends are poorly understood (Mastrofski and Ritti 2000). Nonetheless, even vague goals tend to succeed at some level, directing human activity within organizations toward some "purposive or solidary outcome," to use Aldrich's words (1999, 165; also see Simon 1964). Aldrich argues that major changes in an organization's purposes or goals constitute one important kind of transformation. Transforming an organization's goals entails either expanding or contracting its domain, or changing the breadth of its goals. Starting in the 1890s, for instance, many U.S. police agencies shed their numerous social service tasks, such as finding lost children and housing migrant workers (Monkkonen 1981). Simultaneously, these agencies focused more intently on crime fighting as their primary goal (Fogelson 1977). Taken together, these two changes represented a significant transformation in goals. We examine a number of current movements that represent further transformations in the goals of police organizations.

Boundaries

An organization's boundaries are what separate it from its environment, distinguishing the internal from the external, members from nonmembers. These boundaries are typically not static; they expand and contract in a number of important ways. Organizations can undergo boundary transformations by expanding or contracting their membership, in either nature or number. They can restrict their membership, for instance, by refusing to hire certain types or classes of people. Or they can open up their membership to people who were formerly not eligible. For example, American policing has undergone two waves of gender integration. The first wave, during the early 1900s, was fairly short lived; the second wave, which started during the 1960s, has been more permanent and far-reaching (Owings 1925; Walker 1977). The hiring of females for a variety of sworn and nonsworn positions represents an important boundary transformation in the American policing industry.

Another form of boundary transformation occurs when one organization merges or consolidates with another, or when it adds or divests organizational units. An example of the former type of transformation occurred in 1995 when the New York City Housing Police and Transit Police merged with the New York Police Department. An example of the latter type of transformation occurred in the 1970s and 1980s when police departments around the nation eliminated their domestic intelligence collection units (Donner 1990). In both cases, the boundaries of the police organization shifted, either eliminating or taking on more responsibilities or personnel. We examine the extent to which boundary transformations have occurred in the American policing industry.

Activity systems

According to Aldrich (1999, 166), "Activity systems in organizations are the means by which members accomplish work, which can include processing raw materials, information, or people." We explore three potential kinds of transformations in activity systems: in their administrative apparatuses, in their adoption of technological innovations, and in their organizational behaviors. All organizations experience subtle changes in activity systems over days, weeks, and years. New policies, new leaders, and new environmental stimuli all lead organizations to adapt their activity systems in small (though perhaps important) ways. Transformations constitute more significant shifts in activity systems. We examine the extent to which the American policing industry is experiencing transformations in its activity systems.

Overlap in the three dimensions

Many of the transformations we identify do not fit neatly into one of these three dimensions. Some, for instance, might be considered transformations in more than one dimension. In the 1970s, in the wake of the Watergate scandal, many police agencies dismantled their domestic intelligence collection units or transferred personnel performing those functions to other assignments (Donner 1990). After September 11, 2001, many of these same police agencies scrambled to bolster their intelligence capacities. Research evidence on changes in policing after September 11 is still slim, but anecdotal evidence suggests that recent efforts to reembrace the

---

Police play a crucial risk-management role in defining who is criminal, who is a bad driver, who is mentally ill, and who is dangerous.

---

domestic intelligence function in policing might constitute a new transformation on all three dimensions (Murphy and Plotkin 2003; Rashbaum 2002; U.S. Conference of Mayors 2002). Some police organizations are now expanding their goals to include the timely collection and analysis of terrorist intelligence. Some are creating new positions for intelligence analysts, thereby expanding their occupational boundaries. Some are creating new units and technologies to deal with terrorism, or trying to encourage new competencies among personnel, thereby establishing a potential transformation in activity systems. As the committee's report accurately concludes, the research base is currently not sufficient to determine whether these trends constitute transformations at the industry level.

The trends in domestic intelligence collection illustrate that some transformations cannot easily be forced into just one of the three conceptual dimensions we use here. It may be useful to picture these dimensions as a series of overlapping Venn diagrams. Any individual transformation might fit within just one of the dimensions or in the intersection between either two or three of them. Perhaps the most compelling transformations, those that have the greatest likelihood of reshaping policing, are the ones that have implications for goals, boundaries, and activity systems.

Goals

Several transformations in goals have reshaped the policing industry in recent years and promise to continue doing so in the coming years. According to Aldrich (1999), goal transformations expand or contract an organization's domain and/or change the "breadth of products or services." We explore six areas of potential transformation in goals: the reduction in the domain of public police due to the provision of security by nongovernmental organizations; the changing role of police in preventing, planning for, and responding to domestic and international terrorism; an increasing trend toward militarization among police; an expansion of the police role as information brokers in the risk-management industry; the continuing expansion of policing into the surveillance, security, and socialization of children; and an expansion of the police role in working with communities to solve or mitigate problems. Some of these trends are tangible and readily observable, while others are more subtle or abstract and more difficult to document and track. After exploring six potential goal transformations, we close this section by assessing the extent to which the police research industry is capable of detecting and measuring each one.

Governance of security

While early forms of policing were often delivered by a hodgepodge of public and private entities, public police have dominated the "market" for delivering public safety in the modern era. However, several observers have noted in recent years that public police are losing market share to the rapidly expanding private security industry (Johnston 1992). Bayley and Shearing (1996, 2001) argue that privatization is only the tip of the iceberg—that policing throughout the world is undergoing a substantial restructuring in which a variety of nongovernmental organizations are becoming increasingly responsible for performing policing functions. Bayley and Shearing (2001) conclude that "policing has entered a new era, an era characterized by a transformation in the governance of security." This transformation blurs the lines between public and private policing and constitutes a reduction in the domain of public policing. Jones and Newburn (2002) reject portions of Bayley and Shearing's argument and question the extent of actual transformation. Research evidence, both in the United States and abroad, is insufficient to sort between these two competing claims.

Policing terrorism

A handful of police departments in the United States (most notably, New York's) have had extensive experience in preparing for and investigating terrorism. Until September 11, 2001, however, most agencies viewed the likelihood of a terrorist incident within their jurisdictions as unlikely (Riley and Hoffman 1995). Since

September 11, police agencies have devoted massive effort to preparing for terrorism. Little empirical evidence exists on the nature of the changes they are undergoing, with most of what is known derived from anecdotal evidence and journalistic accounts.

Recent surveys conducted by the U.S. Conference of Mayors (2002) and the Massachusetts Statistical Analysis Center (2002) confirm that a variety of changes are taking place in goals, boundaries, and activity systems. In the Massachusetts survey, only 6.6 percent of police agencies reported making no changes as a result of the September 11 terrorist incidents. From a goals perspective, the changes in policing resulting from September 11 represent an expansion in domain and an increase in the breadth of services and responsibilities. For instance, police are now devoting substantially more attention to disaster planning in concert with other agencies and organizations, a trend that runs counter to their tendency to plan in isolation (Wenger, Quarantelli, and Dynes 1989). They are revamping their domestic and international intelligence-collection efforts (Rashbaum 2002). Furthermore, they are developing new areas of investigative expertise, cooperating much more with federal law enforcement and intelligence agencies, working more closely with the military, increasing their levels of surveillance over their communities, paying more attention to the safety and security of critical infrastructure, and a host of other changes that are likely to have a profound influence on the American policing industry (Murphy and Plotkin 2003).

Militarization

Militarism has always been present to some degree in policing, but some observers note that it is expanding, in both the United States and abroad (Kopel and Blackman 1997; Kraska 1996; McCulloch 2001; Weber 1999). First, police continue to adopt many of the trappings of military organizations, including formal ranks, insignias, uniforms, codes of discipline, organizational structures, equipment, doctrine, and culture.[1] Second, federal law restricting the military from participating in domestic law enforcement functions has become considerably less restrictive over the last two decades. Congress has chipped away at the Posse Comitatus Act of 1878 (18 USC 1385), enabling increased military involvement in civilian law enforcement efforts. Other federal statutes are also beginning to blur the line between police and military. Third, researchers have detected an increase in the number of agencies with police paramilitary units, from 59 percent in 1982, to 78 percent in 1990, to 89 percent in 1995 (Kraska and Cubellis 1997; Kraska and Kappeler 1997). Finally, police are also beginning to rely on a host of nonlethal military technologies intended to augment their communication and surveillance capacities (Haggerty and Ericson 1999). Taken together, these four themes point to an overall increase in militarization among police agencies. Research findings from Australia, together with anecdotal evidence from the United States, suggest that the war on terrorism is likely to enhance this ongoing trend (McCulloch 2001).

Policing risk

Ericson and Haggerty (1997) observe that police agencies have become an increasingly crucial node in the network of institutions responsible for risk management. Their traditional roles are expanding to include collection and dissemination of information. As Maguire and Wells (2002, p. 33) point out, police "are like an army of information soldiers; taken together they contain vast pools of untapped information about the organization and its clients." The important distinction for Ericson and Haggerty is that the police information-processing role is increasingly being shaped by external institutions, including insurance companies, health and welfare organizations, schools, and private firms. Police play a crucial risk-management role in defining who is criminal, who is a bad driver, who is mentally ill, and who is dangerous. While Ericson and Haggerty pose some intriguing ideas, evidence for their assertions is still rather limited, emerging mostly from ethnographic research conducted within police departments and not from the other institutions within the risk-management industry. Katz (2003, p. 485), for instance, examined the processes involved in producing and disseminating data on gang members in a Midwestern police agency. He found serious data errors that are likely to lead to misjudgments about individuals' gang affiliations. These errors were the "product of inadequate communication within the gang unit and between the gang unit and its operating environment." Much more research is needed in this area before we can conclude with any confidence that Ericson and Haggerty have detected an emerging transformation in policing, but their thesis is compelling enough to warrant further investment in carefully designed research.

Socializing children

Police agencies are also expanding their role in securing and socializing our children. Police have always played a role in the lives of children. Police Athletic Leagues, for instance, whose motto is "Filling Playgrounds, Not Prisons," date back to the early 1900s.[2] Police programming in schools has increased with the widespread adoption of Drug Abuse Resistance Education (DARE), Gang Resistance Education and Training (GREAT), and other similar programs that bring police into classrooms. More than 90 percent of police agencies now provide drug-use-prevention programming in schools (Maguire and Mastrofski 2000). There has also been a rapid proliferation in the number of school resource officers. The National Association of School Resource Officers, first established in 1990, now has more than 10,000 members.[3] According to Ericson and Haggerty (1997, p. 8):

> The police help to secure the social boundaries of youth by working in the interstices of institutions that deal more directly with young people. An analysis of police programs in schools reveals that police officers function simultaneously as security officers, risk educators, informant-system operators, and counselors, and that they mobilize students and staff to play these roles as well.

Taken together, these trends imply a systematic broadening of the services that police provide to their communities and therefore constitute another kind of important goal transformation.

Community policing and problem solving

According to some commentators, the community policing and problem-solving movements represent the most significant transformations in the policing industry in the latter half of the twentieth century. One could easily fill a book-length manuscript addressing the evidence on whether this assertion is true; we do not have that luxury here. Because *community policing* is a catchphrase that has been used to describe a potpourri of different strategies, one complication in determining the extent to which it has transformed policing is determining exactly

---

Administrative rules regulating deadly force have reduced its use by police.

---

what it is. Maguire and his colleagues have argued elsewhere that community policing has three primary components: organizational adaptation, community interaction and engagement, and problem solving (Eck and Maguire 2000; Maguire and Uchida 2000). We examine the evidence for organizational adaptation later in a subsection on changes in the administrative apparatuses of police agencies. A large body of research has examined the extent to which community interaction and engagement practices occur in policing, but most of this research was cross-sectional and therefore unable to address change. An equally large body of research has examined the extent to which police organizations have embraced the precepts of problem-oriented policing as outlined by Herman Goldstein (1990), but most of this research was cross-sectional as well.[4]

A handful of multiwave establishment surveys have examined changes in the implementation of community policing during the 1990s (for a review, see Maguire 2002a). In general, these studies report increases nationwide in the number of employees assigned to perform community policing functions and the number of agencies that have implemented various community policing programs. Methodological concerns about these kinds of studies loom large since they are unable to reach valid inferences about the dosage of community policing activities and the depth of philosophical change in agencies claiming to perform these activities (Maguire and Mastrofski 2000). At Harvard University, Mark Moore et al. (1999) conducted intensive case studies of community policing implementation in ten police agencies, eight "high performers" and two "typical" agencies. They found that "while all departments seemed to move pretty far in the direction of increasing the quantity and quality of problem solving efforts, they did less well in developing their capacity for establishing and maintaining community partnerships" (p. 30). These findings are consistent with survey evidence showing that community involvement often lags behind other elements of the community policing movement (Maguire and Katz 2002). Comparative ethnographies of community policing implementation in a cross-section of American police agencies would go a long way toward helping to establish the extent of transformation being inculcated in these agencies as a result of community policing.

Boundaries

Changes in boundaries involve substantial expansions or contractions involving either (1) organizational members or employees (but not "clients") or (2) other organizations. We begin by exploring five potential transformations in the membership boundaries of the American policing industry: overall growth, civilianization, and increasing diversity in the race, gender, and education of the policing workforce. After that, we explore a series of trends influencing the organizational boundaries of the policing industry.

Organizational members

Overall growth. The policing industry is growing not only in the United States but also worldwide. Due to data-quality issues in counting cops, no reliable national data exist that can be used to track changes in police size in the United States over time (Maguire et al. 1998). However, ratios of sworn officers to population can be computed at the agency level. Among agencies for which an accurate ratio can be computed, the median ratio rose from 1.77 sworn officers per 1,000 population in 1975 to 1.98 in 1998.[5] This trend is not unique to the United States. Maguire and Schulte-Murray (2001) found that the ratio of police to population is increasing in nations throughout the world. Just as corporate downsizing represents a contraction of corporate America's boundaries, the growth of the policing industry signals an expansion in the membership boundaries of police organizations. The growth of police relative to population should be considered a basic social indicator representing an expansion of formal social control and is clearly worthy of further investigation.[6]

Civilianization. During the first hundred years of formal, vocational American policing, most police agencies did not employ civilians. For example, among 350 municipal police agencies surveyed by the FBI in 1937, the median percentage civilian was only 2.6 percent. Over time, civilianization in policing has increased steadily. Recent data indicate that about 25 percent of police employees in agencies with a hundred or more employees are civilians.[7] One recent study reported that after years of steady growth, civilianization in large municipal agencies began to level off in the early 1990s but is now inching up again, perhaps due to the availability of federal funding to hire civilians (Maguire et al. 2003).

Civilianization is not just a matter of numbers, however. Traditionally, civilians have been used in two roles. The first role involved relatively unskilled tasks, such as record keeping, maintenance, call taking and dispatch, and clerical duties (King forthcoming). The second traditional role involved skilled "behind the scenes" tasks such as crime mapping and analysis and computer programming and maintenance (King forthcoming). New roles continue to emerge, however (Forst 2000). Some police agencies now employ civilians in high-level leadership positions from which they were formerly excluded as applicants. Civilians are also employed as community liaisons, creating a stable linkage to specific community groups that are ordinarily isolated from police (such as ethnic groups that do not speak English and that are tightly knit and insular, the fundamentally religious, gays and lesbians, and labor groups). A number of agencies also now employ civilians to serve as Public Information Officers (Surette 2001). The future of civilianization may also involve using civilians to process crime scenes, to investigate computer crimes, to respond to particularly dangerous crime scenes (such as covert drug labs or chemical/biological/radiological attacks), and if recent trends in domestic intelligence collection continue to take shape, to spy on us.

Racial diversity. Police officers have become a considerably more diverse lot in recent years, with great strides being made in hiring more minorities. For early police agencies, ethnic diversity involved hiring Italian or Irish officers to police ethnic enclaves (sometimes their own and sometimes not) (Harring 1983). Few agencies employed African Americans as officers, and those that did often chose not to grant them full arrest powers. Overall, the first major wave of racial integration in American policing began in the late 1960s when many police agencies hired African Americans as sworn officers (Alex 1969). According to one study, the percentage of black police officers in the United States rose from about 4 percent in 1973 to 11.3 percent in 1993 (Zhao and Lovrich 1998). According to another study, the percentage of blacks in large police agencies, which are typically located in more diverse communities and therefore have greater proportions of minority officers, rose from 18.4 percent in 1990 to just over 20 percent in 2000. Hispanics in these same agencies increased from 9.2 percent in 1990 to 14.1 percent in 2000 (Reaves and Hickman 2002). Research has shown that these increases in minority employment are often due to court-ordered hiring quotas (Lott 2000; McCrary 2003). While the proportions of minorities employed within police departments still often fail to reach their proportions in the population, there have been significant strides in minority employment in policing.

Gender diversity. Police agencies have also made major strides in enhancing their gender diversity. Except for a handful of notable exceptions, women have entered policing as sworn officers since only the late 1960s. Women had already made considerable inroads into policing as civilians, but police agencies were resistant to hiring them as sworn officers. That picture has changed considerably, though as some critics point out, there is still much room for improvement, particularly with regard to the proportion of women in supervisory or leadership positions (National Center for Women and Policing 2002). The percentage of female sworn officers in large agencies with a hundred or more officers has increased from 2.0 percent in 1972 to 12.7 percent in 2001 (National Center for Women and Policing 2002). Our analysis of a larger sample of agencies from the FBI's Police Employment data shows that the mean percentage of females in sworn positions rose from 3.6 percent in 1975 to 9.7 percent in 2001. A more telling perspective from the same data set is that 25.8 percent of these agencies employed no female sworn officers in 1975; by 2001, this figure was less than 1 percent.[8] Clearly, the number of female police officers is increasing. As the committee's report accurately concludes, however, the effects of these increases on police practice are unknown.

Education. Data on the education levels of American police officers are neither current nor conclusive, but a patchwork of evidence suggests that the policing workforce is becoming increasingly educated (Carter, Sapp, and Stephens 1989). Police agencies have also increased their minimum education requirements. The percentage of officers working in agencies with some college requirements increased from about 10 percent in 1990 to 32 percent in 2000 (Bureau of Justice Statistics 2003b). By 2000, 83 percent of agencies required a high school diploma, 14 percent required some college or a two-year degree, and only 1 percent required a four-year degree (Bureau of Justice Statistics 2003b).[9] In spite of significant progress, the policing field has still fallen well short of meeting a recommendation made twenty-five years ago by the National Advisory Commission on Higher Education for Police Officers: "All police departments should move now to require new recruits to have earned a baccalaureate degree and no police department should require two years of college as the minimum qualifications for police recruits" (Sherman et. al 1978, 14). The policing workforce is likely to become increasingly educated. As the committee's report points out, however, the effects of education on policing practice are still not well understood.

Other organizations

Boundary transformations occur not only within the membership of a police agency but also when the agency's organizational boundaries, or those of other organizations with which it transacts, expand or contract. We explore three classes of organizational boundary transformations.

Organizational deaths, consolidations, and births. Despite the common notion that police organizations are immortal, we now know otherwise. Police agencies have been disbanded with surprising regularity since at least the late 1950s (and likely before). Between 1970 and 1999, at least 105 Ohio police agencies disbanded (King 1999). Even large police agencies such as the Compton Police Department in California (an agency with 103 sworn officers) and New York City's transit, school, and housing police agencies (respectively, the eighth, eighteenth, and twenty-first largest police agencies in terms of full-time sworn employees in 1993) were disbanded during the 1990s (Bureau of Justice Statistics 1996). The

---

Police have long been infatuated with multiple types of technical innovations as far back as the 1800s, with the adoption of uniforms, patrol wagons, and call boxes.

---

demise of a police organization often alters the boundaries for the other police organizations in that particular environmental niche. In most instances, a preexisting agency (usually the county sheriff or the state police) must assume policing duties for the disbanded agency's community. In many instances, surviving agencies hire employees from the disbanded agency and receive some of the disbanded agency's equipment. In this way, new members with considerably different experiences and agency cultures are introduced into existing agencies.

Other times, multiple agencies disband and consolidate into a new agency, or one agency disbands and consolidates within an existing agency. Some consolidations merge two or more police agencies into one, while others form public safety departments by merging police with other emergency services like fire and emergency medical services (Crank 1990). Consolidation has been a topic of scholarly debate since at least the early 1970s (Ostrom, Parks, and Whitaker 1973; Finney 1997), although examples of mergers of police agencies can be found throughout the history of modern policing. While there is a growing body of anecdotal and historical evidence on consolidation, there is no systematic data that would enable us to predict how this phenomenon will affect the landscape of the policing industry.

New police agencies are also sometimes founded. Although many are quite small, the sizes of new agencies vary widely.[10] A recent survey in three states indicates that between 1970 and 1999, fifteen new police agencies were created in

Ohio, while nine were created in Arizona and Nevada (King 1999). New agencies alter the boundaries of preexisting agencies within their niches. They must attract new members, either as new recruits or by attracting current police employees from other agencies. The formation of a new organization presents an opportunity to create an organization unhindered by past arrangements, such as structure and culture (Downs 1967; Stinchcombe 1965). The attitudes and experiences brought by new members, especially new leaders, also shape new organizations (Boeker 1988; Hannan, Baron, and Burton 1999; Tucker, Singh, and Meinhard 1990).

There have been no national studies of organizational births, deaths, and consolidations. Early evidence from pilot studies in three states suggests that deaths far outnumber births. If this trend is similar in other states, and if it continues, the future landscape of American policing might someday look very different, much like the face of corporate America changed after years and years of mergers and acquisitions.

Networks and partnerships. Perhaps now more than ever, police agencies form partnerships with individuals, businesses, government agencies, and other law enforcement agencies as a means of working together toward some common interest. These partnerships are sometimes very loose and informal, based on little more than a handshake and goodwill (Ostrom, Parks, and Whitaker 1978). Other times, they are more formalized and may resemble what David Thacher (forthcoming) calls an "inchoate hierarchy," a developing organization with its own rules, policies, and hierarchy.

Perhaps the best examples in policing of an inchoate hierarchy are multiagency task forces: temporary or semipermanent organizations staffed by members who are also members of other police organizations. Task forces are usually created to deal with some pressing problem that transcends traditional agency jurisdictions (e.g., high-profile criminals, such as serial killers, as well as drug trafficking and terrorist threats). Task forces may be either short lived or long lived. Regardless of their life spans, task forces entail a newly founded organization composed of members from other agencies. Thus, task forces are conglomerations of people who are often trained in different ways, have different perspectives on the problem, and come from different organizational cultures. In 1999, 53 percent of American police agencies reported participating in a multijurisdictional, drug task force (Bureau of Justice Statistics 2003a). After September 11, 2001, the FBI increased the number of Joint Terrorism Task Forces (in which it partners with state and local police agencies) from thirty-five to sixty-six. The U.S. Department of Justice (2003) also recently established ninety-three Anti-Terrorism Advisory Councils to coordinate information sharing among more than 5,000 state and local law enforcement agencies.

Other partnerships do not involve the creation of a new hierarchy or pseudo-organization, but they still cross organizational boundaries. For instance, Hassell (2000) describes a partnership in one city where juvenile probation officers were physically located within the local police department to enhance their collaboration with juvenile detectives. Some partnerships pair police with individuals or organizations located outside the criminal justice system. Under the rubric of problem-oriented policing, for instance, a number of agencies have developed formal or informal interagency partnerships designed to reduce crime, fear, or disorder. These teams often involve housing, zoning, fire, public works, and other local agencies.

Some partnerships occur even less formally, triggered when a police officer attempts to solicit, leverage, or coerce a third party in supervising people or places thought to be criminal or potentially criminal. Buerger and Green Mazerolle (1998) refer to this phenomenon as "third-party policing." It blurs the boundaries between formal social control as performed by paid police officers and other less formal means of social control. Traditionally, informal social control is distributed by a wide range of authorities who are not police, such as parents, teachers, priests, or employers. Third-party policing blurs the distinction between these two forms by enlisting third parties (who traditionally are not paid to exert formal social control) and by convincing them or compelling them (e.g., through threat of civil action) to exercise social control over people (such as tenants and bar patrons) and/or areas (such as rental properties). At present, we know very little about how many police agencies are using some form of third-party policing. Anecdotally, we know that a number of agencies have used civil suits and the threat of civil suits to deal with troublesome properties such as bars, social clubs, and rental properties, but there are no national data on the extent of these practices.

Together, the development of these various forms of networks and partnerships signals a potential transformation in which police organizations appear more open, more transparent, and more cooperative. At the same time, some of these partnerships appear to represent a conscious effort by the police to increase surveillance and control over the citizenry, by expanding their domain or by encouraging others to perform functions that police are not permitted to perform. Unfortunately, national data on the extent to which police organizations are involved in these various networks and partnerships are not available.

Federalization and globalization. Local policing in America is also becoming heavily influenced by federalization and globalization. A task force from the American Bar Association (1998) recently documented the tremendous rise in the federalization of the criminal law. For example, both Project Exile and Project Safe Neighborhoods bring the weight of federal prosecutors to bear on local gun-related crime. Local police agencies work closely with U.S. Drug Enforcement Administration agents so they can take advantage of federal prosecutions that carry longer sentences typically served in out-of-state prisons. Police departments around the country are being investigated for civil rights violations and are entering into consent decrees with the Justice Department to enhance their hiring and promotion practices for women and minorities. The past decade has also seen a massive infusion of federal funding for local law enforcement through a variety of funding programs. Federalization also plays a role in the militarization of the police, discussed earlier, with the Defense Department providing a variety of military equipment and training to state and local police. All of these factors point to an overall increase in federal involvement in local policing (Richman 2000).

American police are also being affected by broader societal trends in globalization (Ward 2000). International terrorism is the most obvious example of how globalization touches home, but numerous others include immigration patterns and transnational investigations. During a recent study, one of us spoke with a small-town New Jersey police officer who was working on an international credit-card fraud case with Turkish police. The globalization of crime has opened up the world for American police. At the same time, the American law enforcement industry is also projecting itself on the world stage (Deflem 2002). Since 1995, for instance, the United States has opened five International Law Enforcement Academies around the world, designed to improve training of local authorities and enhance international cooperation. These academies represent only one of several avenues through which the United States provides training and support to the world's police.

Activity Systems

We could easily write a book on trends in the activity systems of police agencies. Here, we focus briefly on trends within three substantive areas: the administrative apparatuses of police organizations, technological innovation, and organizational behavior.

Administrative apparatus

Police administration has always been influenced by broader trends in management thought. Modern police chiefs are conversant about a variety of management-reform prescriptions in business and government (e.g., Webber 1991). Law enforcement trade journals are filled with exhortations to implement the latest and greatest management fads. No systematic, ongoing, national data sources in policing track the extent to which these changes have taken root. Based on longitudinal data sets assembled from a variety of sources, one study found that during the 1990s, police agencies experienced significant decreases in centralization and administrative intensity, changes encouraged by community policing reformers. At the same time, they did not "flatten" their hierarchies or reduce their levels of specialization, two changes featured prominently in the reform prescriptions (Maguire et al. 2003).

Another recent national study examined the implementation of "Compstat," a popular package of administrative reforms first implemented in New York City in 1994 (Weisburd, Mastrofski, et al. 2001). According to data from a national survey of police agencies, Weisburd, Mastrofski, et al. (2001) found that agencies implementing Compstat differed from those who had not implemented it on three dimensions: they clarified their mission, created or enhanced mechanisms for internal accountability, and instituted data-driven decision making. Other elements of Compstat, such as geographic organization of command and organizational flexibility, did not differ across the two groups of departments. The fieldwork conducted by Weisburd et al. suggests that while Compstat induced some innovations in management, it was not successful in displacing traditional, core policing practices.

The police research industry has produced other scattered findings on changes in the administrative apparatuses of police organizations. Most such findings result from ad hoc research efforts using cross-sectional designs rather than a systematic research agenda implemented longitudinally. Research on both community policing and Compstat has shown that even agencies claiming that they do not do it, still engage in its activities (Maguire and Katz 2002; Weisburd, Mastrofski, et al. 2001). Thus, we cannot assume from cross-sectional data that some policing practice that is thought to be new has been implemented recently. Longitudinal data are necessary to assess change. As a result of a long-term lack of investment in longitudinal research, evidence on changes in the structure and management of police organizations tends to be weak and scattered.

Technological innovation

Technological innovations refer to a range of technology products that are considered state of the art to the police. King (2000) reported that technical innovations bifurcate into those employed predominantly by police managers, such as computer-aided dispatch, and those employed by line officers, such as new firearms or new ways to dispense force. Manning (2003) employs a different classification system, listing five kinds of technological innovations: mobility, training, transformative, analytic, and communicative. Police have long been infatuated with multiple types of technical innovations as far back as the 1800s, with the adoption of uniforms (Monkkonen 1981), patrol wagons, and call boxes (Harring 1983).

At first blush, it appears that new police innovations are merely tools that officers use to perform their usual tasks, and therefore, innovations do not change their core activities. In fact, however, new technologies sometimes change what officers do and can thus alter the activity systems of police organizations. For example, before the adoption of mobile data terminals (MDTs), officers required some visible display of probable cause before stopping a motor vehicle. The installation of MDTs in patrol cars, however, allowed officers to unobtrusively "run" motor vehicles in fishing expeditions for warrants and probable cause (Meehan and Ponder 2002). Access to such information increases the number of people with which the police will have contact, and it also defines the conditions of their interactions. Advances in identification technologies for fingerprints and DNA have also influenced investigative practices.

While acknowledging that MDTs increase the scope of police surveillance activity, Manning (2003, 125) argues that information technology tends to be grafted on "to the extant structure and traditional processes of the police organization, and these organizations have little changed." He concludes more generally that "there is little evidence that thirty years of funding technological innovations has produced much change in police practice or effectiveness" (Manning 2003, 136). While a scattered body of research evidence lends plausibility to Manning's sweeping conclusion, data on the extent of, and especially the consequences of, technological innovation in American police organizations is currently inadequate to confirm or refute it with any empirical precision.

Organizational behavior

Organizational behavior is a catchall phrase that refers to the many behaviors in which an organization and its members engage. In the few pages that remain, we are unable to exhaustively catalog potential transformations in the organizational behavior of American police agencies. Instead, we comment briefly on a handful of behavioral domains and assess the capacity of the police research industry to detect or monitor transformations in these domains.

Egon Bittner noted in 1970 that the key distinction between police and other occupations is that "police are institutions or individuals given the general right to use coercive force by the state within the state's domestic territory" (Klockars 1985, 12). The use of force and other coercive behaviors are core components of police behavior. We explore three specific forms of coercion: use of lethal force, use of nonlethal force, and arrest. Police also engage in an array of other noncoercive behaviors, and we briefly explore some of those as well.

A healthy body of research on the use of deadly force by police has emerged over the past two decades. We now know, for instance, as the committee points out in its report, that administrative rules regulating deadly force have reduced its use by police. The best research on deadly force, however, has taken place within agencies or within communities; therefore, it is not very useful for examining transformations at the industry level. National data on police use of deadly force are collected by two different agencies: the FBI and the National Center for Health Statistics. James Fyfe (2002), as well as several other observers, have argued that both data sources are beset with measurement error and cannot be trusted for comparing agencies. Fyfe (2002) goes so far as to argue that the best data on deadly force are not collected by government agencies or social scientists but by newspapers that collected the data through Freedom of Information Act requests or litigation. Using these various data sources, police researchers can make some limited inferences about trends in deadly force. Fyfe (2002) points out, however, that there are no national data on how often police shoot and miss or wound citizens. It is not unreasonable in a democracy to expect our police agencies to be willing and able to report accurate data on how often they shoot at, wound, or kill people. We endorse the committee's finding that this is a serious deficiency in existing research.

Our understanding of when and why officers use less-than-lethal force has improved considerably over the past several decades, thanks to systematic social observation research and a range of other study methods (McEwen 1996). Although within-agency research on use of force by police has made considerable progress, we still know very little about interagency variation in uses of force. The

International Association of Chiefs of Police (IACP) implemented a voluntary use of force reporting system in 1996. Participating agencies reported their data anonymously to a central archive at IACP. As the committee persuasively argues, this effort suffered from a number of pitfalls and was discontinued in 2001. Because national data on less-than-lethal force do not exist, the policing industry could slowly be increasing (or decreasing) its use of force each year and police researchers would be unable to detect this important trend using existing data systems.

Our overarching recommendation is that the police research industry needs to improve its ability to detect, measure, and monitor trends in the policing industry.

Two alternative research methods could provide promising data on changes in the use of force at the industry level if they were conducted over time. The first would be a regular national survey of a random sample of police officers. The groundwork for such a study has already been laid by the Police Foundation, which recently conducted a telephone survey of a random sample of more than 900 American police officers on abuse of authority (Weisburd, Greenspan, et al. 2001). Longitudinal data from such a study could shed valuable light on changes in their (or their colleagues') propensity to use force. The second would be a regular national survey of a random sample of citizens. Once again, the groundwork for such a study has already been laid by the Bureau of Justice Statistics. In 1999, the bureau conducted a telephone survey titled the Police Public Contact Survey with a random sample of more than 80,000 persons regarding their contacts with police (Langan et al. 2001). This study, if repeated systematically over time, could also provide valuable insights about changes in citizens' experiences with police use of force.

Like the use of force, making an arrest is a concrete expression of the coercive authority of police. The FBI routinely collects arrest data from American police agencies. An audit of these data conducted two decades ago revealed serious measurement problems. The study concluded that using arrest data to compare police agencies is unwise (Sherman and Glick 1984). We are unaware of any factors that might have changed this conclusion since the audit was completed, and therefore, we cannot attach much faith to national arrest statistics.

These traditional measures of police behavior have two problems: first, they conceive of the use of authority as a binary phenomenon rather than a continuous one. Recent research shows that police authority can be conceived of on an ordinal scale that ranges from less to more. For instance, both Klinger (1996) and Brown (2003) have developed formal authority scales used to measure the extent of formal authority exercised by police with an individual suspect or during an encounter. While neither study used police organizations as the unit of analysis, it is not difficult to imagine that the exercise of formal authority might vary significantly across police organizations. Scientific methods for measuring the quantity of formal authority used by police with individuals or during encounters are still developing. As these methods mature, the use of formal authority could conceivably be measured at the organization or the industry level.

Second, traditional measures of police behavior capture only the coercive side of police work. Yet decades of research show that police spend much of their time performing other tasks. Should not we measure these as well? In a section titled "Neglected Dimensions of Police Behavior," the committee makes a useful contribution to discourse on police performance measurement with its argument that current data systems ignore major domains of police behavior. We do not know, for instance, how often the police rely on informal applications of their authority, provide assistance to citizens, mobilize and work with the community, solve community problems, or serve as information brokers to other institutions. Existing aggregate measures of police behavior are beset with measurement problems and neglect major elements of police behavior. The committee makes a persuasive argument that important domains of police behavior are still not being measured systematically. As a result, the capacity of the police research community to detect and monitor industry trends in police behavior is limited.

Discussion and Conclusion

The committee's coverage of the trends we have outlined is inconsistent. Some receive considerable coverage in the report, while others are discussed only briefly or not at all. The committee's review, however, is consistent with the availability of research evidence. Gaps in the report represent gaps in the research. As we have demonstrated, these gaps in the research base are substantial. Filling them represents a challenge for the police research industry, including not only those who carry out the research but those who organize and fund it.

Our major conclusion is that the police research industry is not currently organized or equipped to systematically detect and monitor change in policing. The major modes of research consist of case studies, cross-sectional studies, and studies conducted at the individual level. There is a lack of focus by those who carry out and fund police research on the development of a systematic, cohesive, empirically defensible, longitudinal data-collection strategy at the organization or the industry level. As a result, we are unable to measure, detect, or explain major changes (or continuities) in policing with any scientific confidence. As Lynch (2002, 64) points out, "Some changes in the police industry have taken place in what might be called 'geological' time. Unless you have a reasonably long and constant time series, you will not detect these changes."

What are some of the reasons that the police research community is limited in its capacity to systematically detect and measure trends in the policing industry? First, as we have argued above, many of these trends are mediated through the organizational level; their emergence as an industry-level phenomenon occurs when they diffuse throughout the population of police organizations. As Maguire (2002b) has noted, the volume of research on police organizations is minuscule compared with research on police officers, police work, and police effectiveness. Second, some of these long-term trends are so abstract or subtle that they defy most of our present techniques for seeing or detecting them. For example, testing a hypothesis that police are relying on increasingly more invasive modes of surveillance and control would be very challenging using existing data sources or traditional modes of research. Third, the nature of organizational (and industry) change confounds our ability to detect it. It tends to occur either glacially or as punctuated equilibrium, where long periods of constancy are interrupted by short periods of rapid change. Both of these patterns are almost invisible to short-term investigations of change or cross-sectional research designs.

Our overarching recommendation is that the police research industry needs to improve its ability to detect, measure, and monitor trends in the policing industry. Accomplishing this goal will make police research more relevant to the policing industry. The only way to accomplish it is to collect data that enable such research to take place and analyze it more systematically. We recommend that police researchers, police think tanks, and those who organize and fund police research implement changes designed to ensure the systematic collection and analysis of longitudinal data useful for understanding long-term trends in policing (Maguire 2002a).

In some instances, good data have already been collected but are not frequently assembled and analyzed. For example, the FBI's Police Employees data (Uchida and King 2002) provide information on changes in organizational size and civilianization since the 1930s and on the gender and racial composition of police agencies since the 1960s. These data are available for free through the Inter-university Consortium for Political and Social Research (ICPSR), but they are maintained in separate cross-sections and must be processed separately and then combined to conduct longitudinal analyses. Data collected by the International City/County Management Association (ICMA) also report counts of police employees as well as racial composition, education, and equipment for select years since the 1950s. The ICMA data sets have some of the lowest response rates among establishment surveys of police organizations, and many of them must be purchased (Maguire 2002a). In both cases, these valuable data sets are not used very often to study trends in policing. Perhaps if they were made more readily available or in a more analyzable format, they would be used more frequently.

The major source of organization-level data on American police agencies is the Law Enforcement Management and Administrative Statistics (LEMAS) data series collected by the Bureau of Justice Statistics since 1987. We heartily support the committee's recommendation that the LEMAS series be continued and broadened. Several scholars in recent years have made similar recommendations. For instance, Langworthy (2002) has suggested that the LEMAS "long form" data-collection instrument should be extended to the sample of smaller police agencies surveyed by LEMAS. Maguire and Uchida (2000) recommended treating the existing LEMAS architecture as a platform from which to launch other periodic studies on current issues of interest to scholars and practitioners (such as racial profiling and terrorism).

These existing data collections can also be supplemented and improved, as well as periodically collecting data concerning new issues. Those who manage them should also engage in careful data integrity analyses to ensure the validity and reliability of the data. Several researchers have pointed out flaws or inconsistencies in these data sources that suggest the need for more careful quality-control measures (e.g., Maguire and Uchida 2000; Uchida and King 2002; Walker and Katz 1995).

While it is helpful to look forward, the study of change can also benefit from looking back. Therefore, we also advocate for the collection of historical data from select police agencies. Collecting data on key variables (such as gender integration or the adoption of innovations) over the lives of a sample of police agencies will create small "pooled" cross-sectional and longitudinal data sets. These data will further our understanding of how police agencies change (and resist change) over their life courses. We cannot go back in time to administer surveys, but we can attempt to collect historical data on a limited set of variables from some agencies.

Most of the data that we have discussed so far are collected at the organization level. Yet repeated national surveys of random samples of police officers and citizens can also enhance our ability to detect industry-level trends. Both the Police Foundation's abuse of authority study (Weisburd, Greenspan, et al. 2001) and the Bureau of Justice Statistics' (BJS) police-public contact survey (Langan et al. 2001) are ideal platforms on which to build valuable longitudinal data-collection initiatives. Implementing these studies over time can reveal trends that are otherwise difficult to detect.

Four agencies are well positioned to implement solutions to the problems we have outlined: the FBI, the BJS, the National Institute of Justice (NIJ), and the ICPSR. First, the BJS and the NIJ could provide funding incentives to encourage researchers to pool together multiwave surveys of police agencies as a method for studying change. These could take the form of targeted solicitations for the analysis of existing data. The pooled data could then be made available through the ICPSR to other researchers, thus reducing the transaction costs for analyzing such data. Second, the BJS and the NIJ could also provide incentive programs for scholars to create or assemble historical/longitudinal data sets of police agencies. Once again, the resulting data sets could then be archived at the ICPSR for use by other researchers. Third, the ICPSR could host a summer session on using longitudinal data to draw inferences about trends in the policing industry. Fourth, the FBI and the BJS could both institute fellowships for scholars who specialize in policing data to work alongside agency data-collection staff and statisticians for short periods.

These fellowships would help make the data collections more responsive to scholarly needs, as well as enhance the use of the data for producing new scholarship. Finally, since LEMAS is the principle platform for collecting data on police organizations, we recommend the creation of an advisory board to make recommendations to the BJS staff on revisions to the instrument, sampling procedures, and other basic research decisions.

All of these recommendations are designed to improve the capacity for police research to detect, measure, and monitor trends in the policing industry. We envision a well-rounded police research industry in the future, one that engages in many modes of research at multiple levels. Some researchers will continue to focus on studying individual officers and citizens, police-citizen encounters, and police effectiveness. Some will continue to use case studies, cross-sectional research methods, and surveys of individuals. There is a need for all of these approaches. Yet, in our vision, a sizable segment of the police research community will also focus on measuring and explaining trends in policing at the organization and the industry levels. This investment in larger scale longitudinal research will pay many scholarly dividends, while making police research more relevant to the policing industry.

Notes

1. Critics view the appearance of military styles, symbols, cultures, and structures in policing as a profound shift in the wrong direction (Kopel and Blackman 1997; Kraska 1996; McCulloch 2001; Weber 1999). Others suggest that paramilitary policing styles can be more effective than traditional methods when used correctly (e.g., Waddington 1993) or that some of the threats facing civilian law enforcement agencies today warrant an increased level of cooperation between the military and the police (Brinkerhoff 2002; Klinger and Grossman 2002).

2. http://www.nationalpal.org.

3. http://www.nasro.org/membership.asp.

4. Some purists might object to our use of the terms *problem-solving policing* and *problem-oriented policing* as interchangeable. We acknowledge that there are some differences between these terms, but we do not have the space in this article to address these differences.

5. This analysis used the FBI's Police Employees data and includes agencies serving populations of at least a thousand and employing at least fifty full-time employees in both 1975 and 1998. This left 1,258 agencies with data for both years.

6. Several researchers have pointed out that changes in policing appear linked to an increasing societal tendency to rely on formal social control (e.g., Jones and Newburn 2002; Maguire and Schulte-Murray 2001).

7. We report civilianization ratios for agencies in this size range because computing these ratios for smaller agencies often produces outliers that can be misleading. Data from the 2000 Census of Law Enforcement Agencies (Bureau of Justice Statistics 2003a) reveal that the 1,546 police agencies in the nation with a hundred or more full-time employees had a mean percentage civilian of 24.9 percent (median = 23.2 percent).

8. This analysis relies on 1,108 agencies with 50 or more officers that provided data to the FBI's Police Employees database in 1975 and 2001.

9. In 1959, San Jose, CA, was the only local police agency requiring more than a high school education. San Jose required two years of college education. See the *Municipal Year Book* (1959, vol. 26, p. 434).

10. For instance, the Federal Way Department of Public Safety in Washington was created in 1996 and currently has 116 sworn officers. The Lauderhill Police Department in Florida was created in 1994 and currently employs 103 sworn officers.

References

Aldrich, Howard. 1999. *Organizations evolving*. Thousand Oaks, CA: Sage.

Alex, Nicholas. 1969. *Black in blue: A study of the Negro policeman.* New York: Appleton-Century-Crofts.

American Bar Association. 1998. *The federalization of criminal law*. Washington, DC: American Bar Association, Criminal Justice Section, Task Force on the Federalization of Criminal Law.

Bayley, David H., and Clifford Shearing. 1996. The future of policing. *Law and Society Review* 30:585-606.

———. 2001. *The new structure of policing: Description, conceptualization and research agenda*. Washington, DC: National Institute of Justice.

Boeker, Warren P. 1988. Organizational origins: Entrepreneurial and environmental imprinting at the time of founding. In *Ecological models of organizations*, edited by Glenn R. Carroll, 33-51. Cambridge, MA: Ballinger.

Brinkerhoff, John R. 2002. The Posse Comitatus Act and Homeland Security. *Journal of Homeland Security* (February). http://www.homelandsecurity.org/journal/articles/brinkerhoffpossecomitatus.htm/.

Brown, Robert A. 2003. *Exploring the use of formal authority in police-citizen encounters*. Ph.D. diss., University of Cincinnati, Ohio.

Buerger, Michael, and Lorraine Green Mazerolle. 1998. Third-party policing: A theoretical analysis of an emerging trend. *Justice Quarterly* 15 (2): 301-27.

Bureau of Justice Statistics. 1996. *Law enforcement management and administrative statistics, 1993*. Computer file. Produced and distributed by Inter-university Consortium for Political and Social Research, Ann Arbor, MI.

———. 2003a. *Census of state and local law enforcement agencies, 2000*. Data file. Produced and distributed by Inter-university Consortium for Political and Social Research, Ann Arbor, MI.

———. 2003b. *Local police departments, 2000*. Washington, DC: U.S. Department of Justice.

Carter, David L., Allen D. Sapp, and Darrel W. Stephens. 1989. *The state of police education: Policy direction for the 21st century*. Washington, DC: Police Executive Research Forum.

Committee to Review Research on Police Policy and Practices. 2003. *Fairness and effectiveness in policing: The evidence*. Washington, DC: National Academies Press.

Crank, John P. 1990. Patterns of consolidation among public safety departments, 1987-1988. *Journal of Police Science and Administration* 17 (4): 277-88.

Deflem, Mathieu. 2002. *Policing world society: Historical foundations of international police cooperation*. New York: Oxford University Press.

Donner, Frank. 1990. *Protectors of privilege: Red squads and police repression in urban America*. Berkeley: University of California Press.

Downs, Anthony. 1967. *Inside bureaucracy*. Boston: Little-Brown.

Eck, John, and Edward Maguire. 2000. Have changes in policing reduced violent crime? An assessment of the evidence. In *The crime drop in America*, edited by A. Blumstein and J. Wallman, 207-65. New York: Cambridge University Press.

Ericson, Richard V., and Kevin D. Haggerty. 1997. *Policing the risk society*. Toronto, Canada: University of Toronto Press.

Finney, Miles. 1997. Scale economies and police department consolidation: Evidence from Los Angeles. *Contemporary Economic Policy* 15 (1): 121-27.

Fogelson, Robert M. 1977. *Big city police*. Cambridge, MA: Harvard University Press.

Forst, Brian. 2000. The privatization and civilianization of policing. In vol. 2 of the National Institute of Justice 2000 series *Boundary changes in criminal justice organizations*, edited by Charles M. Friel, 19-79. Washington, DC: National Institute of Justice.

Fyfe, James J. 2002. Too many missing cases: Holes in our knowledge about police use of force. *Justice Research and Policy* 4:87-102.

Goldstein, Herman. 1990. *Problem-oriented policing*. New York: McGraw-Hill.

Haggerty, Kevin, and Richard Ericson. 1999. The militarization of policing in the information age. *The Journal of Military and Political Sociology* 27 (Winter): 233-45.

Hannan, Michael T., James N. Baron, and M. Diane Burton. 1999. Building the iron cage: Determinants of managerial intensity in the early years of organizations. *American Sociological Review* 64:527-47.

Harring, Sidney L. 1983. *Policing a class society: The experience of American cities, 1865-1915*. New Brunswick, NJ: Rutgers University Press.

Hassell, Kimberly D. 2000. *A police probation partnership: One city's response to serious habitual juvenile offending*. Master's thesis, University of Nebraska–Omaha.

Johnston, Les. 1992. *The rebirth of private policing*. London: Routledge.

Jones, Trevor, and Tim Newburn. 2002. The transformation of policing? Understanding current trends in policing systems. *British Journal of Criminology* 42:129-46.

Katz, Charles M. 2003. Issues in the production and dissemination of gang statistics: An ethnographic study of a large Midwestern police gang unit. *Crime & Delinquency* 49 (3): 485-516.

King, William R. 1999. Notes on the demise of Ohio police departments: 105 disbanded and counting. Paper presented at the annual meeting of the Midwestern Criminal Justice Association, Chicago, IL, October.

———. 2000. Measuring police innovation: Issues and measurement. *Policing: An International Journal of Police Strategies & Management* 23 (3): 303-17.

———. Forthcoming. Civilianization. In *Implementing community policing: Lessons from twelve agencies*, edited by E. R. Maguire and W. Wells. Washington, DC: Office of Community Oriented Policing Services.

Klinger, David A. 1996. Quantifying law in police-citizen encounters. *Journal of Quantitative Criminology* 12:391-415.

Klinger, David A., and Dave Grossman. 2002. Who should deal with foreign terrorists on U.S. soil? Socio-legal consequences of September 11 and the ongoing threat of terrorist attacks in America. *Harvard Journal of Law and Public Policy* 25 (2): 815-34.

Klockars, Carl B. 1985. *The idea of police*. Newbury Park, CA: Sage.

Kopel, David, and Paul Blackman. 1997. Can soldiers be peace officers? The Waco disaster and the militarization of American law enforcement period. *Akron Law Review* 30:619-59.

Kraska, Peter B. 1996. Enjoying militarism: Political/personal dilemmas in studying U.S. police paramilitary units. *Justice Quarterly* 13 (3): 405-29.

Kraska, Peter B., and Louis J. Cubellis. 1997. Militarizing Mayberry and beyond: Making sense of American paramilitary policing. *Justice Quarterly* 14 (4): 607-29.

Kraska, Peter B., and Victor E. Kappeler. 1997. Militarizing American police: The rise and normalization of paramilitary units. *Social Problems* 44 (1): 1-18.

Langan, Patrick A., Lawrence A. Greenfeld, Steven K. Smith, Matthew R. Durose, and David J. Levin. 2001. *Contacts between police and the public: Findings from the 1999 national survey*. Washington, DC: Bureau of Justice Statistics.

Langworthy, Robert H. 2002. LEMAS: A comparative organizational research platform. Special issue, *Justice Research and Policy* 4 (Fall): 21-38.

Lott, John R., Jr. 2000. Does a helping hand put others at risk? Affirmative action, police departments, and crime. *Economic Inquiry* 38 (2): 239-77.

Lynch, James P. 2002. Using citizen surveys to produce information on the police: Present and potential uses of the National Crime Victimization Survey. Special issue, *Justice Research and Policy* 4 (Fall): 61-70.

Maguire, Edward R. 2002a. Multiwave establishment surveys of police organizations. Special issue, *Justice Research and Policy* 4 (Fall): 39-60.

———. 2002b. *Organizational structure in American police agencies: Context, complexity, and control*. Albany, NY: SUNY Press.

Maguire, Edward R., and Charles M. Katz. 2002. Community policing, loose coupling, and sensemaking in American police agencies. *Justice Quarterly* 19 (3): 501-34.

Maguire, Edward R., and Stephen D. Mastrofski. 2000. Patterns of community policing in the United States. *Police Quarterly* 3 (1): 4-45.

Maguire, Edward R., and Rebecca Schulte-Murray. 2001. Issues and patterns in the comparative international study of police strength. *International Journal of Comparative Sociology* 42 (1-2): 75-100.

Maguire, Edward R., Y. Shin, J. Zhao, and K. D. Hassell. 2003. Structural change in large police agencies during the 1990s. *Policing: An International Journal of Police Strategies and Management* 26 (2): 251-75.

Maguire, Edward R., J. B. Snipes, C. D. Uchida, and M. Townsend. 1998. Counting cops: Estimating the number of police officers and police agencies in the United States. *Policing: An International Journal of Police Strategies and Management* 21 (1): 97-120.

Maguire, Edward R., and Craig D. Uchida. 2000. Measurement and explanation in the comparative study of police organizations. In *Measurement and analysis of crime and justice*, edited by D. Duffee. Washington, DC: National Institute of Justice.

Maguire, Edward R., and William Wells. 2002. Community policing as communication reform. In *Law enforcement, communication, and community*, edited by Howard Giles, 33-66. Amsterdam: John Benjamins.

Manning, Peter K. 2003. *Policing contingencies*. Chicago: University of Chicago Press.

Massachusetts Statistical Analysis Center. 2002. Fact sheet, the Massachusetts Local Law Enforcement Administrative Survey. *Terrorism*. Boston: Author.

Mastrofski, Stephen D., and R. Richard Ritti. 2000. Making sense of community policing: A theoretical perspective. *Police Practice and Research* 1 (2): 183-210.

McCrary, Justin. 2003. The effect of court-ordered hiring quotas on the composition and quality of police. Paper presented at the 25th Annual APPAM Research Conference, Washington, DC, November 6.

McCulloch, J. 2001. *Blue army: Paramilitary policing in Australia*. Carlton South, Victoria, Australia: Melbourne University Press.

McEwen, Tom. 1996. *National data collection on police use of force*. Washington, DC: U.S. Department of Justice, Bureau of Justice Statistics, and National Institute of Justice.

Meehan, Albert J., and Michael Ponder. 2002. Race and place: The ecology of racial profiling African American motorists. *Justice Quarterly* 19 (3): 401-32.

Monkkonen, Eric. 1981. *Police in urban America: 1860-1920*. Cambridge, UK: Cambridge University Press.

Moore, Mark H., Malcolm Sparrow, and William Spelman. 1996. Innovations in policing: From production lines to job shops. In *Innovation in American government: Challenges, opportunities, and dilemmas*, edited by A. A. Altshuler and R. D. Behn, 274-98. Washington, DC: Brookings Institution.

Moore, Mark H., William Spelman, and Rebecca Young. 1992. Innovations in policing: A test of three different methodologies for identifying important innovations in a substantive field. Unpublished manuscript, Harvard University, John F. Kennedy School of Government.

Moore, Mark H., David Thacher, Francis X. Hartman, Catherine Coles, and Peter Sheingold. 1999. *Case studies of the transformation of police departments: A cross-site analysis*. Working Paper 99-05-16, Harvard University.

Murphy, Gerard R., and Martha R. Plotkin. 2003. *Protecting your community from terrorism: The strategies for local law enforcement series*. Vol. 1: Local-federal partnerships. Washington, DC: Police Executive Research Forum.

National Center for Women and Policing. 2002. Equality denied: The status of women in policing: 2001. Arlington, VA: Author.

Ostrom, Elinor, Roger B. Parks, and Gordon P. Whitaker. 1973. Do we really want to consolidate urban police forces? A reappraisal of some old assertions. *Public Administration Review* 33:423-32.

———. 1978. *Patterns of metropolitan policing*. Cambridge, MA: Ballinger.

Owings, Chloe. 1925. *Women police: A study of the development and status of the women police movement*. New York: Fredrick H. Hitchcock.

Rashbaum, William K. 2002. Terror makes all the world a beat for New York police. *New York Times*, July 22.

Reaves, Brian A., and Matthew J. Hickman. 2002. *Police departments in large cities, 1990-2000*. Washington, DC: Bureau of Justice Statistics.

Richman, Daniel C. 2000. The changing boundaries between federal and local law enforcement. In vol. 2 of the National Institute of Justice 2000 series *Boundary changes in criminal justice organizations*, edited by Charles M. Friel, 81-111. Washington, DC: National Institute of Justice.

Riley, Kevin J., and Bruce Hoffman. 1995. *Domestic terrorism: A national assessment of state and local preparedness*. Santa Monica, CA: Rand.

Sherman, Lawrence W., and Barry D. Glick. 1984. *Quality of police arrest statistics*. Police Foundation Reports, no. 2 (August).

Sherman, Lawrence W., and The National Advisory Commission on Higher Education for Police Officers. 1978. *The quality of police education: A critical review with recommendations for improving programs in higher education*. San Francisco: Jossey-Bass.

Simon, Herbert. 1964. On the concept of organizational goal. *Administrative Science Quarterly* 9:1-22.

Stinchcombe, Arthur. 1965. Social structure and organizations. In *Handbook of organizations*, edited by James G. March, 142-93. Chicago: Rand-McNally.

Surette, Ray. 2001. Public information officers: The civilianization of a criminal justice profession. *Journal of Criminal Justice* 29 (2): 107-17.

Thacher, David. Forthcoming. Interorganizational partnerships as inchoate hierarchies: A case study of the community security initiative. *Administration and Society*.

Tucker, David J., Jitendra Singh, and Agnes Meinhard. 1990. Founding characteristics, imprinting, and organizational change. In *Organizational evolution: New directions*, edited by Jitendra Singh, 182-200. Newbury Park, CA: Sage.

Uchida, Craig D., and William R. King. 2002. Police employee data: Elements and validity. Special issue, *Justice Research and Policy* 4:11-20.

U.S. Conference of Mayors. 2002. *The cost of heightened security in American cities: A 192 city survey*. Washington, DC: Author.

U.S. Department of Justice. 2003. Attorney General John Ashcroft announces changes to anti-terrorism task forces. Press release, September 25.

Waddington, P. A. J. 1993. The case against paramilitarism considered. *British Journal of Criminology* 33 (3): 353-73.

Walker, Samuel. 1977. *A critical history of police reform*. Lexington, MA: Lexington Books.

Walker, Samuel, and Charles M. Katz. 1995. Less than meets the eye: Police department bias-crime units. *American Journal of Police* 14 (1): 29-47.

Ward, Richard H. 2000. The internationalization of criminal justice. In vol. 2 of the National Institute of Justice 2000 series *Boundary changes in criminal justice organizations*, edited by Charles M. Friel, 267-321. Washington, DC: National Institute of Justice.

Webber, Alan M. 1991. Crime and management: An interview With New York City Police Commissioner Lee P. Brown. *Harvard Business Review* 69 (May-June): 111-26.

Weber, Diane Cecilia. 1999. *Warrior cops: The ominous growth of paramilitarism in American police departments*. Cato Institute Briefing Paper 50. Washington, DC: Cato Institute.

Weisburd, David, Rosann Greenspan, Edwin E. Hamilton, Kellie Bryant, and Hubert Williams. 2001. *The abuse of police authority: A national study of issues and attitudes*. Washington, DC: Police Foundation.

Weisburd, David, Stephen Mastrofski, Ann Marie McNally, and Rosann Greenspan. 2001. Compstat and organizational change: Findings from a national survey. Report to the National Institute of Justice.

Wenger, Dennis, E. L. Quarantelli, and Russell R. Dynes. 1989. *Disaster analysis: Police and fire departments*. Newark: University of Delaware, Disaster Research Center.

Zhao, Jihong, and Nicholas Lovrich. 1998. Determinants of minority employment in American municipal police agencies: The representation of African American officers. *Journal of Criminal Justice* 26 (4): 267-77.

What Can Police Do to Reduce Crime, Disorder, and Fear?

By
DAVID WEISBURD
and
JOHN E. ECK

The authors review research on police effectiveness in reducing crime, disorder, and fear in the context of a typology of innovation in police practices. That typology emphasizes two dimensions: one concerning the *diversity of approaches*, and the other, the *level of focus*. The authors find that little evidence supports the standard model of policing—low on both of these dimensions. In contrast, research evidence does support continued investment in police innovations that call for greater focus and tailoring of police efforts, combined with an expansion of the tool box of policing beyond simple law enforcement. The strongest evidence of police effectiveness in reducing crime and disorder is found in the case of geographically focused police practices, such as hot-spots policing. Community policing practices are found to reduce fear of crime, but the authors do not find consistent evidence that community policing (when it is implemented without models of problem-oriented policing) affects either crime or disorder. A developing body of evidence points to the effectiveness of problem-oriented policing in reducing crime, disorder, and fear. More generally, the authors find that many policing practices applied broadly throughout the United States either have not been the subject of systematic research or have been examined in the context of research designs that do not allow practitioners or policy makers to draw very strong conclusions.

Keywords: police; evaluations; crime; disorder; hot spots; problem-oriented policing; community policing

The past decade has been the most innovative period in American policing. Such approaches as community policing, problem-oriented policing, hot-spots policing, and broken-windows policing either emerged in the 1990s or came to be widely adopted by police agencies at that time. The changes in American

David Weisburd is a professor of criminology at the Hebrew University Law School and a professor of criminology and criminal justice at the University of Maryland–College Park. He is also a senior fellow at the Police Foundation in Washington, D.C.

John E. Eck is a professor in the Division of Criminal Justice at the University of Cincinnati.

DOI: 10.1177/0002716203262548

policing were dramatic. From an institution known for its conservatism and resistance to change, policing suddenly stood out as a leader in criminal justice innovation. This new openness to innovation and widespread experimentation in new practices were part of a renewed confidence in American policing that could be found among not only police professionals but also scholars and the general public. While there is much debate over what caused the crime drop of the 1990s, many police executives, police scholars, and lay people looked to new policing practices as a primary explanation (Bratton 1998; Eck and Maguire 2000; Kelling and Sousa 2001).

At the same time that many in the United States touted the new policing as an explanation for improvements in community safety, many scholars and police professionals identified the dominant policing practices of earlier decades as wasteful and ineffective. This criticism of the "standard model" of policing was part of a more general critique of the criminal justice system that emerged as early as the mid-1970s (e.g., see Martinson 1974). As in other parts of the criminal justice system, a series of studies seemed to suggest that such standard practices as random preventive patrol or rapid response to police calls for service had little impact on crime or on fear of crime in American communities (e.g., see Kelling et al. 1974; Spelman and Brown 1981). By the 1990s, the assumption that police practices were ineffective in combating crime was widespread (Bayley 1994; Gottfredson and Hirschi 1990), a factor that certainly helped to spawn rapid police innovation at that time.

In this article, we revisit the central assumptions that have underlain recent American police innovation. Does the research evidence support the view that standard models of policing are ineffective in combating crime and disorder? Do elements of the standard model deserve more careful study before they are abandoned as methods of reducing crime or disorder? Do recent police innovations hold greater promise of increasing community safety, or does the research evidence suggest that they are popular but actually ineffective? What lessons can we draw from research about police innovation in reducing crime, disorder, and fear over the last two decades? Does such research lead to a more general set of recommendations for American policing or for police researchers?

Our article examines these questions in the context of a review of the research evidence about what works in policing. Our focus is on specific elements of community safety: crime, fear, and disorder. We begin by developing a typology of police practices that is used in our article to organize and assess the evidence about

NOTE: Our review of police practices in this paper derives from a subcommittee report on police effectiveness that was part of a larger examination of police research and practices undertaken by the National Academy of Sciences and chaired by Wesley G. Skogan. We cochaired the subcommittee charged with police effectiveness which also included David Bayley, Ruth Peterson, and Lawrence Sherman. While we draw heavily from that review, our analysis also extends the critique and represents our interpretation of the findings. Our review has benefited much from the thoughtful comments of Carol Petrie and Kathleen Frydl of the National Academy of Sciences. We also want to thank Nancy Morris and Sue-Ming Yang for their help in preparation of this paper.

police effectiveness. We then turn to a discussion of how that evidence was evaluated and assessed. What criteria did we use for distinguishing the value of studies for coming to conclusions about the effectiveness of police practices? How did we decide when the evidence was persuasive enough to draw more general statements about specific programs or strategies? Our review of the evidence follows. Our approach is to identify what existing studies say about the effects of core police practices. Having summarized the research literature in this way, we conclude with a more general synthesis of the evidence reviewed and a discussion of its implications for police practice and research on policing.

The Standard Model of Policing and Recent Police Innovation: A Typology of Police Practices

Over the past three decades, scholars have increasingly criticized what has come to be considered the standard model of police practices (Bayley 1994; Goldstein 1990; Visher and Weisburd 1998). This model relies generally on a "one-size-fits-all" application of reactive strategies to suppress crime and continues to be the dominant form of police practices in the United States. The standard model is based on the assumption that generic strategies for crime reduction can be applied throughout a jurisdiction regardless of the level of crime, the nature of crime, or other variations. Such strategies as increasing the size of police agencies, random patrol across all parts of the community, rapid response to calls for service, generally applied follow-up investigations, and generally applied intensive enforcement and arrest policies are all examples of this standard model of policing.

Because the standard model seeks to provide a generalized level of police service, it has often been criticized as focused more on the means of policing or the resources that police bring to bear than on the effectiveness of policing in reducing crime, disorder, or fear (Goldstein 1979). Accordingly, in the application of preventive patrol in a city, police agencies following the standard model will often measure success in terms of whether a certain number of patrol cars are on the street at certain times. In agencies that seek to reduce police response times to citizen calls for service, improvements in the average time of response often become a primary measure of police agency success. In this sense, using the standard model can lead police agencies to become more concerned with how police services are allocated than whether they have an impact on public safety.

This model has also been criticized because of its reliance on the traditional law enforcement powers of police in preventing crime (Goldstein 1987). Police agencies relying upon the standard model generally employ a limited range of approaches, overwhelmingly oriented toward enforcement, and make relatively little use of institutions outside of policing (with the notable exception of other parts of the criminal justice system). "Enforcing the law" is a central element of the standard model of policing, suggesting that the main tools available to the police, or legitimate for their use, are found in their law enforcement powers. It is no coinci-

FIGURE 1
DIMENSIONS OF POLICING STRATEGIES

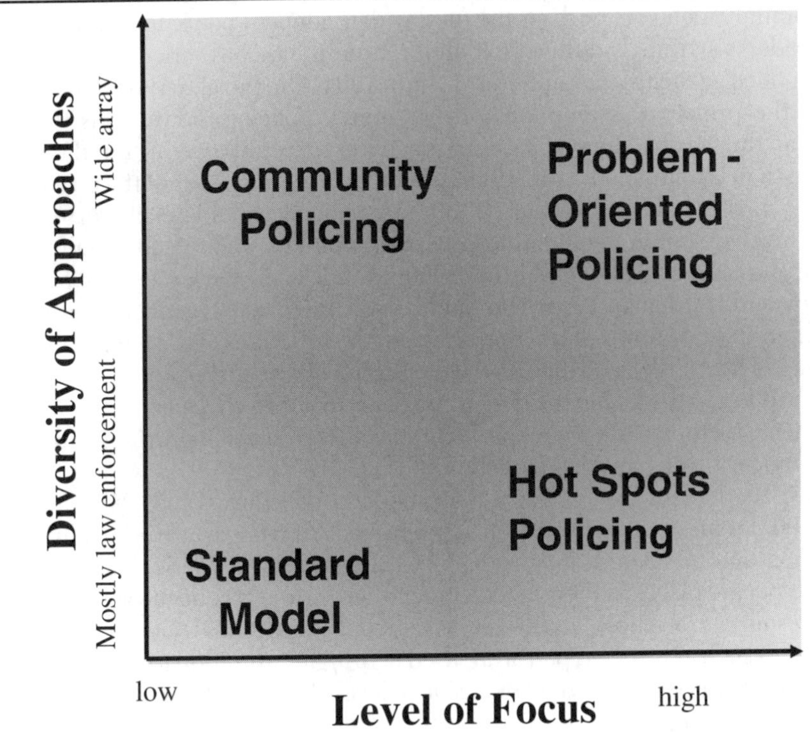

dence that police departments are commonly referred to as "law enforcement agencies." In the standard model of policing, the threat of arrest and punishment forms the core of police practices in preventing and controlling crime.

Recent innovations in policing have tended to expand beyond the standard model of policing along two dimensions. Figure 1 depicts this relationship. The vertical axis of the figure, *diversity of approaches*, represents the content of the practices employed. Strategies that rely primarily on traditional law enforcement are low on this dimension. The horizontal axis, *level of focus*, represents the extent of focus or targeting of police activities. Strategies that are generalized and applied uniformly across places or offenders score low on this dimension. Innovations in policing over the last decade have moved outward along one or both of these dimensions. This point can be illustrated in terms of three of the dominant trends in innovation over the last two decades: community policing, hot-spots policing, and problem-oriented policing. We note at the outset that in emphasizing specific components of these innovations, we are trying to illustrate our typology, although in practice, the boundaries between approaches are seldom clear and often overlap in their applications in real police settings. We will discuss this point in fuller detail in our examination of specific strategies later in our article.

Community policing, perhaps the most widely adopted police innovation of the last decade, is extremely difficult to define: Its definition has varied over time and among police agencies (Eck and Rosenbaum 1994; Greene and Mastrofski 1988). One of the principal assumptions of community policing, however, is that the police can draw from a much broader array of resources in carrying out the police function than is found in the traditional law enforcement powers of the police. For example, most scholars agree that community policing should entail greater community involvement in the definition of crime problems and in police activities to prevent and control crime (Goldstein 1990; Skolnick and Bayley 1986; Weisburd, McElroy, and Hardyman 1988). Community policing suggests a reliance on a more community-based crime control that draws on the resources of the public as well as the police. Thus, it is placed high on the dimension of diversity of approaches in our typology. It lies to the left on the dimension of level of focus because when community policing is employed without problem solving (see later), it provides a common set of services throughout a jurisdiction.

Hot-spots policing (Braga 2001; Sherman and Weisburd 1995; Weisburd and Braga 2003) represents an important new approach to crime control that illustrates innovation on our second dimension, level of focus. It demands that the police identify specific places in their jurisdictions where crime is concentrated and then focus resources at those locations. When only traditional law enforcement approaches such as directed patrol are used in bringing attention to such hot spots, hot-spots policing is high on the dimension of level of focus but low on that of diversity of approaches.

Problem-oriented policing (Goldstein 1990) expands beyond the standard model in terms of both focus and the tools that are used. Problem-oriented policing, as its name suggests, calls for the police to focus on specific problems and to fit their strategies to the problems identified. It thus departs from the generalized one-size-fits-all approach of the standard model and calls for tailor-made and focused police practices. But in defining those practices, problem-oriented policing also demands that the police look beyond their traditional law enforcement powers and draw upon a host of other possible methods for addressing the problems they define. In problem-oriented policing, the tool box of policing might include community resources or the powers of other government agencies.

Evaluating the Evidence

Before we turn to what our review tells us about the standard model of policing and recent police innovation, it is important to lay out the criteria we used in assessing the evidence we reviewed. There is no hard rule for determining when studies provide more reliable or valid results, or any clear line to indicate when there is enough evidence to come to an unambiguous conclusion. Nonetheless, social scientists generally agree on some basic guidelines for assessing the strength of the evidence available. Perhaps the most widely agreed-upon criterion relates to what is often referred to as internal validity (Sherman et al. 2002; Weisburd, Lum, and Petrosino 2001). Research designs that allow the researcher to make a stronger link between the interventions or programs examined and the outcomes observed are generally considered to provide more valid evidence than are designs that provide for a more ambiguous connection between cause and effect. In formal terms, the former designs are considered to have higher internal validity. In reviewing studies, we used internal validity as a primary criterion for assessing the strength of the evidence provided.

Using the standard model can lead police agencies to become more concerned with how police services are allocated than whether they have an impact on public safety.

Researchers generally agree that randomized experiments provide a higher level of internal validity than do nonexperimental studies (see, e.g., Boruch, Victor, and Cecil 2000; Campbell and Boruch 1975; Cook and Campbell 1979; Farrington 1983; Feder and Boruch 2000; Shadish, Cook, and Campbell 2002; Weisburd 2003). In randomized experiments, people or places are randomly assigned to treatment and control or comparison groups. This means that all causes, except treatment itself, can be assumed to be equally distributed among the groups. Accordingly, if an effect for an intervention is found, the researcher can conclude with confidence that the cause was the intervention itself and not some other confounding factor.

Another class of studies, referred to here as quasi-experiments, typically allow for less confidence in making a link between the programs or strategies examined and the outcomes observed (Cook and Campbell 1979). Quasi-experiments generally fall into three classes. In the first class, the study compares an "experimental" group with a control or comparison group, but the subjects of the study are not randomly assigned to the categories. In the second class of quasi-experiments, a long series of observations is made before the treatment, and another long series of observations is made after the treatment. The third class of quasi-experiments combines the use of a control group with time-series data. This latter approach is generally seen to provide the strongest conclusions in quasi-experiment research.

Quasi-experimental designs are assumed to have a lower level of internal validity than are randomized experimental studies, however, because the researcher can never be certain that the comparison conditions are truly equivalent.

Finally, studies that rely only on statistical controls—generally termed *nonexperimental* or *correlational* designs—are often seen to lead to the weakest level of internal validity (Cook and Campbell 1979; Sherman et al. 1997). In nonexperimental research, neither researchers nor policy makers intentionally vary treatments to test for outcomes. Rather, researchers observe natural variation in outcomes and examine the relationships between that variation and police practices. For example, when trying to determine if police staffing levels influence crime, researchers might examine the relationship between staffing levels and crime rates across cities. The difficulty with this approach is apparent: other factors may influence crime and may also be confounded with staffing levels. To address this concern, researchers attempt to control for these other factors statistically. It is generally agreed, however, that causes unknown or unmeasured by the researcher are likely to be a serious threat to the internal validity of these correlational studies (Feder and Boruch 2000; Kunz and Oxman 1998; Pedhazer 1982).

In our review, we rely strongly on these general assessments of the ability of research to make statements of high internal validity regarding the practices evaluated. However, we also recognize that other criteria are important in assessing the strength of research. While academics generally recognize that randomized experiments have higher internal validity than nonrandomized studies, a number of scholars have suggested the results of randomized field experiments can be compromised by the difficulty of implementing such designs (Cornish and Clarke 1972; Eck 2002; Pawson and Tilley 1997). Accordingly, in assessing the evidence, we also took into account the integrity of the implementation of the research design.

Even if a researcher can make a very strong link between the practices examined in a specific study and their influence on crime, disorder, or fear, if one cannot make inferences from that study to other jurisdictions or police practices more generally, then the findings will not be very useful. Moreover, most social scientists agree that caution should be used in drawing strong policy conclusions from a single study, no matter how well designed (Manski 2003; Weisburd and Taxman 2000). For these reasons, we took into account such additional factors related to our ability to generalize from study findings in drawing our conclusions.

What Works in Policing Crime, Disorder, and Fear of Crime

Below, we review the evidence on what works in policing using the criteria outlined above. In organizing our review, we rely on our typology of police practices and thus divide our discussion into four sections, representing the four broad types of police approaches suggested in our discussion of Figure 1. For each type, we begin with a general proposition that summarizes what the research literature tells us about the effectiveness of that approach in reducing crime, disorder, and fear of crime.

Proposition 1: The standard model of policing has relied on the uniform provision of police resources and the law enforcement powers of the police to prevent crime and disorder across a wide array of crimes and across all parts of the jurisdictions that police serve. Despite the continued reliance of many police agencies on these standard practices, little evidence exists that such approaches are effective in controlling crime and disorder or in reducing fear of crime.

In our review of the standard model of policing, we identified five broad strategies that have been the focus of systematic research over the last three decades: (1) increasing the size of police agencies; (2) random patrol across all parts of the community; (3) rapid response to calls for service; (4) generalized investigations of crime; and (5) generally applied intensive enforcement and arrest policies.

Increasing the size of police agencies

Evidence from case studies in which police have suddenly left duty (e.g., police strikes) shows that the absence of police is likely to lead to an increase in crime (Sherman and Eck 2002). While these studies are generally not very strong in their design, their conclusions are consistent. But the finding that removing all police will lead to more crime does not answer the primary question that most scholars and policy makers are concerned with—that is, whether marginal increases in the number of police officers will lead to reductions in crime, disorder, or fear. The evidence in this case is contradictory and the study designs generally cannot distinguish between the effects of police strength and the factors that ordinarily are associated with police hiring such as changes in tactics or organizational structures. Most studies have concluded that variations in police strength over time do not affect crime rates (Chamlin and Langworthy 1996; Eck and Maguire 2000; Niskanen 1994; van Tulder 1992). However, two recent studies using more sophisticated statistical designs suggest that marginal increases in the number of police are related to decreases in crime rates (Levitt 1997; Marvell and Moody 1996).

Random patrol across all parts of the community

Random preventive patrol across police jurisdictions has continued to be one of the most enduring of standard police practices. Despite the continued use of random preventive patrol by many police agencies, the evidence supporting this practice is very weak, and the studies reviewed are more than a quarter century old. Two studies, both using weaker quasi-experimental designs, suggest that random preventive patrol can have an impact on crime (Dahmann 1975; Press 1971). A much larger scale and more persuasive evaluation of preventive patrol in Kansas City found that the standard practice of preventive patrol does not reduce crime, disorder, or fear of crime (Kelling et al. 1974). However, while this is a landmark study, the validity of its conclusions has also been criticized because of methodological flaws (Larson and Cahn 1985; Minneapolis Medical Research Foundation 1976; Sherman and Weisburd 1995).

Rapid response to calls for service

A third component of the standard model of policing, rapid response to calls for service, has also not been shown to reduce crime or even to lead to increased chances of arrest in most situations. The crime-reduction assumption behind rapid response is that if the police get to crime scenes rapidly, they will apprehend offenders, thus providing a general deterrent against crime. No studies have been done of the direct effects of this strategy on disorder or fear of crime. The best evidence concerning the effectiveness of rapid response comes from two studies conducted in the late 1970s (Kansas City Police Department 1977; Spelman and Brown 1981). Evidence from five cities examined in these two studies consistently shows that most crimes (about 75 percent at the time of the studies) are discovered some time after they have been committed. Accordingly, offenders in such cases have had plenty of time to escape. For the minority of crimes in which the offender and the victim have some type of contact, citizen delay in calling the police blunts whatever effect a marginal improvement in response time might provide.

Generally applied follow-up investigations of crimes

No studies to date examine the direct impact of generalized improvements in police investigation techniques on crime, disorder, or fear of crime. Nonetheless, it has been assumed that an increase in the likelihood of a crime's being solved through arrest would lead to a deterrence or incapacitation effect. Research suggests, however, that the single most important factor leading to arrest is the presence of witnesses or physical evidence (Greenwood, Chaiken, and Petersilia 1977; Eck 1983)—factors that are not under the control of the police and are difficult to manipulate through improvements in investigative approaches.

Generally applied intensive enforcement and arrests

Tough law enforcement strategies have long been a staple of police crime-fighting. We reviewed three broad areas of intensive enforcement within the standard model: disorder policing, generalized field interrogations and traffic enforcement, and mandatory and preferred arrest policies in domestic violence.

Disorder policing. The model of intensive enforcement applied broadly to incivilities and other types of disorder has been described recently as "broken windows policing" (Kelling and Coles 1996; Kelling and Sousa 2001) or "zero tolerance policing" (Bowling 1999; Cordner 1998; Dennis and Mallon 1998; Manning 2001). While the common perception is that enforcement strategies (primarily arrest) applied broadly against offenders committing minor offenses lead to reductions in serious crime, research does not provide strong support for this proposition. For example, studies in seven cities that were summarized by Skogan (1990, 1992) found no evidence that intensive enforcement reduced disorder, which went up despite the special projects that were being evaluated. More recent claims of the effects of disorder policing based on crime declines in New York City have also been strongly challenged because they are confounded with either other organizational changes in New York (notably Compstat; see Eck and Maguire 2000), other changes such as the crack epidemic (see Bowling 1999; Blumstein 1995), or more general crime trends (Eck and Maguire 2000). One correlational study by Kelling and Sousa (2001) found a direct link between misdemeanor arrests and more serious crime in New York, although limitations in the data available raise questions about the validity of these conclusions.

Generalized field interrogations and traffic enforcement. Limited evidence supports the effectiveness of field interrogations in reducing specific types of crime, though the number of studies available is small and the findings are mixed. One strong quasi-experimental study (Boydstun 1975) found that disorder crime decreased when field interrogations were introduced in a police district. Whitaker et al. (1985) report similar findings in a correlational study of crime and the police in sixty neighborhoods in Tampa, Florida; St. Louis, Missouri; and Rochester, New York. Researchers have also investigated the effects of field interrogations by examining variations in the intensity of traffic enforcement. Two correlational studies suggest that such interventions do reduce specific types of crime (Sampson and Cohen 1988; J. Q. Wilson and Boland 1979). However, the causal link between enforcement and crime in these studies is uncertain. In a more direct investigation of the relationship between traffic stops and crime, Weiss and Freels (1996) compared a treatment area in which traffic stops were increased with a matched control area. They found no significant differences in reported crime for the two areas.

Mandatory arrest policies for domestic violence. Mandatory arrest in misdemeanor cases of domestic violence is now required by law in many states. Consistent with the standard model of policing, these laws apply to all cities in a state, in all areas of the cities, for all kinds of offenders and situations. Research and public interest in mandatory arrest policies for domestic violence was encouraged by an important experimental study in Minneapolis, Minnesota (Sherman and Berk 1984a, 1984b), which found reductions in repeat offending among offenders who were arrested as opposed to those who were counseled or separated from their partners. This study led to a series of replications supported by the National Institute of Justice. These experiments found deterrent effects of arrest in two cities and no effect of arrest in three other cities (Berk et al. 1992; Dunford 1990; Dunford, Huizinga, and Elliot 1990; Hirschel and Hutchinson 1992; Pate and Hamilton 1992; Sherman et al. 1991), suggesting that the effects of arrest will vary by city, neighborhood, and offender characteristics (see also Sherman 1992; Maxwell, Garner, and Fagan 2001, 2002).

Proposition 2: Over the past two decades, there has been a major investment on the part of the police and the public in community policing. Because community policing involves so many different tactics, its effect as a general strategy cannot be evaluated. Overall, the evidence does not provide strong support for the position that community policing approaches impact strongly on crime or disorder. Stronger support is found for the ability of community policing tactics to reduce fear of crime.

Police practices associated with community policing have been particularly broad, and the strategies associated with community policing have sometimes changed over time. Foot patrol, for example, was considered an important element of community policing in the 1980s but has not been a core component of more recent community policing programs. Consequently, it is often difficult to determine if researchers studying community policing in different agencies at different times are studying the same phenomena. One recent correlational study that

The research available suggests that when the police partner more generally with the public, levels of citizen fear will decline.

attempts to assess the overall impact of federal government investment for community policing found a positive crime control effect of "hiring and innovative grant programs" (Zhao, Scheider, and Thurman 2002); however, a recent review of this work by the General Accounting Office (2003) has raised strong questions regarding the validity of the findings.

Studies do not support the view that community meetings (Wycoff and Skogan 1993), neighborhood watch (Rosenbaum 1989), storefront offices (Skogan 1990; Uchida, Forst, and Annan 1992), or newsletters (Pate and Annan 1989) reduce crime, although Skogan and Hartnett (1995) found that such tactics reduce community perceptions of disorder. Door-to-door visits have been found to reduce both crime (see Sherman 1997) and disorder (Skogan 1992). Simply providing information about crime to the public, however, does not have crime prevention benefits (Sherman 1997).

As noted above, foot patrol was an important component of early community policing efforts. An early uncontrolled evaluation of foot patrol in Flint, Michigan, concluded that foot patrol reduced reported crime (Trojanowicz 1986). However, Bowers and Hirsch (1987) found no discernable reduction in crime or disorder due to foot patrols in Boston. A more rigorous evaluation of foot patrol in Newark also found that it did not reduce criminal victimizations (Police Foundation 1981). Nonetheless, the same study found that foot patrol reduced residents' fear of crime.

Additional evidence shows that community policing lowers the community's level of fear when programs are focused on increasing community-police interaction. A series of quasi-experimental studies demonstrate that policing strategies characterized by more direct involvement of police and citizens, such as citizen contract patrol, police community stations, and coordinated community policing, have a negative effect on fear of crime among individuals and on individual level of concern about crime in the neighborhood (Brown and Wycoff 1987; Pate and Skogan 1985; Wycoff and Skogan 1986).

An aspect of community policing that has only recently received systematic research attention concerns the influences of police officer behavior toward citizens. Citizen noncompliance with requests from police officers can be considered a form of disorder. Does officer demeanor influence citizen compliance? Based on systematic observations of police-citizen encounters in three cities, researchers found that when officers were disrespectful toward citizens, citizens were less likely to comply with their requests (Mastrofski, Snipes, and Supina 1996; McCluskey, Mastrofski, and Parks 1999).

Proposition 3: There has been increasing interest over the past two decades in police practices that target very specific types of criminals and crime places. In particular, policing crime hot spots has become a common police strategy for addressing public safety problems. While only weak evidence suggests the effectiveness of targeting specific types of offenders, a strong body of evidence suggests that taking a focused geographic approach to crime problems can increase policing effectiveness in reducing crime and disorder.

While the standard model of policing suggests that police activities should be spread in a highly uniform pattern across urban communities and applied uniformly across the individuals subject to police attention, a growing number of police practices focus on allocating police resources in a focused way. We reviewed research in three specific areas: (1) police crackdowns, (2) hot-spots policing, and (3) focus on repeat offenders.

Police crackdowns

There is a long history of police crackdowns that target particularly troublesome locations or problems. Such tactics can be distinguished from more recent hot-spots policing approaches (described below) in that they are temporary concentrations of police resources that are not widely applied. Reviewing eighteen case studies, Sherman (1990) found strong evidence that crackdowns produce short-term deterrent effects, though research is not uniformly in support of this proposition (see, e.g., Annan and Skogan 1993; Barber 1969; Kleiman 1988). Sherman (1990) also reports that crackdowns did not lead to spatial displacement of crime to nearby areas in the majority of studies he reviewed.

Hot-spots policing

Although there is a long history of efforts to focus police patrols (Gay, Schell, and Schack 1977; O. W. Wilson 1967), the emergence of what is often termed *hot-spots policing* is generally traced to theoretical, empirical, and technological innovations in the 1980s and 1990s (Weisburd and Braga 2003; Braga 2001; Sherman and Weisburd 1995). A series of randomized field trials shows that policing that is focused on hot spots can result in meaningful reductions in crime and disorder (see Braga 2001).

The first of these, the Minneapolis Hot Spots Patrol Experiment (Sherman and Weisburd 1995), used computerized mapping of crime calls to identify 110 hot spots of roughly street-block length. Police patrol was doubled on average for the experimental sites over a ten-month period. The study found that the experimental as compared with the control hot spots experienced statistically significant reductions in crime calls and observed disorder. In another randomized experiment, the Kansas City Crack House Raids Experiment (Sherman and Rogan 1995a), crackdowns on drug locations were also found to lead to significant relative improvements in the experimental sites, although the effects (measured by citizen calls and offense reports) were modest and decayed in a short period. In yet another randomized trial, however, Eck and Wartell (1996) found that if the raids were immediately followed by police contacts with landlords, crime prevention benefits could be reinforced and would be sustained for long periods. More general crime and disorder effects are also reported in two randomized experiments that take a more tailored, problem-oriented approach to hot-spots policing (Braga et al. 1999; Weisburd and Green 1995a, because of their use of problem-solving approaches, we discuss them in more detail in the next section). Nonexperimental studies provide similar findings (see Hope 1994; Sherman and Rogan 1995b).

The effectiveness of the hot-spots policing approach has strong empirical support. Such approaches would be much less useful, however, if they simply displaced crime to other nearby places. While measurement of crime displacement is complex and a matter of debate (see, e.g., Weisburd and Green 1995b), a number of the studies reported above examined immediate geographic displacement. In the Jersey City Drug Market Analysis Experiment (Weisburd and Green 1995a), for example, displacement within two block areas around each hot spot was measured. No significant displacement of crime or disorder calls was found. Importantly, however, the investigators found that drug-related and public-morals calls actually declined in the displacement areas. This "diffusion of crime control benefits" (Clarke and Weisburd 1994) was also reported in the New Jersey Violent Crime Places experiment (Braga et al. 1999), the Beat Health study (Green Mazerolle and Roehl 1998), and the Kansas City Gun Project (Sherman and Rogan 1995b). In each of these studies, no displacement of crime was reported, and some improvement in the surrounding areas was found. Only Hope (1994) reports direct displacement of crime, although this occurred only in the area immediate to the treated locations and the displacement effect was much smaller overall than the crime prevention effect.

Focusing on repeat offenders

Two randomized trials suggest that covert investigation of high-risk, previously convicted offenders has a high yield in arrests and incarceration per officer per hour, relative to other investments of police resources (Abrahamse and Ebener 1991; Martin and Sherman 1986). It is important to note, however, that these evaluations examined the apprehension effectiveness of repeat-offender programs not the direct effects of such policies on crime. However, a recent study—The Boston Ceasefire Project (Kennedy, Braga, and Piehl 1996)—which used a multiagency and problem-oriented approach (referred to as a "pulling levers" strategy), found a reduction in gang-related killings as well as declines in other gun-related events when focusing on youth gangs (Kennedy et al. 2001).

Another method for identifying and apprehending repeat offenders is "antifencing," or property sting, operations, where police pose as receivers of stolen property and then arrest offenders who sell them stolen items (see Weiner, Chelst, and Hart 1984; Pennell 1979; Criminal Conspiracies Division 1979). Although a number of evaluations were conducted of this practice, most employed weak research designs, thus making it difficult to determine if such sting operations reduce crime. There seems to be a consensus that older and criminally active offenders are more likely to be apprehended using these tactics as compared with more traditional law enforcement practices, but they have not been shown to have an impact on crime (Langworthy 1989; Raub 1984; Weiner, Stephens, and Besachuk 1983).

Proposition 4: Problem-oriented policing emerged in the 1990s as a central police strategy for solving crime and disorder problems. There is a growing body of research evidence that problem-oriented policing is an effective approach for reducing crime, disorder, and fear.

Research is consistently supportive of the capability of problem solving to reduce crime and disorder. A number of quasi-experiments going back to the mid-1980s consistently demonstrates that problem solving can reduce fear of crime (Cordner 1986), violent and property crime (Eck and Spelman 1987), firearm-related youth homicide (Kennedy et al. 2001), and various forms of disorder, including prostitution and drug dealing (Capowich and Roehl 1994; Eck and Spelman 1987; Hope 1994). For example, a quasi-experiment in Jersey City, New Jersey, public housing complexes (Green Mazerolle et al. 2000) found that police problem-solving activities caused measurable declines in reported violent and property crime, although the results varied across the six housing complexes studied. In another example, Clarke and Goldstein (2002) report a reduction in thefts of appliances from new home construction sites following careful analysis of this problem by the Charlotte-Mecklenburg Police Department and the implementation of changes in building practices by construction firms.

Two experimental evaluations of applications of problem solving in hot spots suggest its effectiveness in reducing crime and disorder.[1] In a randomized trial with Jersey City violent crime hot spots, Braga et al. (1999) report reductions in property and violent crime in the treatment locations. While this study tested problem-solving approaches, it is important to note that focused police attention was brought only to the experimental locations. Accordingly, it is difficult to distinguish between the effects of bringing focused attention to hot spots and that of such focused efforts being developed using a problem-oriented approach. The Jersey City Drug Market Analysis Experiment (Weisburd and Green 1995a) provides more direct support for the added benefit of the application of problem-solving approaches in hot-spots policing. In that study, a similar number of narcotics

The effectiveness of the hot-spots policing approach has strong empirical support.

detectives were assigned to treatment and control hot spots. Weisburd and Green (1995a) compared the effectiveness of unsystematic, arrest-oriented enforcement based on ad hoc target selection (the control group) with a treatment strategy involving analysis of assigned drug hot spots, followed by site-specific enforcement and collaboration with landlords and local government regulatory agencies, and concluding with monitoring and maintenance for up to a week following the intervention. Compared with the control drug hot spots, the treatment drug hot spots fared better with regard to disorder and disorder-related crimes.

Evidence of the effectiveness of situational and opportunity-blocking strategies, while not necessarily police based, provides indirect support for the effectiveness of problem solving in reducing crime and disorder. Problem-oriented policing has been linked to routine activity theory, rational choice perspectives, and situational crime prevention (Clarke 1992a, 1992b; Eck and Spelman 1987). Recent reviews of prevention programs designed to block crime and disorder opportunities in small places find that most of the studies report reductions in target crime and disorder events (Eck 2002; Poyner 1981; Weisburd 1997). Furthermore, many of these efforts were the result of police problem-solving strategies. We note that many of the studies reviewed employed relatively weak designs (Clarke 1997; Weisburd 1997; Eck 2002).

TABLE 1
SYNTHESIS OF FINDINGS ON POLICE EFFECTIVENESS RESEARCH

Police Strategies That . . .	Are Unfocused	Are Focused
Apply a diverse array of approaches, including law enforcement sanctions.	**Inconsistent or weak evidence of effectiveness** Impersonal community policing, for example, newsletters **Weak to moderate evidence of effectiveness** Personal contacts in community policing Respectful police-citizen contacts Improving legitimacy of police Foot patrols (fear reduction)	**Moderate evidence of effectiveness** Problem-oriented policing **Strong evidence of effectiveness** Problem solving in hot spots
Rely almost exclusively on law enforcement sanctions	**Inconsistent or weak evidence of effectiveness** Adding more police General patrol Rapid response Follow-up investigations Undifferentiated arrest for domestic violence	**Inconsistent or weak evidence of effectiveness** Repeat offender investigations **Moderate to strong evidence of effectiveness** Focused intensive enforcement Hot-spots patrols

Discussion

We began our article with a series of questions about what we have learned from research on police effectiveness over the last three decades. In Table 1, we summarize our overall findings using the typology of police practices that we presented earlier. One of the most striking observations in our review is the relatively weak evidence there is in support of the standard model of policing—defined as low on both of our dimensions of innovation. While this approach remains in many police agencies the dominant model for combating crime and disorder, we find little empirical evidence for the position that generally applied tactics that are based primarily on the law enforcement powers of the police are effective. Whether the strategy examined was generalized preventive patrol, efforts to reduce response time to citizen calls, increases in numbers of police officers, or the introduction of generalized follow-up investigations or undifferentiated intensive enforcement activities, studies fail to show consistent or meaningful crime or disorder prevention benefits or evidence of reductions in citizen fear of crime.

Of course, a conclusion that there is not sufficient research evidence to support a policy does not necessarily mean that the policy is not effective. Given the continued importance of the standard model in American policing, it is surprising that so little substantive research has been conducted on many of its key components. Preventive patrol, for example, remains a staple of American police tactics. Yet our knowledge about preventive patrol is based on just a few studies that are more than two decades old and that have been the subject of substantial criticism. Even in cases where a larger number of studies are available, like that of the effects of adding more police, the nonexperimental designs used for evaluating outcomes generally make it difficult to draw strong conclusions.

This raises a more general question about our ability to come to strong conclusions regarding central components of the standard model of policing. With the exception of mandatory arrest for domestic violence, the evidence we review is drawn from nonexperimental evaluations. These studies are generally confounded in one way or another by threats to the validity of the findings presented. Indeed, many of the studies in such areas as the effects of police hiring are correlational studies using existing data from official sources. Some economists have argued that the use of econometric statistical designs can provide a level of confidence that is almost as high as randomized experiments (Heckman and Smith 1995). We think that this confidence is not warranted in police studies primarily because of the lack of very strong theoretical models for understanding policing outcomes and the questions of validity and reliability that can be raised about official police data. But what does this mean for our ability to come to strong conclusions about police practices that are difficult to evaluate using randomized designs, such as increasing the numbers of police or decreasing response time?

A simple answer to this question is to argue that our task is to improve our methods and data over time with the goal of improving the validity of our findings. In this regard, some recent research on police strength has tried to advance methods in ways likely to improve on prior conclusions (e.g., see Levitt 1997). We think this approach is important for coming to strong conclusions not only about the effectiveness of the standard model of policing but also about recent police innovation. But, more generally, we think experimental methods can be applied much more broadly in this area, as in other areas of policing. For example, we see no reason why the addition of police officers in federal government programs that offer financial assistance to local police agencies could not be implemented experimentally. While the use of experimental methods might be controversial in such cases, the fact that we do not know whether marginal increases in police strength are effective at reducing crime, disorder, or fear suggests the importance and legitimacy of such methods.

While we have little evidence indicating the effectiveness of standard models of policing in reducing, crime, disorder, or fear of crime, the strongest evidence of police effectiveness in our review is found in the cell of our table that represents focused policing efforts. Studies that focused police resources on crime hot spots provide the strongest collective evidence of police effectiveness that is now available. A series of randomized experimental studies suggests that hot-spots policing is effective in reducing crime and disorder and can achieve these reductions without significant displacement of crime control benefits. Indeed, the research evidence suggests that the diffusion of crime control benefits to areas surrounding treated hot spots is stronger than any displacement outcome.

The two remaining cells of the table indicate the promise of new directions for policing in the United States; however, they also illustrate once more the tendency for widely adopted police practices to escape systematic or high-quality investigation. Community policing has become one of the most widely implemented approaches in American policing and has received unprecedented federal government support in the creation of the Office of Community Oriented Policing Services and its grant program for police agencies. Yet in reviewing existing studies, we could find no consistent research agenda that would allow us to assess with strong confidence the effectiveness of community policing. Given the importance of community policing, we were surprised that more systematic study was not available. As in the case of many components of the standard model, research designs of the studies we examined were often weak, and we found no randomized experiments evaluating community policing approaches.

While the evidence available does not allow for definitive conclusions regarding community policing strategies, we do not find consistent evidence that community policing (when it is implemented without problem-oriented policing) affects either crime or disorder. However, the research available suggests that when the police partner more generally with the public, levels of citizen fear will decline. Moreover, growing evidence demonstrates that when the police are able to gain wider legitimacy among citizens and offenders, the likelihood of offending will be reduced.

There is greater and more consistent evidence that focused strategies drawing on a wide array of non–law-enforcement tactics can be effective in reducing crime and disorder. These strategies, found in the upper right of the table, may be classed more generally within the model of problem-oriented policing. While many problem-oriented policing programs employ traditional law enforcement practices, many also draw on a wider group of strategies and approaches. The research available suggests that such tools can be effective when they are combined with a tactical philosophy that emphasizes the tailoring of policing practices to the specific characteristics of the problems or places that are the focus of intervention. While the primary evidence in support of the effectiveness of problem-oriented policing is nonexperimental, initial experimental studies in this area confirm the effectiveness of problem-solving approaches and suggest that the expansion of the toolbox of policing practices in combination with greater focus can increase effectiveness overall.

Conclusions

Reviewing the broad array of research on police effectiveness in reducing crime, disorder, and fear rather than focusing in on any particular approach or tactic provides an opportunity to consider policing research in context and to assess what the cumulative body of knowledge we have suggests for policing practices in the coming decades. Perhaps the most disturbing conclusion of our review is that knowledge of many of the core practices of American policing remains uncertain.

Many tactics that are applied broadly throughout the United States have not been the subject of systematic police research nor have they been examined in the context of research designs that allow practitioners or policy makers to draw very strong conclusions. We think this fact is particularly troubling when considering the vast public expenditures on such strategies and the implications of their effectiveness for public safety. American police research must become more systematic and more experimental if it is to provide solid answers to important questions of practice and policy.

But what should the police do given existing knowledge about police effectiveness? Police practice has been centered on standard strategies that rely primarily on the coercive powers of the police. There is little evidence to suggest that this standard model of policing will lead to communities that feel and are safer. While police agencies may support such approaches for other reasons, there is not consistent scientific evidence that such tactics lead to crime or disorder control or to reductions in fear. In contrast, research evidence does support continued investment in police innovations that call for greater focus and tailoring of police efforts and for the expansion of the toolbox of policing beyond simple law enforcement. The strongest evidence is in regard to focus and surrounds such tactics as hot-spots policing. Police agencies now routinely rely on such approaches (Weisburd et al. 2001; Weisburd and Lum 2001), and the research suggests that such reliance is warranted. Should police agencies continue to encourage community- and problem-oriented policing? Our review suggests that community policing (when it is not combined with problem-oriented approaches) will make citizens feel safer but will not necessarily impact upon crime and disorder. In contrast, what is known about the effects of problem-oriented policing suggests its promise for reducing crime, disorder, and fear.

Note

1. An early experimental hot-spots study that tested problem solving at high crime-call addresses did not show a significant crime or disorder reduction impact (Buerger 1994; Sherman 1990). However, Buerger, Cohn, and Petrosino (1995) argue that there was insufficient dosage across study sites to produce any meaningful treatment impact.

References

Abrahamse, Allan F., and Patricia A. Ebener. 1991. An experimental evaluation of the Phoenix repeat offender program. *Justice Quarterly* 8 (2): 141-68.

Annan, Sampson O., and Wesley G. Skogan. 1993. *Drug enforcement in public housing: Signs of success in Denver.* Washington, DC: Police Foundation.

Barber, R. N. 1969. Prostitution and the increasing number of convictions for rape in Queensland. *Australian and New Zealand Journal of Criminology* 2 (3): 169-74.

Bayley, David H. 1994. *Police for the future.* New York: Oxford University Press.

Berk, Richard A., Alec Campbell, Ruth Klap, and Bruce Western. 1992. Bayesian analysis of the Colorado Springs spouse abuse experiment. *Journal of Criminal Law and Criminology* 83 (1): 170-200.

Blumstein, Alfred. 1995. Youth violence, guns and the illicit-drug industry. *Journal of Criminal Law and Criminality* 86:10-36.

Boruch, Robert, Timothy Victor, and Joe Cecil. 2000. Resolving ethical and legal problems in randomized studies. *Crime and Delinquency* 46 (3): 330-53.

Bowers, William, and Jon H. Hirsch. 1987. The impact of foot patrol staffing on crime and disorder in Boston: An unmet promise. *American Journal of Policing* 6 (1): 17-44.

Bowling, Benjamin. 1999. The rise and fall of New York murder. *British Journal of Criminology* 39 (4): 531-54.

Boydstun, John. 1975. *The San Diego field interrogation experiment*. Washington, DC: Police Foundation.

Braga, Anthony A. 2001. The effects of hot spots policing on crime. *The Annals of American Political and Social Science* 578:104-25.

Braga, Anthony A., David Weisburd, Elin J. Waring, Lorraine Green Mazerolle, William Spelman, and Francis Gajewski. 1999. Problem-oriented policing in violent crime/places: A randomized controlled experiment. *Criminology* 37 (3): 541-80.

Bratton, William J. 1998. Crime is down in New York City: Blame the police. In *Zero tolerance: Policing a free society*, edited by William J. Bratton and Norman Dennis. London: Institute of Economic Affairs Heath and Welfare Unit.

Brown, Lee P., and Mary Ann Wycoff. 1987. Policing Houston: Reducing fear and improving service. *Crime and Delinquency* 33:71-89.

Buerger, Michael E. 1994. The problems of problem-solving: Resistance, interdependencies, and conflicting interests. *American Journal of Police* 13 (3): 1-36.

Buerger, Michael E., Ellen G. Cohn, and Anthony J. Petrosino. 1995. Defining the "hot spots of crime": Operationalizing theoretical concepts for field research. In *Crime and place*, edited by John Eck and David Weisburd. Monsey, NY: Criminal Justice Press.

Campbell, Donald T., and Robert Boruch. 1975. Making the case for randomized assignment to treatments by considering the alternatives: Six ways in which quasi-experimental evaluations in compensatory education tend to underestimate effects. In *Evaluation and experiment: Some critical issues in assessing social programs*, edited by Carl A. Bennett and Arthur A. Lumsdaine. New York: Academic Press.

Capowich, George E., and Janice A. Roehl. 1994. Problem-oriented policing: Actions and effectiveness in San Diego. In *Community policing: Testing the promises*, edited by Dennis P. Rosenbaum. Thousand Oaks, CA: Sage.

Chamlin, Mitchell B., and Robert Langworthy. 1996. The police, crime, and economic theory: A replication and extension. *American Journal of Criminal Justice* 20 (2): 165-82.

Clarke, Ronald V. 1992a. Situational crime prevention: Theory and practice. *British Journal of Criminology* 20:136-47.

———. 1992b. *Situational crime prevention: Successful case studies*. Albany, NY: Harrow and Heston.

———. 1997. *Situational crime prevention: Successful case studies*. 92nd ed. New York: Harrow and Heston.

Clarke, Ronald V., and Herman Goldstein. 2002. Reducing theft at construction sites: Lessons from a problem-oriented project. In *Analysis for crime prevention*, edited by Nick Tilley. Monsey, NY: Criminal Justice Press.

Clarke, Ronald V., and David Weisburd. 1994. Diffusion of crime control benefits: Observations on the reverse of displacement. *Crime Prevention Studies* 2:165-84.

Cook, Thomas, and Donald Campbell. 1979. *Quasi-experimentation: Design and analysis issues*. Chicago: Rand McNally.

Cordner, Gary W. 1986. Fear of crime and the police: An evaluation of a fear-reduction strategy. *Journal of Police Science and Administration* 14 (3): 223-33.

———. 1998. Problem-oriented policing vs. zero-tolerance. In *Problem-oriented policing*, edited by Tara O'Connor Shelly and Anne C. Grant. Washington, DC: Police Executive Research Forum.

Cornish, Derek B., and Ronald V. Clarke. 1972. *Home office research studies, number 15: The controlled trial in institutional research: Paradigm or pitfall for penal evaluators?* London: Her Majesty's Stationery Office.

Criminal Conspiracies Division. 1979. *What happened: An examination of recently terminated anti-fencing operations—A special report to the administrator.* Washington, DC: Law Enforcement Assistance Administration, U.S. Department of Justice.

Dahmann, Judith S. 1975. *Examination of Police Patrol Effectiveness*. McLean, VA: Mitre Corporation.

Dennis, Norman, and Ray Mallon. 1998. Confident policing in Hartlepool. In *Zero tolerance: Policing a free society*, edited by William J. Bratton and Norman Dennis. London: Institute of Economic Affairs Heath and Welfare Unit.

Dunford, Franklin W. 1990. System-initiated warrants for suspects of misdemeanor domestic assault: A pilot study. *Justice Quarterly* 7 (1): 631-54.

Dunford, Franklin W., David Huizinga, and Delbert S. Elliot. 1990. Role of arrest in domestic assault: The Omaha police experiment. *Criminology* 28 (2): 183-206.

Eck, John E. 1983. *Solving crime: A study of the investigation of burglary and robbery*. Washington, DC: Police Executive Research Forum.

———. 2002. Preventing crime at places. In *Evidence-based crime prevention*, edited by Lawrence W. Sherman, David Farrington, Brandon Welsh, and Doris Layton MacKenzie, 241-94. New York: Routledge.

Eck, John E., and Edward Maguire. 2000. Have changes in policing reduced violent crime? An assessment of the evidence. In *The crime drop in America*, edited by Alfred Blumstein and Joel Wallman. New York: Cambridge University Press.

Eck, John E., and Dennis Rosenbaum. 1994. The new police order: Effectiveness, equity and efficiency in community policing. In *Community policing: Testing the promises*, edited by Dennis P. Rosenbaum. Thousand Oaks, CA: Sage.

Eck, John E., and William Spelman. 1987. *Problem solving: Problem oriented policing in Newport news*. Washington, DC: Police Executive Research Forum.

Eck, John E., and Julie Wartell. 1996. *Reducing crime and drug dealing by improving place management: A randomized experiment: Report to the San Diego Police Department*. Washington, DC: Crime Control Institute.

Farrington, David. 1983. Randomized studies in criminal justice. *Crime and justice: An annual review of research*, vol. 4, edited by Michael Tonry and Norval Morris. Chicago: University of Chicago Press.

Feder, Lynette, and Robert Boruch. 2000. The need for randomized experimental designs in criminal justice settings. *Crime and Delinquency* 46 (3): 291-94.

Gay, William G., Theodore H. Schell, and Stephen Schack. 1977. *Prescriptive package: Improving patrol productivity, volume I routine patrol*. Washington, DC: Office of Technology Transfer, Law Enforcement Assistance Administration.

General Accounting Office. 2003. *Technical assessment of Zhao and Thurman's 2001 Evaluation of the effects of COPS grants on crime*. Retrieved September 3, 2003, from http://www.gao.gov/new.items/d03867r.pdf.

Goldstein, Herman. 1979. Improving policing: A problem oriented approach. *Crime and Delinquency* 24:236-58.

———. 1987. Toward community-oriented policing: Potential, basic requirements and threshold questions. *Crime and Delinquency* 33 (1): 6-30.

———. 1990. *Problem-oriented policing*. New York: McGraw-Hill.

Gottfredson, Michael, and Travis Hirschi. 1990. *A general theory of crime*. Palo Alto, CA: Stanford University Press.

Greene, Jack R., and Stephen D. Mastrofski, eds. 1988. *Community policing: Rhetoric or reality*. New York: Praeger.

Green Mazerolle, Lorraine, Justin Ready, William Terrill, and Elin Waring. 2000. Problem-oriented policing in public housing: The Jersey City evaluation. *Justice Quarterly* 17 (1): 129-58.

Green Mazerolle, Lorraine, and Jan Roehl. 1998. *Civil remedies and crime prevention*. Munsey, NJ: Criminal Justice Press.

Greenwood, Peter W., Jan Chaiken, and Joan Petersilia. 1977. *The criminal investigation process*. Lexington, MA: D.C. Heath.

Heckman, James, and Jeffrey A. Smith. 1995. Assessing the case for social experimentation. *Journal of Economic Perspectives* 9 (2): 85-110.

Hirschel, David J., and Ira W. Hutchinson. 1992. Female spouse abuse and the police response: The Charlotte, North Carolina experiment. *Journal of Criminal Law and Criminology* 83 (1): 73-119.

Hope, Tim. 1994. Problem-oriented policing and drug market locations: Three case studies. In *Crime prevention studies*, vol. 2, edited by Ronald V. Clarke. Monsey, NY: Criminal Justice Press.

Kansas City Police Department. 1977. *Response time analysis*. Kansas City, MO: Kansas City Police Department.

Kelling, George, and Catherine M. Coles. 1996. *Fixing broken windows: Restoring order and reducing crime in our communities*. New York: Free Press.

Kelling, G., and W. H. Sousa Jr. 2001. *Do police matter? An analysis of the impact of New York City's Police Reforms Civic Report* 22. New York: Manhattan Institute for Policy Research.

Kelling, George, Tony Pate, Duane Dieckman, and Charles Brown. 1974. *The Kansas City preventive patrol experiment: Technical report*. Washington, DC: Police Foundation.

Kennedy, David M., Anthony A. Braga, and Anne Morrison Piehl. 1996. *Youth gun violence in Boston: Gun markets, serious youth offenders, and a use reduction strategy*. Boston, MA: John F. Kennedy School of Government, Harvard University.

Kennedy, David M., Anthony A. Braga, Anne Morrison Piehl, and Elin J. Waring. 2001. *Reducing gun violence: The Boston Gun Project's Operation Ceasefire*. Washington, DC: U.S. National Institute of Justice.

Kleiman, Mark. 1988. Crackdowns: The effects of intensive enforcement on retail heroin dealing. In *Street-level drug enforcement: Examining the issues*, edited by Marcia Chaiken. Washington, DC: National Institute of Justice.

Kunz, Regina, and Andrew Oxman. 1998. The unpredictability paradox: Review of empirical comparisons of randomized and non-randomized clinical trials. *British Medical Journal* 317:1185-90.

Langworthy, Robert H. 1989. Do stings control crime? An evaluation of a police fencing operation. *Justice Quarterly* 6 (1): 27-45.

Larson, Richard C., and Michael F. Cahn. 1985. *Synthesizing and extending the results of police patrols*. Washington, DC: U.S. Government Printing Office.

Levitt, Steven D. 1997. Using election cycles in police hiring to estimate the effect of police on crime. *American Economic Review* 87 (3): 270-90.

Manning, Peter K. 2001. Theorizing policing: The drama and myth of crime control in the NYPD. *Theoretical Criminology* 5 (3): 315-44.

Manski, Charles F. 2003. Credible research practices to inform drug law enforcement. *Criminology and Public Policy* 2 (3): 543-56.

Martin, Susan E., and Lawrence W. Sherman. 1986. Selective apprehension: A police strategy for repeat offenders. *Criminology* 24 (1): 155-73.

Martinson, Robert. 1974. What works? Questions and answers about prison reform. *Public Interest* 35:22-54.

Marvell, Thomas B., and Carlisle E. Moody. 1996. Specification problems, police levels, and crime rates. *Criminology* 34 (4): 609-46.

Mastrofski, Stephen D., Jeffrey B. Snipes, and Anne E. Supina. 1996. Compliance on demand: The public response to specific police requests. *Journal of Research in Crime and Delinquency* 3:269-305.

Maxwell, Christopher D., Joel D. Garner, and Jeffrey A. Fagan. 2001. *The effects of arrest on intimate partner violence: New evidence from the spouse assault replication program, research in Brief NCJ 188199*. Washington, DC: National Institute of Justice.

———. 2002. The preventive effects of arrest on intimate partner violence: Research, policy, and theory. *Criminology and Public Policy* 2 (1): 51-95.

McCluskey, John D., Stephen D. Mastrofski, and Roger B. Parks. 1999. To acquiesce or rebel: Predicting citizen compliance with police requests. *Police Quarterly* 2:389-416.

Minneapolis Medical Research Foundation, Inc. 1976. Critiques and commentaries on evaluation research activities—Russell Sage reports. *Evaluation* 3 (1-2): 115-38.

Niskanen, William. 1994. Crime, police, and root causes. *Policy Analysis* 218. Washington, DC: Cato Institute.

Pate, Anthony M., and Sampson O. Annan. 1989. *The Baltimore community policing experiment: Technical report*. Washington, DC: Police Foundation.

Pate, Anthony M., and Edwin E. Hamilton. 1992. Formal and informal deterrents to domestic violence: The Dade County spouse assault experiment. *American Sociological Review* 57:691-98.

Pate, Anthony M., and Wesley G. Skogan. 1985. *Coordinated community policing: The Newark experience. Technical report*. Washington, DC: Police Foundation.

Pawson, Ray, and Nick Tilley. 1997. *Realistic evaluation*. Beverly Hills, CA: Sage.

Pedhazur, Elazar J. 1982. *Multiple regression in behavioral research: Explanation and prediction*. New York: Hold, Rinehart and Winston.

Pennell, Susan. 1979. Fencing activity and police strategy. *Police Chief* (September): 71-75.

Police Foundation. 1981. *The Newark foot patrol experiment*. Washington, DC: Police Foundation.

Poyner, Barry. 1981. Crime prevention and the environment—Street attacks in city centres. *Police Research Bulletin* 37:10-18.

Press, S. James. 1971. *Some effects of an increase in police manpower in the 20th precinct of New York City*. New York: New York City Rand Institute.

Raub, Richard A. 1984. Effects of antifencing operations on encouraging crime. *Criminal Justice Review* 9 (2): 78-83.

Rosenbaum, Dennis. 1989. Community crime prevention: A review and synthesis of the literature. *Justice Quarterly* 5 (3): 323-95.

Sampson, Robert J., and Jacqueline Cohen. 1988. Deterrent effects of the police on crime: A replication and theoretical extension. *Law and Society Review* 22 (1): 163-89.

Shadish, William R, Thomas Cook, and Donald Campbell. 2002. *Experimental and quasi-experimental designs*. Boston: Houghton Mifflin.

Sherman, Lawrence W. 1990. Police crackdowns: Initial and residual deterrence. In *Crime and justice: A review of research*, vol. 12, edited by Michael Tonry and Norval Morris. Chicago: University of Chicago Press.

———. 1992. *Policing domestic violence: Experiments and dilemmas*. New York: Free Press.

———. 1997. Policing for prevention. In *Preventing crime: What works, what doesn't, what's promising—A report to the attorney general of the United States*, edited by Lawrence W. Sherman, Denise Gottfredson, Doris MacKenzie, John Eck, Peter Reuter, and Shawn Bushway. Washington, DC: United States Department of Justice, Office of Justice Programs.

Sherman, Lawrence W., and Richard A. Berk. 1984a. *Specific deterrent effects of arrest for domestic assault Minneapolis*. Washington, DC: National Institute of Justice.

———. 1984b. Specific deterrent effects of arrest for domestic assault. *American Sociological Review* 49 (2): 261-72.

Sherman, Lawrence W., and John E. Eck. 2002. Policing for prevention. In *Evidence based crime prevention*, edited by Lawrence W. Sherman, David Farrington, and Brandon Welsh. New York: Routledge.

Sherman, Lawrence W., David P. Farrington, Brandon C. Welsh, and Doris Layton MacKenzie. 2002. *Evidence-based crime prevention*. New York: Routledge.

Sherman, Lawrence W., Denise Gottfredson, Doris Layton MacKenzie, John E. Eck, Peter Reuter, and Shawn Bushway. 1997. *Preventing crime: What works, what doesn't, what's promising—A report to the attorney general of the United States*. Washington, DC: United States Department of Justice, Office of Justice Programs.

Sherman, Lawrence W., and Dennis P. Rogan. 1995a. Deterrent effects of police raids on crack houses: A randomized, controlled, experiment. *Justice Quarterly* 12 (4): 755-81.

———. 1995b. Effects of gun seizures on gun violence: "Hot spots" patrol in Kansas City. *Justice Quarterly* 12 (4): 673-93.

Sherman, Lawrence W., Janell D. Schmidt, Dennis P. Rogan, Patrick R. Gartin, Ellen G. Cohn, Dean J. Collins, and Anthony R. Bacich. 1991. From initial deterrence to long-term escalation: Short custody arrest for poverty ghetto domestic violence. *Criminology* 29 (4): 1101-30.

Sherman, Lawrence W., and David Weisburd. 1995. General deterrent effects of police patrol in crime "hot spots:" A randomized, controlled trial. *Justice Quarterly* 12 (4): 625-48.

Skogan, Wesley G. 1990. *Disorder and decline*. New York: Free Press.

———. 1992. *Impact of policing on social disorder: Summary of findings*. Washington, DC: U.S. Department of Justice, Office of Justice Programs.

Skogan, Wesley G., and Susan M. Hartnett. 1995. *Community policing Chicago style: Year two*. Chicago: Illinois Criminal Justice Information Authority.

Skolnick, Jerome H., and David H. Bayley. 1986. *The new blue line: Police innovation in six American cities*. New York: Free Press.

Spelman, William, and Dale K. Brown. 1981. *Calling the police: A replication of the citizen reporting component of the Kansas City response time analysis*. Washington, DC: Police Executive Research Forum.

Trojanowicz, Robert. 1986. Evaluating a neighborhood foot patrol program: The Flint, Michigan project. In *Community crime prevention: Does it work?* edited by Dennis Rosenbaum. Beverly Hills, CA: Sage.

Uchida, Craig, Brian Forst, and Sampson O. Annan. 1992. *Modern policing and the control of illegal drugs: Testing new strategies in two American cities*. Washington, DC: National Institute of Justice.

van Tulder, Frank. 1992. Crime, detection rate, and the police: A macro approach. *Journal of Quantitative Criminology* 8 (1): 113-31.

Visher, Christy, and David Weisburd. 1998. Identifying what works: Recent trends in crime. *Crime, Law and Social Change* 28:223-42.

Weiner, Kenneth, Kenneth Chelst, and William Hart. 1984. Stinging the Detroit criminal: A total system perspective. *Journal of Criminal Justice* 12:289-302.

Weiner, Kenneth, Christine K. Stephens, and Donna L. Besachuk. 1983. Making inroads into property crime: An analysis of the Detroit anti-fencing program. *Journal of Police Science and Administration* 11 (3): 311-27.

Weisburd, David. 1997. *Reorienting crime prevention research and policy: From the causes of criminality to the context of crime*. Washington, DC: U.S. Government Printing Office.

———. 2003. Ethical practice and evaluation of interventions in crime and justice: The moral imperative for randomized trials. *Evaluation Review* 27:336-54.

Weisburd, David, and Anthony A. Braga. 2003. Hot spots policing. In *Crime prevention: New approaches*, edited by Helmut Kury and Obergerfeld Fuchs. Mainz, Germany: Weisner Ring.

Weisburd, David, and Lorraine Green. 1995a. Policing drug hot spots: The Jersey City drug market analysis experiment. *Justice Quarterly* 12 (4): 711-35.

———. 1995b. Assessing immediate spatial displacement: Insights from the Minneapolis hot spot experiment. In *Crime and place: Crime prevention studies*, vol. 4, edited by John E. Eck and David Weisburd. Monsey, NY: Willow Tree Press.

Weisburd, David, and Cynthia Lum. 2001. Translating research into practice: Reflections on the diffusion of crime mapping innovation. Retrieved September 5, 2003, from http://www.ojp.usdoj.gov/nij/maps/Conferences/01conf/Papers.html

Weisburd, David, Cynthia Lum, and Anthony Petrosino. 2001. Does research design affect study outcomes in criminal justice? *Annals of American Political and Social Science* 578:50-70.

Weisburd, David, Stephen Mastrofski, Anne Marie McNally, and Rosann Greenspan. 2001. *Compstat and organizational change: Findings from a national survey*. Washington, DC: National Institute of Justice.

Weisburd, David, Jerome McElroy, and Patricia Hardyman. 1988. Challenges to supervision in community policing: Observations on a pilot project. *American Journal of Police* 7 (2): 29-50.

Weisburd, David, and Faye Taxman. 2000. Developing a multi-center randomized trial in criminology: The case of HIDTA. *Journal of Quantitative Criminology* 16 (3): 315-39.

Weiss, Alexander, and Sally Freels. 1996. Effects of aggressive policing: The Dayton traffic enforcement experiment. *American Journal of Police* 15 (3): 45-64.

Whitaker, Gordon P, Charles Phillips, Peter Haas, and Robert Worden. 1985. Aggressive policing and the deterrence of crime. *Law and Policy* 7 (3): 395-416.

Wilson, James Q., and Barbara Boland. 1979. The effect of police on crime. *Law and Society Review* 12 (3): 367-90.

Wilson, O. W. 1967. *Crime prevention—Whose responsibility?* Washington, DC: Thompson Book.

Wycoff, Mary Ann, and Wesley G. Skogan. 1986. Storefront police offices: The Houston field test. In *Community crime prevention: Does it work?* edited by Dennis Rosenbaum. Beverly Hills, CA: Sage.

———. 1993. *Community policing in Madison: Quality from the inside, out*. Washington, DC: Police Foundation.

Zhao, Jihong, Matthew C. Scheider, and Quint Thurman. 2002. Funding community policing to reduce crime: Have COPS grants made a difference? *Criminology and Public Policy* 2 (1): 7-32.

Lawful Policing

By
WESLEY G. SKOGAN
and
TRACEY L. MEARES

Police compliance with the law is one of the most important aspects of a democratic society. Americans expect the police to enforce laws to promote safety and to reduce crime, victimization, and fear, but no one believes that the police should have unlimited power to do so. We expect police to enforce laws fairly according to law and rules that circumscribe their enforcement powers. The existence of these rules justify the claim that police are a rule-bound institution engaged in the pursuit of justice and the protection of individual liberties, as well as the battle against crime. This article reviews research on the extent to which police follow laws and rules, especially constitutional criminal procedure rules, addressing seizures, searches, interrogations, and deadly force. Also reviewed is research pertaining to police adherence to rules governing excessive force, corruption, and racial profiling.

Keywords: constitutionality; interrogation; search and seizure; excessive force; corruption

As the National Research Council's report *Fairness and Effectiveness in Policing: The Evidence* (hereafter referred to as the "committee's report") points out, police compliance with the law is one of the most important aspects of a democratic society. The committee reviewed research on police compliance with the U.S.

Wesley G. Skogan has been a faculty member at Northwestern University since 1971 and holds joint appointments with the political science department and the Institute for Policy Research. His research focuses on the interface between the public and the legal system. Much of this research has examined public encounters with institutions of justice, in the form of crime prevention projects and community-oriented policing. His most recent books on policing are On the Beat: Police and Community Problem Solving *(Westview, 1999) and* Community Policing, Chicago Style *(Oxford University Press, 1997). They are both empirical studies of Chicago's community policing initiative. His 1990 book* Disorder and Decline *examined public involvement in these programs, their efficacy, and the issues involved in police-citizen cooperation in order maintenance. This book won a prize from the American Sociological Association. He is also the author of two lengthy reports in the Home Office Research Series examining citizen contact*

DOI: 10.1177/0002716204263637

Constitution, state laws, and the policies and standards of their own organizations. The existence of these rules justify the claim that police are a rule-bound institution engaged in the pursuit of justice and the protection of individual liberties, as well as the battle against crime. Although the authority of the state granted to police to enforce the laws is circumscribed by the various types of laws we review here, it is also the case that the exercise of police power in the United States takes place largely at the discretion of individual officers. The decision to make a traffic stop or issue a ticket, to make an arrest or issue a stern warning, or to use force to accomplish any of these things is in the hands of officers on the street.

Everything about policing makes this exercise of discretion hard to monitor and control. The organization under which officers work struggles to keep control of its field force. Most police officers work alone or with a partner—not under the constant gaze of an assembly-line foreman. Police officers go out into the night heavily armed, and we know little about what they do there except what they report on pieces of paper that they sometimes fill out to document their activities. Many of the encounters police officers have occur under potentially troublesome circumstances. The individuals whom officers meet during these encounters include alleged offenders, drunks, the homeless, and prostitutes—those with "spoiled" identities. The complaints these individuals may have about their treatment by officers may not be taken very seriously. Because police work outside the public eye, they routinely have opportunities to engage in a laundry list of corrupt activities. Moreover, it is difficult to punish such misbehavior due to the civil service protections afforded police as public employees. In many regions of the country, policing is unionized, and provisions of the labor agreement can further bind the hands of top management when it comes to supervising, rewarding, disciplining, and firing employees.

---

and satisfaction with policing in Britain. Other articles on police-citizen issues include "The Impact of Community Policing on Neighborhood Residents: A Cross-Site Analysis" in Rosenbaum's The Challenge of Community Policing. *He chaired the National Research Council's Committee to Review Research on Police Policies and Practices.*

Tracey L. Meares graduated from the University of Illinois with a B.S. in general engineering in 1988. She then obtained her J.D. with honors from The Law School at The University of Chicago in 1991. After clerking for the Honorable Harlington Wood Jr. of the U.S. Court of Appeals for the Seventh Circuit, she was an Honors Program Trial Attorney for the U.S. Department of Justice in the Antitrust Division. In 1994, she joined the law faculty of The University of Chicago as an assistant professor. In 1999, she accepted a joint appointment as a research fellow at the American Bar Foundation. Her research brings insights from sociological theory and contemporary poverty research to the analysis of criminal law policy. A related group of writings explores the impact of the evolution of law enforcement policy on constitutional criminal procedure, of which "The Coming Crisis of Criminal Procedure," 86 Georgetown Law Journal *1153 (1998) (with Dan Kahan), is a notable example. She is also involved in a large empirical study funded by the Catherine T. and John D. MacArthur Foundation of cooperation between churches (predominantly black) and the police on Chicago's West Side. In "Place and Crime," 73* Chicago-Kent Law Review *669 (1998), she offers a foundational framework for exploring the questions posed by this research, but the work, both theoretical and empirical, is ongoing. She was a member of the National Research Council's Committee to Review Research on Police Policies and Practices.*

In addition to this long list of factors, many of the recent innovations reviewed in the committee's report recognize, celebrate, and extend this operational independence. The foundational premise underlying both problem-solving policing and community policing is that community and crime-related problems vary tremendously from place to place and that their causes and solutions are highly contextual. In such contexts, we expect police to use good judgment rather than enforce the letter of the law in order to produce good results. Decentralizing, reducing hierarchy, granting officers more independence, and trusting in their professionalism are the organizational reforms of choice today, not tightening up the management screws to further constrain officer discretion. This is especially true when "we," the segment of the public that has not traditionally had antagonistic relationship with the police, are the ones demanding better outcomes from policing.

Most police officers are honest and stay out of serious trouble for their entire careers. Most citizens who come into contact with the police are satisfied with the experience, even when they were on the receiving end of an investigation.

Somehow, this witches' brew of authority and autonomy usually works out. Most police officers are honest and stay out of serious trouble for their entire careers. Most citizens who come into contact with the police are satisfied with the experience, even when they were on the receiving end of an investigation. There is evidence that it has been working out better and better over time. In a paper reviewing trends in American policing over the course of the twentieth century, historian Samuel Walker (2001a) concludes that police at century's end are better trained, more professional, less likely to use excessive or fatal force, and more effective than they were in previous decades.

But, inevitably, it sometimes does not work out. Police are what the British call "the sharp end of the stick" when it comes to regulating the social and economic relationships in society. Their capacity to use force authoritatively and take lives lawfully in the course of regulating our lives uniquely defines *the police*. We are then led to the task of constructing legal and organizational mechanisms for hemming in the exercise of police discretion and ensuring that it is exercised in accordance with law and public policy. Just how to construct and enforce such rules can be a difficult puzzle. It is not easy to impose these rules, and it is not easy to make them work. This article presents an overview of what is known about the nature and extent of police lawfulness and about the effectiveness of mechanisms to control it. The evidence that it summarizes is documented in detail in the committee's report. Here, we present our main conclusions about this research and our judgments about its implications for policies aimed at ensuring police lawfulness.

How Police Get in Trouble

Since 1934, the Supreme Court has regularly reviewed the practices of local police. Like many early cases, *Brown v. Mississippi* (297 U.S. 278, 1935) evoked the Court's twin concern with racial discrimination—Brown was a black man—and egregious police conduct, in this instance the extraction of a confession through torture. Later cases erected a dense network of rules delimiting police power to stop people on the street, conduct searches, question them in custody, and listen in on their conversations. Taken together, these cases establish what we now recognize as modern constitutional criminal procedure: rules that provide the link between constitutional principles and the daily actions of the police. On their face, these rules greatly constrain the authority of the police. Social scientists know, of course, that pronouncing a rule does not automatically make it so. They are not self-enforcing, and individual officers have to learn and actually follow them. Where they do not, police can get in trouble, and this section reviews what we know about the lawfulness of police activities in the line of duty in several key areas. Neither are the more mundane laws that govern police corruption automatically effective, and corruption is another way that police get in trouble.

Interrogations

Brown involved the lawfulness of an interrogation. It was followed by a line of cases reviewing under the due process clause of the Constitution the appropriate and voluntary nature of police questioning of suspects and taking of confessions. *Miranda v. Arizona* (372 US. 436, 1966), one of the best-known and most thoroughly researched Supreme Court decisions, represents a break in this sort of decision making. Rather than reviewing the voluntarism of Miranda's confession under due process principles, the Court imposed on police via the Fifth Amendment responsibility for delivering the famous four-part warning, which is familiar to any regular viewer of television drama, to any suspect during a custodial interrogation. In fact, *Miranda*'s four-part warning may be the best-known element of criminal procedure. Initially, the *Miranda* decision was criticized for "hamstringing" police in the pursuit of criminals, but in *Dickerson v. United States* (120 S. Ct. 2326, 2000), even a Supreme Court that might have threatened the ruling decided instead that it "has become embedded in routine police practice to the point where the warnings have become part of our national culture (p. 2336)."

Miranda presented a natural case for social research. It involves a clearly observable requirement (the four warnings) that might be followed or ignored, and its critics posed a hypothesis to be tested (it would hamstring the police). The studies that followed paint an ironic picture of *Miranda* in action: it seems that the police follow the rule, and it does not have much effect.

The first big study of *Miranda* did not actually come to that complete conclusion. Donald Black and Albert Reiss Jr. had a large field study of police operations under way when the decision was announced. They added the warning to the checklist of things their observers were looking for as they rode along with officers. They found that the required warnings were frequently not given when police arrested suspects, but they also found that for felonies, there was typically alternate physical evidence and eyewitness testimony that police could rely on (Black and Reiss 1967). Subsequent studies have almost universally found high levels of verbal compliance with this constitutional requirement, so it is likely that the low compliance rate they observed was an artifact of the timing of the Black and Reiss project. For example, Leo (1996) observed detectives at work and found essentially 100 percent compliance with the letter of the law.

Other studies have confirmed the other Black and Reiss conclusion: in routine cases, confessions are rarely the only evidence available for submission to the prosecutor. This is one of the factors that has mitigated the impact of *Miranda*, belying the early charge that it would severely undercut the crime-fighting effectiveness of the police. The reason that the existence of nonconfessional evidence can undercut the sting of *Miranda*'s exclusionary rule in situations in which police do follow *Miranda*'s prescriptions is that *Miranda*'s exclusionary rule requires that only a tainted confession be excluded from trial, not other evidence. Another mitigating influence on *Miranda*'s bite is the strategic manner in which police deliver the message. Leo noted how police presented the four warnings in ways that encouraged suspects to waive their rights. Terms like *perfunctory* and *superficial* are used by researchers to describe police delivery. Cassell and Hayman (1996) also observed a number of "noncustodial" interviews that took place (technically, legally) without warnings, presumably in an attempt to skirt the requirement. In a summary, Meares and Harcourt (2000) concluded that in practice, *Miranda* may reduce the number of confessions between 4 and 16 percent, but the availability of other evidence means that its real impact is considerably lower than that range.

Searches and seizures

Seizing people and searching them and their properties are basic law enforcement tools. Searches and seizures are vital to removing weapons and contraband from the street, building criminal cases, and potentially preventing crime. But searches and seizures can also be extremely problematic for police. While Americans recognize that searches and seizures are necessary tools for police to do their jobs of maintaining order and responding to criminal events, Americans have always feared the misuse of these intrusions by the state into their lives. The Fourth Amendment speaks directly to "the right of the people to be secure in their persons, houses, papers and effects, against unreasonable searches." Through its interpretation of the Fourth Amendment, the Supreme Court has established concepts such as "probable cause" and "reasonable suspicion" in criminal procedure cases as the standard for justifying different types of searches and seizures.

The principal tool for enforcing judicially imposed injunctions against unreasonable police conduct is the exclusionary rule, which applies both to state and federal prosecutions. A deterrence model underlies the logic of the decision: the rule that a demonstrably bad guy can earn a "get out of jail free card" if the evidence required to convict him (perhaps a seized gun or trunk load of drugs) was obtained improperly is supposed to keep police and prosecutors in line.

Research in this area attempts to document the extent of police propriety and the factors associated with rule bending versus rule minding. Much of it has been reactive to changes in legal standards. A large body of research was stimulated by the Supreme Court's decision in *Mapp v. Ohio* (367 U.S. 643, 1961) to extend the Fourth Amendment exclusionary rule to the states. More appeared in the wake of follow-up search-and-seizure cases. These include *Terry v. Ohio* (392 U.S. 1, 1968), which justifies pat-down searches under the rubric of Fourth Amendment reasonableness by sanctioning them so long as police could demonstrate reasonable suspicion; *United States v. Calandra* (414 U.S. 338, 1974), which balances the exclusion of evidence against its deterrent effect; and *United States v. Leon* (486 U.S. 897, 1984), which permits the use of evidence obtained faultily but in good faith. Because they have been reactive, there are few before-and-after studies assessing the impact of these new rules for police conduct, even though many of them read as if that were their goal.

Search-and-seizure actions by individual officers have been examined in a variety of ways. Researchers have ridden with detectives or interviewed them in the stationhouse, passed out questionnaires to uniformed officers, and observed encounters between the police and the public in the field. Collectively, these studies indicate that police mostly follow the rules, but sometimes, they do not. Officers know the rules, but they sometimes skirt constitutional standards because they want to deter crime by incarcerating the truly guilty. Or if deterrence is not their immediate goal, officers sometimes bend rules because they simply want an individual that they have identified as a lawbreaker to get his or her "due" in a sort of retributive justice sense. Officers can be quite strategic in pursuing these goals, including risking a bit of censure when they have other forms of evidence to fall back on if their actions are challenged. Several studies found that officers intent on seizing contraband, disrupting illicit networks, or asserting their authority on the street freely violated the rules because their goal was not principally to secure an individual conviction.

One of the most recent of these studies involved observations of what happens when police confront citizens in the field. The study (Gould and Mastrofski forthcoming) documents that field searches are fairly uncommon. Trained observers in two cities spent in total more than 2,800 hours in the field observing 12,000 police-citizen encounters. During this period, they observed just 115 searches. About 30 percent were judged to be unconstitutional, but only 10 percent of those (and just 3 percent of all searches) involved what they classified as egregious police misconduct. About 7 percent of suspects who were arrested or cited were searched improperly. Most improper searches occurred when officers were looking for drugs, a finding that is consistent with earlier work on detective practices. Most of the observed violations involved frisking suspect's outer clothing and were not particularly invasive. The authors describe the officers involved as "respectful, even solicitous," and not distinguishable by their attitudes or other behaviors. Most of the rule violations arose during encounters that did not ultimately lead to an arrest or citation, so no record of them was left behind.

Another large study examined the lawfulness of street encounters in New York City. The New York Office of the Attorney General (1999) analyzed forms that are supposed to be completed by officers when they conduct a stop and frisk. On their face, the stops described there were judged to violate *Terry* standards 14 percent of the time (Fagan and Davies 2000). Two measures were also used to test whether there was racial bias in the stops themselves. One compared stops by race with the race of the neighborhood in which they occurred, while the other made a similar adjustment for the racial makeup of arrests in the area as a proxy for who the troublemakers there were. Both analyses suggested that African Americans were disproportionately stopped.

Researchers have used case files to assess the magnitude of search-and-seizure issues and their aggregate consequences at the system level. To assess the cost of excluding evidence of guilt, studies have counted lost convictions and concluded that they are not particularly frequent. Sutton's (1986) study tracked a large sample of cases in seven cities. He found that search warrants were rarely used, judges gave only perfunctory review of warrant applications, and the participants subverted the process by fabricating evidence when necessary. Other researchers have done pre-post studies of the impact of *Leon* and found no impact on police practices (Uchida and Bynum 1991).

Excessive and lethal force

The use of force is so integral to the police role that a common definition of the term *police* is the body that is lawfully authorized to exercise deadly force against citizens. As a price for holding a virtual monopoly over this power, there are standards for the use of force, standards that are too often violated. In the United States, use of deadly force has been a major source of conflict between minority groups and the police. Numerous studies have demonstrated large discrepancies between the rate at which African Americans are shot and killed by the police and the comparable rate for whites. One found that between 1950 and 1960, African Americans were killed by Chicago police at a rate of 16.1 per 100,000, compared with a rate of 2.1 per 100,000 for whites (Robin 1963).

The constitutional rule adopted by the Court to circumscribe the use of deadly force by police officers is found in *Tennessee v. Garner* (471 U.S. 1, 1985). In this case, the Supreme Court overturned a permissive fleeing-felon rule that allowed police officers to use "all the means necessary to effect an arrest" of even an unarmed fleeing felon. The case arose from the killing of a fifteen-year-old African American male in suburban Memphis, and it was imbued with racial tensions. Interestingly, few of the states whose statutes on this matter did not comply with the Court's ruling were willing to change them; the states relied instead on departments to change their policies and procedures. Generally, police are now authorized to use force in self-defense or when a life is in danger, when certain forcible felons flee, or when other means have been exhausted. Both deadly force and excessive force claims are also grounds for civil suits under state tort law and federal civil rights laws.

Officers know the rules, but they sometimes skirt constitutional standards because they want to deter crime by incarcerating the truly guilty.

This is a difficult research area. There is no national repository of data on police use of force, and access to local records is difficult. Virtually every study has been based on the records of one or a small number of local police departments. Official case files inevitably present a situation in which every incentive exists for the organization to present a favorable version of events. Studies conducted in agencies that voluntarily open their records to researchers probably represent those that are most confident of their professionalism. Studies of agencies that are forced to open their records because of suits alleging use of excessive force, or through freedom of information suits by media organizations, tend to find more racial disparity in the use of force, great deals of disparity in the use of deadly force, and higher rates of shootings of racial minorities that appear to be questionable (Fyfe 2002). For example, Meyer (1980) found that African Americans in Los Angeles were more often unarmed when they were shot, and Fyfe (1982) found that African Americans in Memphis were more often shot in circumstances that were not as threatening to the officer.

One firm conclusion that can be drawn from this research is that rates of police use of force and deadly force are highly variable. In a recent study, Fyfe (2002) analyzed the results of a project conducted by the *Washington Post*. Using freedom of information requests and suits, they assembled data on fatal police shootings in fifty-one large municipal and county police and sheriff's departments during 1990 to 2000. Fatal shootings rates for county police departments varied by a factor of 14, while for city departments, the ratio of shootings from top to bottom was 8:1

and among sheriff's departments it was almost 6:1. In a seven-city study by Milton et al. (1977), the top to bottom ratio was also 6:1. Another general conclusion is that most police use of force is nonfatal. In one six-agency study, only 17 percent of "potentially volatile encounters" (a high-risk sample of incidents) led to the use of force, and most of the force was confined to threats, use of restraints, weaponless tactics, and control holds (Garner and Maxwell 1999). A final conclusion is that there is usually considerable racial disparity in the use of force and often in the use of fatal force. Many see such disparities in the exercise of force lying at the core of challenges to the legitimacy of American policing in the twenty-first century.

There is also evidence of the positive effects of legal and administrative efforts to control police use of force. Many before-and-after studies of changes in department rules or leadership find evidence that management makes a difference. In a study of the use of force by the New York Police Department, Fyfe (1979) found that a policy change by the agency led to a precipitous drop in shootings by officers there. He also found that New York City police rarely shot unarmed people. Sparger and Giacopassi (1992) conducted a follow-up study in Memphis, the jurisdiction in which the *Garner* decision originated, and found a dramatic reduction in racial disparities in police shootings in the post-*Garner* period. Tennenbaum (1994) concluded that *Garner* reduced fatal police shootings by about sixty per year.

Corruption

The previous sections reviewed research in which the disjuncture between police activity and legal standards ostensibly and typically were grounded in the officers' desire to pursue public ends. However, police also deviate from the law for personal gain. Corruption is to a certain extent endemic in police departments because of the attractive opportunities officers can face when deciding when and how to enforce the law. The range of what constitutes corruption is a wide one and, at the lower end, depends on department policies. "Police discounts" for meals and haircuts fall at one end of the continuum, which widens to include the sale of inside information, accepting bribes not to enforce the law or to testify falsely, and even payoffs to secure advancement within the department. Corruption may be proactive, as when officers seek out and rob street drug dealers, or reactive to offers large and small from community members. Some researchers include so-called noble-cause corruption in their inventories. This includes investigating, arresting, and "testi-lying" people who are "deserving" of punishment, whatever the "legal niceties." It is not clear, however, whether including these practices increases our ability to understand the scope and frequency of corruption for gain or if it just muddies the concept. Other important distinctions are whether corruption is organized or freelance work, if it is widespread or found only in isolated pockets, if it permeates management ranks or is confined to street officers, and if it is linked to more widespread political corruption or is largely confined to police ranks.

Corruption is not only hard to control but also hard to study systematically. Much of what we know in any detailed fashion flows from investigations and testimony collected by commissions set up in response to public uproar over revelations of corruption. New York City provides a treasure trove of these reports, including those of the Knapp Commission (City of New York 1973) and the Mollen Commission (City of New York 1994). Sherman (1978) used media reports and investigatory material like these commission reports to develop comparative case studies of corruption and reform efforts in four cities. He concluded that corruption was highly organized before it surfaced in public view. Another approach is to survey officers. While self-report surveys are unlikely to uncover revelations of any but the smallest scale side benefits of serving the public, Klockars et al. (2000) and others have demonstrated that it is quite fruitful to ask police about the practices of others in their agency, the "climate of opinion" among their peers concerning corruption, their awareness of the rules concerning misconduct, their support for imposing discipline, and their (hypothetical) willingness to report various kinds of misconduct internally. For example, Klockars et al. (2000) surveyed officers in thirty American police departments and found that, overall, a majority would not report a colleague who engaged in the least serious misbehavior (e.g., accepting free meals and discounts) but that they would report someone who engaged in behaviors judged to be at intermediate or high levels of seriousness (e.g., accepting kickbacks from an auto repair shop for referrals, turning in a lost wallet while keeping the cash from that wallet). Their study also found that police departments varied considerably in the climate of integrity.

Surveys have also asked the general public whether they had been required to bribe public officials, including the police, and these open an alternative window into the extent of that problem. Some of these, conducted in a number of countries, lend a comparative aspect to experiences with police corruption. Unfortunately, no studies have compared police with any other occupation's corruption rate, for this would provide a useful avenue for testing hypotheses involving some of the reputedly unique features of police work.

What seems to lead to corruption? As noted above, many of the most important explanations are systemic in character. History provides evidence of the importance of very broad social and regulatory factors, for probably no event had a greater corrupting effect on police and the American political system generally than did the passage of a constitutional amendment prohibiting the manufacture and sale of alcoholic beverages in the 1920s. Today's equivalent is drugs. Police work combines high discretion with low-visibility decision making in an environment that can be awash with tempting opportunities and an ample supply of "regular" citizens willing to offer up even more. The drug dealers, prostitutes, and others that officers routinely deal with can be robbed or abused with relative impunity. Narcotics units are especially prone to problems because of the very large sums of money and drugs that come their way, the willingness of both buyers and sellers in the marketplace to pay bribes to avoid regulation, and the very low visibility of the many discretionary decisions that are made on a daily basis by investigators and their supervisors (U.S. General Accounting Office 1998; Manning and Redlinger 1977). Officers whose opportunities for career advancement have come to an end may be more prone to being on the take. Corruption is very much facilitated by tolerance—or at least passive unresponsiveness—by peer officers in the organization. Integrity, on the other hand, can be measured by officers' support for the rules, their belief that internal complaints will be investigated fully and fairly, and their willingness to report misconduct (Klockars et al. 2000). The public's standards concerning what constitutes intolerable corruption may set an upper boundary on how out of hand corruption may get, and the views of the politicians who represent them are probably even more directly important. The aggressiveness of local and federal prosecutors, and the intrusiveness of the media, also determine how much can go on before heads start to roll.

Racial profiling

No controversy in law enforcement today has received more attention than racial profiling. There is no ready agreement on what the term means, however. While the law enforcement community has defined *racial profiling* as the practice of stopping citizens solely or exclusively because of their race, many others use the term to refer to police using race in any way in deciding whom to stop or search, except in the instance when race is part of a specific description of a wanted offender. Police have defended the legitimacy of considering race along with other factors with respect to their decision to stop, search, or otherwise engage citizens, arguing that consideration of race in decision making is justified by statistics demonstrating that racial minorities make up a disproportionate number of suspects arrested, convicted, and sentenced nationwide. This stance was quickly challenged by the observation that this proved only that the criminal justice system targeted black male offenders. While this debate continues, there can be little doubt that the term *racial profiling* and the offense known as *driving while black* have become a part of the nation's lexicon. And it seems that the threat of global terrorism will keep the debate alive.

The problem of racial profiling is inextricably intertwined with the fact that police officers have a great deal of discretion in performing their job. Key Supreme Court decisions have further increased the range of police discretion in ways that are relevant to the racial profiling controversy. *Ohio v. Robinette* (519 U.S. 33, 1996) made it easier for police to talk suspects into consenting to a search of their person or vehicle. *Whren v. United States* (517 U.S. 806, 1996) holds that police can make traffic stops to investigate suspicions that have nothing to do with the traffic offense for which the stop was made—so long as there is an offense. These are known as "pretextual traffic stops."

Given that police must make determinations as to how to perform their job, it is not surprising that their judgments could be influenced by racial, ethnic, or gender stereotypes. At some point, this becomes a lawfulness issue, although debate over where the boundary begins and the appropriate penalties continues. For example, a bill introduced (but not passed) during the 107th Congress (*Racial Profiling Pro-*

hibition Act of 2001, HR 1907, 107th Cong., 2nd sess.) defined racial profiling as the consideration of race "to any degree or in any fashion" by an officer when deciding whom to stop or search, except when race is part of a specific description of an offender who committed a crime. The penalties that have been considered include losing federal highway funds and other federal grants. On various hit lists are the Edward Byrne Memorial State and Local Law Enforcement Assistance Programs; the "Cops on the Beat" program under part Q of title I of the Omnibus Crime Control and Safe Streets; and the Local Law Enforcement Block Grant program of the Department of Justice.

The road to police reform is largely an internal one, featuring training, supervision, internal inspections, performance measures, and policy making.

The legal handle for judicial intervention to restrict racial profiling is the constitutional injunction against depriving persons of their rights, privileges, or immunities because of their race, a "legally protected" social category. In the federal system, the Justice Department is authorized to investigate allegations of a pattern or practice of discrimination, and it can file civil litigation against police agencies found not to be in compliance with the Constitution.

However, there is just as much controversy over the extent of racial profiling as there is over its definition or any other part of this issue. The lack of definitional clarity, combined with serious flaws in methods for assessing profiling, make it difficult to identify with any confidence how much of it there is, who is doing it, or whether it is increasing or decreasing in the face of new policies. A large number of agencies are now engaged in new data collection documenting their activities; some of this is voluntary, while many are doing so in the face of municipal or state requirements. But detecting a "pattern of profiling" (whatever that is defined to be) presents difficult data and analytic issues. Studies of the accuracy with which officers complete the forms they are supposed to use to record stops, and the accuracy with which they guess citizens' races, do not point in a hopeful direction. Furthermore, the racial distribution of stops, citations, and even searches does not in itself demonstrate much. Profiling can be identified only by comparing the frequency of encounters to some baseline, a denominator that yields an interpretable stop rate. Some have compared traffic stops by race to the population composition of the neighborhoods in which they were made. This has little to do with the population at risk of being stopped, or even better, the offending population at risk of being apprehended. There have been attempts to standardize stop counts by the racial distribution of drivers, in the expectation that everyone speeds. Traffic offending is not randomly distributed, however, and not all police-initiated encounters involve only traffic offenses. Studies have used the racial distribution of arrests in the area, and even counts of the racial distribution of drivers timed to be actually exceeding the speed limit, to estimate the relative size of offending populations. However, it is clear that the cheap and simple denominators do not adequately represent the population at risk of being stopped and that the effort and expense required to generate more focused and localized measures is far beyond the scope of policing agencies. It is not even clear that the population at risk is the most appropriate baseline measure. To develop policies to address the problem, it is not enough simply to gather information about those stopped; therefore, another way to measure profiling activity might be to focus on the group doing the stopping—police. Common sense suggests that the problem of racial profiling, however defined, is different if a small isolated number of officers are stopping individuals as opposed to a large dispersed group (Walker 2001c). Other strategies that have been proposed for eliminating racial profiling, including in-car video cameras, have not been evaluated.

How Police Can Get Out of Trouble

In the view of the committee, the road to police reform is largely an internal one, featuring training, supervision, internal inspections, performance measures, and policy making. At this level, controlling police behavior is a management problem. For example, a department's use of force policy includes the types of weapons that are made available to officers, the rules for their use, training in weapon safety, reporting requirements when they are employed, procedures for reviewing the appropriateness of their use in an "after-action" report, and the kinds of sanctions that can be imposed for their misuse.

To date, however, little research has examined the effectiveness of managerial strategies to secure officer compliance with department policies. As noted earlier, some the best evidence comes from studies of the use of lethal force, which has shown that administrative changes and determined leadership can reduce shootings by police. Changes in policies governing high-speed pursuits can reduce their number and save lives. Randomized experiments in responding to domestic violence have demonstrated along the way that careful training and supervision can change how officers handle those cases, whatever the eventual findings regarding their effectiveness. Research on corruption points to the importance of leadership, internal accountability, training, internal inspections, and a willingness to challenge informal practices and peer tolerance.

Otherwise, there is not much research on internal police control processes. In particular, virtually no research has studied police internal inspection bureaus, which are increasingly called professional standards units. They are recognized by police leaders to play a critical role in keeping their organizations in line, but little is known about the organization, management, and staffing of these units. Nor is much known about the investigative procedures used or patterns of discipline. Interestingly, unlike the private sector, virtually no research has focused on systems for rewarding good officer performance, through pay or perquisites. Traditionally, police management consists of overseeing subordinates until they break a rule in the book and then punishing them. It is essentially negative, with little in their management kitbag but sanctions for noncompliance; hence, the emphasis on internal inspections to ensure compliance with rules.

If internal processes could be effective at controlling police misconduct, why are so many departments demonstrably lacking effective internal controls? One problem is that there are contrary political and organizational pressures. Calls to get tough on crime can drown out concern about excessive police zeal. In fact, one controversial feature of the committee report itself is that it tried to attend to research on police lawfulness as well as their crime-fighting effectiveness. Public-sector workers, including police and firefighters, are usually well organized on the political front, with independent links to powerful local politicians, state legislators, and the governor's office. Attempts to reform their organizations thus can lead to a tough political fight. In many cities, police departments operate with a significant degree of autonomy, protected by law and order rhetoric, labor agreements, and the political clout of their employees. Calls for administrative reform can seem to fall on deaf ears, when they do not have to listen. Instead, we tend to get individualized, short-term responses to widespread, systemic problems.

In reaction to the perceived inability of departments to manage themselves, external pressure can be mounted in an attempt to reign in police. We have emphasized internal management efforts because ultimately processes have to be put into motion inside the organization to make those changes. In the end, these processes make up the "transmission belt" by which external pressures translate into internal change, and in our judgment, they should be the central focus of reform efforts. Without engaging these, most externally imposed solutions to lawfulness problems will not be very effective.

For example, prosecutors can bring criminal charges against individual police officers accused of using excessive force or engaging in acts of corruption. In addition to exacting justice in that case, we can hope that the message that initiating a prosecution sends sets in motion deterrent processes leading to general changes in behavior within the organization. However, the committee concluded that this is an extremely limited vehicle for changing police organizations. Few cases are brought forward by internal inspectors, prosecutors are wary of indicting the police officers on whom they depend, intent is difficult to document in excessive force cases, it is difficult to convince judges and juries to convict, and the best evidence is that the few sentences that are actually imposed in these cases are light.

The odds of effecting organizational change through civil suits are only a little better. In most states, individual victims can sue police for damages, and federal rules are in place that allow similar cases to be brought. To a certain extent, civil rights and civil liberties groups have begun to use the civil process, again to both right individual wrongs and force organizational reform. Although they can be difficult to win, these cases can elicit fairly substantial individual payments. Their deterrent impact is muted, however, because legal fees and judgments are paid by the city's taxpayers not by individual officers or even (typically) out of the department's own budget. The limited research on this point also suggests that departments often do not take meaningful disciplinary action against the officers

---

Calls to get tough on crime can drown out concern about excessive police zeal.

---

involved, even when they are found at fault in civil court. There is also little evidence of structural changes in big-city police organizations as a result of damage payments, despite the public lamentations of mayors and city council members over their cost. It is a cost of doing business, and in actuality, the cost amounts to only a small fraction of municipal budgets. Patton (1993, 767) concluded that in Los Angeles, the cost of civil suits is considered "a reasonable price for the presumed deterrent effect of the department's most violent responses to lawbreaking."

A very limited number of agencies have been swept up in federal "pattern-and-practice" suits initiated by the civil rights division of the Department of Justice. Congress empowers the department to conduct investigations and to bring suits against departments that routinely deprive persons of rights, privileges, or immunities secured or protected by the Constitution. Three features of these cases promise that they may have more impact than the usual criminal and civil suits. First, the pattern-and-practice language of the act enables litigation against the general practices of a police department, as opposed to identifying and holding a single officer culpable for unlawful actions. Second, the settlement agreements that arise from these cases include implementing agreed-upon best practices in new training, internal investigations, use of potentially lethal equipment, and incident reporting. These are the mechanisms for making change in police organizations. Third, there is continued supervision of the settlement agreements. In every case, a court-appointed monitor watches over its implementation, and in some cities (including Pittsburgh and Cincinnati), universities or nonprofit research groups monitor the effectiveness of the decrees in resolving the problems that led to them in the first place. Often, consent decrees require the collection of systematic data on departmental practices, increasing their transparency. Most have focused on police use of force, but the federal settlement with the New Jersey State Police required the collection of data on traffic stops, and these have been used to monitor for racial disparities. In other words, although they are not numerous, pattern-and-practice settlements are designed to activate the internal organizational mechanisms that we identified at the outset as crucial for sustaining true organizational change.

Citizen-complaint review agencies provide another form of external control of the police. There has been a steady growth in the number of citizen-complaint review agencies in the United States over the past twenty years. By 2001, there were slightly more than a hundred such agencies (Walker 2001b). Virtually all of them are created by local ordinances. They take a variety of forms, and this count used a broad definition that included any procedure where there is some input, however limited, by persons who are not sworn officers in the review of citizen complaints against police officers. Some of these agencies have original jurisdiction for receiving and investigating citizen complaints. Others play an auditing or monitoring function, generally overseeing the internal investigatory actions of departments. They take so many forms and responsibilities that it is difficult to say much in general about them, and the committee's review indicated that so little systematic research on these agencies has taken place that their impact is unknown. Their appearance reflects a widely enough held belief that police internal affairs units, in varying degrees, discourage complaints, fail to investigate complaints thoroughly and fairly, and fail to discipline officers who are found to have committed misconduct. Police and their supporters in turn deny that excessive force is a problem and argue that police departments are better equipped to investigate complaints internally, for no one outside the organization can really understand police work.

Conclusion

The National Research Council's report on policing, *Fairness and Effectiveness in Policing: The Evidence*, emphasizes fairness for a reason. People expect the police to enforce laws to promote safety; to reduce crime, victimization, and fear; and to redress wrongs, but no one believes that the police should have unlimited power to prevent, reduce, or deter crime. In a democratic society, fundamental principles of liberty and justice require the circumscription of the authority of the state to enforce laws. It is police adherence to the rules that limit their power that informs at least one notion of the legitimacy of police operation. The research reviewed here goes some way to demonstrating—at least according to available research—that police tend to obey the law. The more important, and perhaps deeper, question is whether adherence to these rules is enough to establish the legitimacy of a key government institution.

References

Black, Donald, and Albert J. Reiss Jr. 1967. Interrogation and the criminal process. *The Annals of the American Academy of Political and Social Science* 374:47-57.

Cassell, Paul G., and Bret S. Hayman. 1996. Dialog on *Miranda*-police interrogation in the 1990s: An empirical study of the effects of *Miranda*. *UCLA Law Review* 43:840-929.

City of New York, Commission to Investigate Allegations of Police Corruption. 1973. *The Knapp Commission report on police corruption*. New York: George Braziller.

City of New York, Commission to Investigate Allegations of Police Corruption and the Anti-Corruption Procedures of the Police Department. 1994. *Mollen Commission report*. New York: Mollen Commission.

Fagan, Jeffrey, and Garth Davies. 2000. Street stops and broken windows: Terry, race and disorder in New York City. *Fordham Urban Law Journal* 28:457-82.

Fyfe, James J. 1979. Administrative interventions on police shooting discretion: An empirical examination. *Journal of Criminal Justice* 7:309-23.

———. 1982. Blind justice: Police shootings in Memphis. *Journal of Criminal Law and Criminology* 73:702-22.

———. 2002. Too many missing cases: Holes in our knowledge about police use of force. *Justice Research and Policy* 4:87-102.

Garner, Joel H., and Christopher D. Maxwell. 1999. Measuring the amount of force used by and against the police in six jurisdictions. In *Use of force by police: Overview of national and local data*, edited by Jeremy Travis, Jan M. Chaiken, and Robert J. Kaminski, 25-44. Washington, DC: National Institute of Justice and Bureau of Justice Statistics.

Gould, Jon B., and Stephen D. Mastrofski. Forthcoming. Suspect searches: Assessing police behavior under the U.S. Constitution. *Criminology and Public Policy*.

Klockars, Carl B., Sanja Kutnjak Ivkovich, William E. Harver, and Maria R. Haberfeld. 2000. *The measurement of police integrity*. Washington, DC: National Institute of Justice.

Leo, Richard. 1996. The impact of *Miranda* revisited. *Journal of Criminal Law and Criminology* 86:621-93

Manning, Peter K., and Lawrence J. Redlinger. 1977. Invitational edges of corruption: Some consequences of narcotics law enforcement. In *Drugs and politics*, edited by Paul Rock, 279-310. Rutgers, NJ: Transaction Books.

Meares, Tracey L., and Bernard E. Harcourt. 2000. Transparent adjudication and social science research in constitutional criminal procedure. *Journal of Criminal Law and Criminology* 90:733-69.

Meyer, Marshall W. 1980. Police shootings of minorities: The case of Los Angeles. *The Annals of the American Academy of Political and Social Science* 452:98-110.

Milton, Catherine H., Jeanne W. Halleck, James Lardner, and Gary Albrecht. 1977. *Police use of deadly force*. Washington, DC: Police Foundation.

New York Office of the Attorney General. 1999. *The New York City Police Department's "stop & frisk" practice: A report from the Office of the Attorney General*. New York: Author.

Patton, Alison L. 1993. The endless cycle of abuse: Why 42 U.S.C. § 1983 is ineffective in deterring police brutality. *Hastings Law Journal* 44:753-68.

Robin, Gerald. 1963. Justifiable homicide by police officers. *Journal of Criminal Law, Criminology, and Police Science* 54:225-54.

Sherman, Lawrence W. 1978. *Scandal and reform: Controlling police corruption*. Berkeley: University of California Press.

Sutton, Peter. 1986. Fourth Amendment in action: An empirical view of the search warrant process. *Criminal Law Bulletin* 22:405-29.

Sparger, Jerry R., and David J. Giacopassi. 1992. Memphis revisited: A reexamination of police shootings after the *Garner* decision. *Police Quarterly* 9:211-25.

Tennenbaum, Abraham N. 1994. The influence of the *Garner* decision on police use of lethal force. *Journal of Criminal Law and Criminology* 85:241-60.

Uchida, Craig D., and Timothy S. Bynum. 1991. Search warrants, motions to suppress, and "lost cases": The effects of the exclusionary rule in seven jurisdictions. *Journal of Criminal Law and Criminology* 81:1034-66.

U.S. General Accounting Office. 1998. *Law enforcement: Information on drug-related police corruption.* Washington, DC: Author.

Walker, Samuel. 2001a. The trees and the forest: Reflections on whether American policing has improved over time. Unpublished manuscript, University of Nebraska–Omaha.

———. 2001b. *Police accountability: The role of citizen oversight.* Belmont, CA: Wadsworth.

———. 2001c. Problems with traffic stop data and an early warning system solution. *Justice Research and Policy* 3:63-95.

Enhancing Police Legitimacy

By
TOM R. TYLER

This article makes three points. First, the police need public support and cooperation to be effective in their order-maintenance role, and they particularly benefit when they have the voluntary support and cooperation of most members of the public, most of the time. Second, such voluntary support and cooperation is linked to judgments about the legitimacy of the police. A central reason people cooperate with the police is that they view them as legitimate legal authorities, entitled to be obeyed. Third, a key antecedent of public judgments about the legitimacy of the police and of policing activities involves public assessments of the manner in which the police exercise their authority. Such procedural-justice judgments are central to public evaluations of the police and influence such evaluations separately from assessments of police effectiveness in fighting crime. These findings suggest the importance of enhancing public views about the legitimacy of the police and suggest process-based strategies for achieving that objective.

Keywords: police; legitimacy; compliance; trust and confidence

Public Cooperation with the Police

One way to approach the relationship between the police and the public is to consider how the public impacts on the effectiveness of the police in their efforts to combat crime and maintain social order. Traditional discussions of the effective exercise of legal authority have focused on the ability of legal authorities to shape the behavior of the people within the communities they police. The ability of the police to secure compliance with their directives and with the law more generally—the ability to be authoritative—is widely identified as one key

Tom R. Tyler is a professor of psychology at New York University. His work is concerned with the dynamics of authority in groups and organizations. His books include Why People Obey the Law *(1990),* Social Justice in a Diverse Society *(1997), and* Cooperation in Groups *(2000).*

DOI: 10.1177/0002716203262627

indicator of their viability as authorities (Easton 1975; Fuller 1971). To be effective as maintainers of social order, in other words, the police must be widely obeyed (Tyler 1990). This obedience must occur both during personal encounters between police officers and members of the public (Tyler and Huo 2002) and in people's everyday law-related behavior (Tyler 1990).

While compliance is widespread, it can never be taken for granted. Studies of policing suggest that "although deference to legal authorities is the norm, disobedience occurs with sufficient frequency that skill in handling the rebellious, the disgruntled, and the hard to manage—or those potentially so—have become the street officer's performance litmus test" (Mastrofski, Snipes, and Supina 1996, 272; also see Sherman 1993). Studies of police encounters with members of the public suggest overall noncompliance rates of around 20 percent (Mastrofski, Snipes, and Supina 1996; McCluskey, Mastrofski, and Parks 1999).

Furthermore, it is difficult to gain compliance solely via the threat of use or force (Tyler 1990, 1997b, 1997c). The police need for people to both accept their decisions and follow the law at least in part because they choose to do so (Easton 1975; Parsons 1967; Sarat 1977; Tyler 1990). Why is such voluntary compliance important? Although the police represent the threat of force and carry guns and clubs with them, it is impractical for the police to be everywhere all of the time. The police must rely upon widespread, voluntary law-abiding behavior to allow them to concentrate their resources on those people and situations in which compliance is difficult to obtain. This is first true in personal encounters. When people comply in the immediate presence of the police but later return to noncompliance (since "citizens who acquiesce at the scene can renege"; Mastrofski, Snipes, and Supina 1996, 283), the police have difficulty maintaining order in the long term. In addition, the people in the community need to defer to the law in their everyday behavior. When people widely ignore the law, the resources of the police quickly become inadequate to the maintenance of order. In both situations, the police benefit from widespread, voluntary deference.

In addition to the importance of gaining compliance with the law, more recent discussions of crime and social disorder emphasize the important role of public cooperation to the success of police efforts to fight crime by preventing crime and disorder and bringing offenders to account for wrongdoing (Sampson, Raudenbush, and Earls 1997). The public supports the police by helping to identify criminals and by reporting crimes. In addition, members of the public help the police by joining together in informal efforts to combat crime and address community problems, whether it is by working in "neighborhood watch" organizations or by attending community-police meetings. As was the case with compliance, these cooperative efforts are largely voluntary in character, and the police are not generally in a position to reward members of the public for their aid. Instead, the police rely on willing public cooperation with police efforts to control crime and community disorder.

Legitimacy

The value of voluntary cooperation and support from the public raises the question of how such cooperation and support can be created and maintained (Tyler and Blader 2000). Traditionally, the focus in policing has been on instrumental models of policing. For example, compliance with the law has been viewed as being motivated through the creation of a credible risk that people will be caught and punished for wrongdoing, that is, "by manipulating an individual's calculus regarding whether crime pays in the particular instance" (Meares 2000, 396). Similarly, public cooperation in fighting crime is motivated by evidence that the police are performing effectively in their efforts to control crime and urban disorder.

Evidence suggests that these instrumental perspectives are inadequate models with which to explain public cooperation. In the case of sanction threat and compliance, the findings of research support the argument that sanction risks do shape compliance behavior (Nagin 1998), but the magnitude of their influence is typically small. For example, based on a review of research on the influence of deterrence on drug use, MacCoun (1993) estimates that variations in the certainty and severity of punishment account for only approximately 5 percent in the variance in drug-related behavior, a finding consistent with the suggestion of Paternoster (1987) that "perceived certainty [of punishment] plays virtually no role in explaining deviant/criminal conduct (191)" (also see Paternoster et al. 1983). The low level of this relationship may be due to the difficulties that the police have bringing the risk of being caught and punished for wrongdoing to high-enough levels to effectively influence public behavior (Ross 1982; Robinson and Darley 1995, 1997). This evidence suggests that deterrence is an inadequate basis for securing compliance with the law.

In the case of police effectiveness in fighting crime, evidence suggests that police innovations in the management of police services may have contributed to the widespread declines in crime reported in major American cities during recent decades (Kelling and Coles 1996; Silverman 1999). Furthermore, indicators show increasing professionalism in policing, including declining rates of complaints against the police and lower levels of excessive police use of force against community residents. However, studies of the public and public views about and cooperation with the police suggest that the public's reactions to the police are again only loosely linked to police effectiveness in fighting crime, suggesting that police performance is an insufficient basis for gaining the cooperation of the public.

How can the police encourage public cooperation and support? To have an effective strategy for encouraging cooperation, people need to have additional reasons for cooperating beyond instrumental assessments of police performance. One alternative perspective is linked to the recognition that people have internalized values upon which the police might draw to secure compliance and to gain cooperation (Sherman 1993; Tyler 1990). A key value that people hold is their widespread support for the legitimacy of the police—the belief that the police are entitled to call upon the public to follow the law and help combat crime and that members of the public have an obligation to engage in cooperative behaviors. When people feel that an authority is legitimate, they authorize that authority to determine what their behavior will be within a given set of situations. Such an authorization of an authority "seem[s] to carry automatic justification. . . . Behaviorally, authorization obviates the necessity of making judgments or choices. Not only do normal moral principles become inoperative, but—particularly when the actions are explicitly ordered—a different type of morality, linked to duty to obey superior orders, tends to take over" (Kelman and Hamilton 1989, 16). People, in other words, feel responsible for following the directives of legitimate authorities (French and Raven 1959; Merelman 1966).

When people feel that an authority is legitimate, they authorize that authority to determine what their behavior will be within a given set of situations.

The roots of the modern use of legitimacy are usually traced to the writings of Weber (1968). Weber argued that the ability to issue commands that will be obeyed did not rest solely on the possession or ability to deploy power. In addition, there were rules and authorities that people would voluntarily obey. These rules and authorities possessed the quality of legitimacy, the belief by others that they ought to be obeyed. Weber's framing of the issue of legitimacy is important because his articulation of the question of why people obey authorities defines the modern focus of social science perspectives on legitimacy. In addition, he distinguished this issue from the philosophical question of why people ought to obey, which is central to discussions within law and political philosophy (Beetham 1991).

The argument that people's feelings about their internal obligation to obey social norms and rules also shape their behavior is equally central to the writings of Freud (Hoffman 1977) and Durkheim (1947, 1986), although these authors focused on people's moral values. This legitimacy argument is not particular to the police. On the contrary, legitimacy is suggested to be central to the exercise of all forms of authority. For example, Selznick's classic examination of authority in industrial settings argues that "there is a demand that rules be legitimate, not only in emanating from established authority, but also in the manner of their formulation, in the way they are applied, and in their fidelity to agreed-upon institutional purposes. . . . [The] obligation to obey has some relation to the quality of the rules and the integrity of their administration" (Selznick 1969, 29).

A legitimacy-based strategy of policing increases cooperation with the law by drawing on people's feelings of responsibility and obligation. The advantage of such a strategy lies in its ability to facilitate voluntary cooperation. To the degree that cooperation is motivated by personal values, it is self-regulatory and does not depend upon the ability of the authorities to effectively deploy incentives or sanctions to secure desired public behavior. In such a society, only minimal levels of societal resources are needed to maintain social order, and those resources can be redirected toward meeting other needs (Tyler 2001a; Tyler and Darley 2000). Furthermore, such voluntary deference is more reliable than instrumentally motivated compliance because it does not vary as a function of the circumstances or situation involved. Driving up to a stop sign on a deserted road at night, internal values motivate a person to stop, even when the possibility of punishment for law-breaking behavior is minimal.

The key empirical issue underlying a legitimacy-based strategy of policing is whether people's views about the legitimacy of the law and the police actually shape their cooperative behavior. The importance of legitimacy has been examined on two distinct levels: first, in studies of everyday interactions with police officers; and second, on the community level, with people evaluating the characteristics of their community police force—irrespective of whether they have had personal experience with police officers.

Studies of the influence of legitimacy typically assess people's views about the legitimacy of the police in three ways. First, people are asked about their sense of obligation to obey the police and the law, for example, whether they feel that "people should obey the law even if it goes against what they think is right" and that "disobeying the law is seldom justified." When asked questions of this type, Americans are generally found to express a strong sense of obligation to defer to law and to legal authorities. Second, legitimacy has been assessed by asking about institutional trust and confidence. People are asked, for example, which statements they agree with: "The police are generally honest"; "I respect the police"; and "I feel proud of the police." Finally, legitimacy is sometimes measured by assessing feelings about the police.

When they have personal experiences with the police, people sometimes have to decide whether to accept outcomes that they do not regard as desirable, or even as fair. The key question is whether their views about the legitimacy of the police in general, and/or of the particular officers with whom they are dealing, shape this willingness. Tyler and Huo (2002) studied this question using a sample of 1,656 residents of Los Angeles and Oakland. They found that two factors shaped the willingness to accept decisions: the degree to which the decisions were regarded as favorable and fair and the degree to which the police were generally regarded as legitimate authorities. These two factors were of approximately equal importance.

Tyler and Huo (2002, and reviewed in this volume) further found that the degree to which people generally viewed the police as legitimate influenced the basis upon which they decided whether to accept decisions. People could potentially accept decisions because those decisions were favorable or fair. They could also accept them because they believed that the police had acted appropriately when dealing with them—that is, due to procedural justice. Procedural justice will be discussed in more detail in the next section. Process-based reactions benefit the police, however, because they cannot always provide desirable outcomes, but it is almost always possible to behave in ways that people experience as being fair. The key finding of this study of personal experiences was that when people generally viewed the police as legitimate authorities, people's decisions about whether to accept police decisions were more strongly based upon evaluations of the procedural justice of police actions. Hence, having prior legitimacy facilitated the task of the police by leading people to assess police actions in more heavily procedural terms.

These studies do not examine the impact of legitimacy on whether people help the police. We might anticipate, for example, that people who viewed the police as more legitimate would be more willing to help them during personal encounters by, for example, volunteering information about conditions in the neighborhood or the identity or location of wrongdoers. Similarly, they might be more willing to volunteer to attend police-community meetings.

Legitimacy might also have an important influence on everyday compliance with the law. Much of peoples' law-related behavior occurs outside the immediate presence of legal authorities, although some possibility of sanctions always exists. Theories of legitimacy predict that in such settings, people's feelings of obligation will shape their behavior, leading to deference to the law. Tyler (1990) tested this argument in a study of the attitudes and behaviors of the residents of Chicago. He found that legitimacy has a significant influence on the degree to which people obeyed the law. Furthermore, that influence was distinct from and greater in magnitude than the influence of estimates of the likelihood of being caught and punished for wrongdoing. These findings suggest that as predicted by theories of legitimacy, people's views about the legitimacy of authorities influence the degree to which people obey the law in their everyday lives.

More recently, Sunshine and Tyler (2003) replicated this test of the influence of legitimacy on compliance within two samples of the residents of New York City. In both studies, they also found that the legitimacy of the police significantly influenced compliance with the law. Their study also extended consideration of the influence of legitimacy to a second area of concern: cooperation with the police. They found that those residents who viewed the police as more legitimate were more willing to cooperate with them both by reporting crimes or identifying criminals and by engaging in community activities to combat the problems of crime.

These findings support the basic premise of legitimacy theories. People are more willing to cooperate with legal authorities when they believe that those authorities are legitimate. This includes both deferring to their decisions during personal encounters and generally obeying legal rules in their everyday lives. Furthermore, people are more cooperative in helping the police to deal with crime in their communities when they view the police as legitimate. Hence, as anticipated in the work of Weber, legitimacy does represent a basis upon which authorities can act that is distinct from the possession or use of power and resources.

Legitimacy-based policing has clear advantages for the police and the community. When people act based upon their feelings of obligation and responsibility, they are engaging in self-regulatory behavior. Society and social authorities benefit from the occurrence of such behavior because it does not depend upon the maintenance of a credible system of deterrence or upon the quality of police performance. Studies suggest that the maintenance of such a system is always costly and inefficient, and in times of financial difficulty or crisis, when public cooperation is most clearly needed, it poses special difficulties for authorities.

One reason for focusing on issues of legitimacy at this time is that recent evidence shows public mistrust and lack of confidence in the law and the legal authorities (Tyler 1997a, 1998). For example, in 2002, the National Institute of Justice (NIJ) found that only 27 percent of Americans expressed "a great deal" of confidence in the criminal justice system. Within this broad category, the police have traditionally received high ratings. For example, in this same study, 59 percent expressed "a great deal" of confidence in the police. This is consistent with the suggestion that it is the courts that are the particular target of public dissatisfaction. In 1998, the General Social Survey found that only 22 percent of Americans expressed "a great deal" of confidence in the courts.

While the higher levels of confidence expressed in the police are encouraging from the perspective of a legitimacy-based approach to policing, a second troubling aspect of public views is the finding that there is a striking racial gap in views about legal authorities. For example, in a 2001 study conducted by the NIJ, 63 percent of whites expressed a great deal of confidence in the police, as compared with 31 percent of African Americans. In the case of the overall criminal justice system, 27 percent of whites expressed a great deal of confidence, as compared with 22 percent of African Americans.

The argument that legitimacy is a key antecedent to public cooperation with the police highlights the importance of being able to create and maintain a climate of public opinion in which community residents generally view the police as legitimate authorities. Given that perspective on policing, it is important to take seriously the evidence of public dissatisfaction and mistrust and to ask how legitimacy can be enhanced.

Enhancing Police Legitimacy: The Influence of Procedural Justice

Given the important role that legitimacy can play in determining the level of public cooperation with the police, it is important to try to understand how the police shape public views about their legitimacy. Public views about the legitimacy of the police might, for example, be the result of public assessments of police performance, in terms of either the ability of the police to create a credible sanction risk for wrongdoers or the effectiveness of the police in fighting crime and urban disorder. To the extent that this is true, the already-outlined importance of legitimacy would not have new or novel implications for policing. To enhance their legitimacy, the police would need to effectively combat crime and apprehend wrongdoers.

An alternative perspective on legitimacy is provided by the literature on procedural justice. That literature argues that the legitimacy of authorities and institutions is rooted in public views about the appropriateness of the manner in which the police exercise their authority. In other words, people are viewed as evaluating authorities by assessing whether they use fair procedures when engaging in policing activities. These procedural judgments are distinct from judgments about the effectiveness, valence, or fairness of the outcomes of those activities.

When people act based upon their feelings of obligation and responsibility, they are engaging in self-regulatory behavior.

As in the case of legitimacy, the key empirical issue is whether people consider procedural-justice issues when making inferences about the legitimacy of the police. Studies of people's evaluations of all types of authorities—police officers, judges, political leaders, managers, and teachers—have all provided strong support for the basic procedural-justice argument. When people are dealing with authorities or institutions, their evaluations of legitimacy are primarily linked to assessments of the fairness of the authority's or the institution's procedures. Such procedural-justice assessments are consistently found to be more strongly linked to legitimacy judgments than are the evaluations of their effectiveness or the valence or fairness of the outcomes they deliver (Lind and Tyler 1988; Tyler 1990, 2000a; Tyler et al. 1997; Tyler and Smith 1997).

In the case of personal experiences, studies find that when authorities act in ways that people experience as being fair, people are more willing to voluntarily accept the authorities' decisions (Kitzman and Emery 1993; Lind et al. 1993; MacCoun et al. 1988; Wissler 1995). These field studies confirm the findings of the earlier experimental findings of social psychological research (Thibaut and Walker 1975). Procedural-justice judgments are found to have an especially important role in shaping adherence to agreements over time. Pruitt et al. (1993) studied the factors leading those involved in disputes to adhere to mediation agreements over time and found that the procedural fairness of the initial mediation setting was a central determinant of adherence six months later. A second study suggested that procedural justice encourages long-term obedience to the law. Paternoster et al.

(1997) found that spouse abusers were less likely to commit future abuses when they experienced procedural justice with the police during an initial encounter.

These findings also receive support in the context of encounters between police and members of the public. Tyler and Huo (2002) found that procedural-justice judgments shaped people's willingness to accept the decisions made by police officers and are more important than are judgments about the favorability or fairness of the outcomes of the encounter. Similarly, Mastrofski, Snipes, and Supina (1996) and McCluskey, Mastrofski, and Parks (1999) found that the experience of disrespect from the police reduces compliance. This is consistent with the finding by Casper, Tyler, and Fisher (1988) that the satisfaction of felony defendants with their experiences with the police and courts was strongly linked to their assessments of the fairness of the process by which their cases were handled.

In a recent study of police encounters with community residents in two American cities that involved both interviews and observational analysis, McCluskey (2003) used a wide variety of indicators of procedural justice and found that five aspects of procedural justice influenced the willingness to comply with police requests for self-control. In particular, he found that

> holding all else constant, citizens who receive respectful treatment from authorities are almost twice as likely to comply, and those receiving disrespectful treatment are nearly twice as likely to rebel. If the citizen's voice is terminated by the police they are more than twice as likely to rebel against the police request for self-control. If the police demonstrate their commitment to making an informed decision by seeking information about the presenting situation, citizens are more than twice as likely to comply with the phase 1 request for self-control (p. 91).

The impact of procedural justice is greatest early in the encounter, and at that time, "the likelihood of citizen compliance is strongly affected by procedurally just tactics" (p. 114).

These findings suggest that procedural justice has a broad impact upon people's reactions to their experiences with the police. In particular, people's willingness to buy into and voluntarily accept decisions that may require them to accept outcomes that they do not want, or to engage in self-control over their actions, is enhanced by the judgment that one has been treated fairly by the police. Furthermore, evidence shows that this deference continues over time and shapes people's law-related behavior in the future. These findings suggest that the procedural justice that members of the public experience during their personal encounters with the police has both immediate and long-term behavior effects. It is also important to note, however, that procedural justice is not always found to be important. For example, McClusky (2003) did not find that procedural justice mattered when people were stopped by the police on the street and asked for identification, and Hickman and Simpson (2003) found that receiving procedurally fair treatment from the police did not encourage the victims of domestic violence to report future violent incidents to the police. Hence, procedural justice often, but not always, facilitates favorable reactions to policing activities.

Research further suggests that procedural justice during a personal encounter with the police influences views about the legitimacy of the police. Tyler (1990) demonstrated that the procedural justice of a personal experience with the police shaped general views about the legitimacy of the law, a finding replicated by Tyler and Huo (2002). Similarly, Tyler, Casper, and Fisher (1989) found that the procedural justice of their case disposition process shaped the views of felony defendants about the legitimacy of the criminal justice system and of the law.

More recently, Barnes (1999) has examined the influence of procedural justice in a Reintegrative Shaming Experiments (RISE)–based study of 900 Australians arrested for intoxicated driving. In a field experiment, these drivers had their cases referred to traditional courts or diversionary conferences. These conferences, designed using restorative-justice ideals, were viewed by participants as procedurally fairer. As procedural-justice models would predict, those who attended such conferences expressed more positive views about the legitimacy of the legal system than did those who went to court. They also expressed stronger intentions to obey the law in the future. Whether these differences lead to differences in actual behavior over time is unclear (Sherman 2003).

Of course, not all members of the community have personal contact with the police. It is also important to consider people's general views about the police and policing activities in their communities. Based upon a secondary analysis of prior surveys, Tyler (2001b) argued that procedural-justice judgments play a central role in shaping people's views about the legitimacy of the police and the courts. The findings of the four surveys reviewed by Tyler (2001b) suggest that people consider both performance in controlling crime and procedural fairness when evaluating the police and the courts. The major factor, however, is consistently found to be the fairness of the manner in which the police and the courts are believed to treat citizens. For example, in a study of Oakland residents living in high-crime areas, it was found that the primary factor shaping overall evaluations of the police was the quality of their treatment of community residents (which explained 26 percent of the unique variance in evaluations), with a secondary influence of performance evaluations (which explained 5 percent of the unique variance).

Sunshine and Tyler (2003) find support for this argument in two surveys of the residents of New York City. In both studies, the key antecedent of legitimacy was procedural justice. Those community residents who thought that the police exercised their authority in fair ways were also more willing to comply with the law and to cooperate with the police. Even in more coercive settings, like prisons, cooperation is found to be linked to procedural justice (Sparks, Bottoms, and Hay 1996).

What Is Procedural Justice?

Studies have identified a wide variety of issues that influence the degree to which people evaluate a procedure's fairness. Furthermore, it has been found that the importance of procedural criteria varies depending upon the setting (Tyler

1988). However, studies consistently point to several elements as key to people's procedural-justice judgments.

Participation is one key element. People are more satisfied with procedures that allow them to participate by explaining their situations and communicating their views about situations to authorities. This participation effect explains, for example, why mediation procedures are popular (Adler, Hensler, and Nelson 1983; McEwen and Maiman 1981) and settlement conferences are not (Lind et al. 1990). It suggests to police officers the importance of allowing people to have input before they make decisions about how to handle a problem. Interestingly, being able to control the outcome is not central to feeling that one is participating (Heinz and Kerstetter 1979). What people want is to feel that their input has been solicited and considered by decision makers, who can then frame their concerns into an appropriate resolution (Conley and O'Barr 1990).

People are more satisfied with procedures that allow them to participate by explaining their situations and communicating their view about situations to authorities.

A second key element is neutrality. People think that decisions are being more fairly made when authorities are unbiased and make their decisions using objective indicators, not personal views. As a consequence, evidence of evenhandedness and objectivity enhances perceived fairness. Basically, people are seeking a level playing field in which no one is unfairly advantaged. Because people are seldom in a position to know what the correct or reasonable outcome is, they focus on evidence that the decision-making procedures by which outcomes are arrived at show evidence of fairness. Transparency provides an opportunity to make that judgment, while evidence of factuality and lack of bias suggest that those procedures are fair.

Third, people value being treated with dignity and respect by legal authorities. The quality of interpersonal treatment is consistently found to be a distinct element of fairness, separate from the quality of the decision-making process. Above and beyond the resolution of their problems, people value being treated with politeness and having their rights acknowledged. The importance of interpersonal treatment is emphasized in studies of alternative dispute resolution procedures, which suggest that people value evidence that authorities "took the litigants and the dispute seriously," "after all, the trial was in all likelihood one of the most meticulous, most individualized interactions that the litigant had ever experienced in the course of his or her contacts with government agencies" (Lind et al. 1990). Their treatment during this experience carries for them important messages concerning their social status, their self-worth, and their self-respect. In other words, reaffirming one's sense of his or her standing in the community, especially in the wake of events that demean status, such as crime victimization or being publicly stopped and questioned by the police, can be a key issue to people dealing with legal authorities.

Finally, people feel that procedures are fairer when they trust the motives of decision makers. If, for example, people believe that authorities care about their well-being and are considering their needs and concerns, they view procedures as fairer. People are seldom able to judge the actions of authorities with specialized expertise (doctors, judges, police officers, etc.) since people lack the training and experience to know if the actions taken were reasonable and sufficient. Hence, they depend heavily upon their inferences about the intentions of the authority. If the authorities are viewed as having acted out of a sincere and benevolent concern for those involved, people infer that the authorities' actions were fair. Authorities can encourage people to view them as trustworthy by explaining their decisions and justifying and accounting for their conduct in ways that make clear their concern about giving attention to people's needs.

Why is trust such a key issue? Tyler (1990) found that the people he interviewed acknowledged that unfair treatment was widespread when people dealt with the police and courts. Nonetheless, over 90 percent predicted that if they had contact with the police or courts in the future, they would receive fair treatment. People, in other words, have a strong desire to view the authorities as benevolent and caring. This view is directly tested during a personal encounter with those authorities, and people's views are powerfully shaped by whether they do, in fact, receive the behavior they expect from the police or courts.

Ethnic Group Differences

These findings suggest that the roots of public trust and confidence in the police lie in public views about how the police exercise their authority. Given the already-noted ethnic group differences in trust and confidence, it is important to consider whether the argument outlined applies equally to the members of all ethnic groups.

Tyler and Huo (2002) address this issue directly in their study of the acceptance of decisions made by the police. Their findings suggest that procedural justice is an equally important issue to the members of three major ethnic groups: whites, African Americans, and Hispanics. Tyler (1994, 2000b) suggests that this finding is broader in scope. His analysis suggests that the importance of procedural justice is maintained across ethnicity, gender, income, education, age, ideology, and political party. As a result, a process-based approach to policing is an ideal way to bridge ethnic and other social divisions in society.

The Idea of a Law-abiding Society

The distinction between risk/gain estimates, performance evaluations, and legitimacy as antecedents of behavior highlights the possibility of two types of legal culture. The first is a culture that builds public compliance on the basis of people's judgments about police performance. Such a society depends upon the ability of legal authorities to create and maintain a credible presence by combating crime and punishing wrongdoers. The studies outlined demonstrate that while instrumental issues are important, it is difficult for legal authorities to sustain a viable legal system simply based upon performance.

The important role played by legitimacy in shaping people's law-related behavior indicates the possibility of creating a law-abiding society in which citizens have the internal values that lead to voluntary deference to the law and to the decisions of legal authorities such as the police. Such a society is based upon the willing consent and cooperation of citizens. That cooperation develops from people's own feelings about appropriate social behavior and is not linked to the risks of apprehension and punishment or to the estimates of the nature and magnitude of the crime problem that people estimate to exist in their social environment. Tyler (2001a) refers to such a society as a law-abiding society. The studies outlined make clear that such a society is possible in the sense that if people think authorities are legitimate, they are more likely to obey and to cooperate with authorities (Tyler 2003; Tyler and Blader 2000).

A law-abiding society cannot be created overnight through changes in the allocation of resources within government agencies, changes that would alter the expected gains and/or risks associated with cooperation. It depends upon the socialization of appropriate social and moral values among children and the enhancement of those values among adults. Evidence suggests that a core element to the creation and enhancement of such social values is the judgment that legal authorities exercise their authority following fair procedures. This is true both during personal experiences with the police and the courts, where people are found to be more willing to accept decisions that are fairly made, and in general evaluations of the police and courts, where people are found to comply with the law and support the police and courts as institutions when they think that these same institutions generally exercise authority fairly.

References

Adler, Patricia, Deborah Hensler, and Charles E. Nelson. 1983. *Simple justice: How litigants fare in the Pittsburgh Court arbitration program*. Santa Monica, CA: RAND.

Barnes, Geoffrey C. 1999. *Procedural justice in two contexts: Testing the fairness of diversionary conferences for intoxicated drivers*. Ph.D. diss., University of Maryland.

Beetham, David. 1991. *The legitimation of power*. Atlantic Highlands, NJ: Humanities Press.

Casper, Jonathan D., Tom R. Tyler, and Bonnie Fisher. 1988. Procedural justice in felony cases. *Law and Society Review* 22:483-507.

Conley, John M., and William M. O'Barr. 1990. *Rules versus relationships*. Chicago: University of Chicago Press.

Durkheim, Emile. 1947. *The division of labor.* Translated by George Simpson. New York: Free Press.

———. 1986. *Moral education*. Translated by Paul Fauconnet and Herman Schnurer. New York: Free Press.

Easton, David. 1975. A reassessment of the concept of political support. *British Journal of Political Science* 5:435-57.

French, John R. P., and Bertrand Raven. 1959. The bases of social power. In *Studies in social power*, edited by Dorwin Cartwright. Ann Arbor: University of Michigan Press.

Fuller, Lon. 1971. Human interaction and the law. In *The rule of law*, edited by Robert P. Wolff. New York: Simon and Schuster.

Heinz, Anne M., and Wayne A. Kerstetter. 1979. Pretrial settlement conference: Evaluation of a reform in plea bargaining. *Law and Society Review* 13:349-66.

Hickman, Laura J., and Sally S. Simpson. 2003. Fair treatment or preferred outcome? The impact of police behavior on victim reports of domestic violence incidents. *Law and Society Review* 37:607-34.

Hoffman, Martin. 1977. Moral internalization: Current theory and research. *Advances in Experimental Social Psychology* 10:85-133.

Kelling, George L., and Catherine M. Coles. 1996. *Fixing broken windows*. New York: Touchstone.

Kelman, Herbert C., and V. Lee Hamilton. 1989. *Crimes of obedience*. New Haven, CT: Yale University Press.

Kitzman, Katherine M., and Robert E. Emery. 1993. Procedural justice and parents' satisfaction in a field study of child custody dispute resolution. *Law and Human Behavior* 17:553-67.

Lind, E. Allan, Carol T. Kulik, Maureen Ambrose, and Maria de Vera Park. 1993. Individual and corporate dispute resolution. *Administrative Science Quarterly* 38:224-51.

Lind, E. Allan, Robert J. MacCoun, Patricia A. Ebener, William L. F. Felstiner, Deborah R. Hensler, Judith Resnik, and Tom R. Tyler. 1990. In the eye of the beholder: Tort litigants' evaluations of their experiences in the civil justice system. *Law and Society Review* 24:953-96.

Lind, E. Allan, and Tom R. Tyler. 1988. *The social psychology of procedural justice*. New York: Plenum.

MacCoun, Robert J. 1993. Drugs and the law: A psychological analysis of drug prohibition. *Psychological Bulletin* 113:497-512.

MacCoun, Robert J., E. Allan Lind, Deborah R. Hensler, D. L. Bryant, and Patricia A. Ebener. 1988. *Alternative adjudication: An evaluation of the New Jersey automobile arbitration program*. Santa Monica, CA: RAND.

Mastrofski, Stephen D., Jeffrey B. Snipes, and Anne E. Supina. 1996. Compliance on demand: The public's responses to specific police requests. *Journal of Crime and Delinquency* 33:269-305.

McCluskey, John D. 2003. *Police requests for compliance: Coercive and procedurally just tactics*. New York: LFB Scholarly Publishing.

McCluskey, John D., Stephen D. Mastrofski, and Roger B. Parks. 1999. To acquiesce or rebel: Predicting citizen compliance with police requests. *Police Quarterly* 2:389-416.

McEwen, Craig A., and Richard J. Maiman. 1981. Small claims mediation in Maine. *Maine Law Review* 33:237-68.

Meares, Tracey L. 2000. Norms, legitimacy, and law enforcement. *Oregon Law Review* 79:391-415.

Merelman, Richard J. 1966. Learning and legitimacy. *American Political Science Review* 60:548-61.

Nagin, Daniel S. 1998. Criminal deterrence research at the outset of the twenty-first century. In vol. 23 of *Crime and justice: A review of research*, edited by Michael Tonry, 1-42. Chicago: Chicago University Press.

Parsons, Talcott. 1967. Some reflections on the place of force in social process. In *Sociological theory and modern society*, edited by Talcott Parsons. New York: Free Press.

Paternoster, Raymond. 1987. The deterrent effect of the perceived certainty and severity of punishment. *Justice Quarterly* 4:173-217.

Paternoster, Raymond, Ronet Brame, Robert Bachman, and Lawrence W. Sherman. 1997. Do fair procedures matter? *Law and Society Review* 31:163-204.

Paternoster, Raymond, Linda E. Saltzman, Gordon P. Waldo, and Theodore G. Chiricos. 1983. Perceived risk and social control: Do sanctions really deter? *Law and Society Review* 17:457-79.

Pruitt, Dean G., Robert S. Peirce, Neil B. McGillicuddy, Gary L. Welton, and Lynn M. Castrianno. 1993. Long-term success in mediation. *Law and Human Behavior* 17:313-30.

Robinson, Paul H., and John M. Darley. 1995. *Justice, liability, and blame: Community views and the criminal law*. Boulder, CO: Westview.

———. 1997. The utility of desert. *Northwestern University Law Review* 91:453-99.

Ross, H. Lawrence. 1982. *Deterring the drinking driver: Legal policy and social control*. Lexington, MA: Heath.

Sampson, Robert J., Stephen Raudenbush, and Felton Earls. 1997 Neighborhoods and violent crime. *Science* 277:918-24.

Sarat, Austin. 1977. Studying American legal culture. *Law and Society Review* 11:427-88.

Selznick, Philip. 1969. *Law, society, and industrial justice*. New York: Russell Sage.

Sherman, Lawrence W. 1993. Defiance, deterrence, irrelevance: A theory of the criminal sanction. *Journal of Research in Crime and Delinquency* 30:445-73.

———. 2003. Reason with emotion: Reinventing justice with theories, innovations, and research. *Criminology* 41:1-37.

Silverman, Eli B. (1999). *NYPD battles crime: Innovative strategies in policing*. Evanston, IL: Northwestern University Press.

Sparks, Richard, Anthony Bottoms, and Will Hay. 1996. *Prisons and the problem of order*. Oxford, UK: Clarendon.

Sunshine, Jason, and Tom R. Tyler. 2003. The role of procedural justice and legitimacy in shaping public support for policing. *Law and Society Review* 37:513-48.

Thibaut, John W., and Laurens Walker. 1975. *Procedural justice: A psychological analysis*. Hillsdale, NJ: Lawrence Erlbaum.

Tyler, Tom R. 1988. What is procedural justice? Criteria used by citizens to assess the fairness of legal procedures. *Law and Society Review* 22:103-35.

———. 1990. *Why people obey the law*. New Haven, CT: Yale University Press.

———. 1994. Governing amid diversity: Can fair decision-making procedures bridge competing public interests and values? *Law and Society Review* 28:701-22.

———. 1997a. Citizen discontent with legal procedures. *American Journal of Comparative Law* 45:869-902.

———. 1997b. Compliance with intellectual property laws: A psychological perspective. *Journal of International Law and Politics* 28:101-15.

———. 1997c. Procedural fairness and compliance with the law. *Swiss Journal of Economics and Statistics* 133:219-40.

———. 1998. Public mistrust of the law: A political perspective. *University of Cincinnati Law Review* 66:847-76.

———. 2000a. Social justice: Outcome and procedure. *International Journal of Psychology* 35:117-25.

———. 2000b. Multiculturalism and the willingness of citizens to defer to law and to legal authorities. *Law and Social Inquiry* 25 (3): 983-1019.

———. 2001a. Trust and law abidingness: A proactive model of social regulation. *Boston University Law Review* 81:361-406.

———. 2001b. Public trust and confidence in legal authorities: What do majority and minority group members want from legal authorities? *Behavioral Sciences and the Law* 19:215-35.

———. 2003. Procedural justice, legitimacy, and the effective rule of law. In vol. 30 of *Crime and justice—A review of research*, edited by M. Tonry, 431-505. Chicago: University of Chicago Press.

Tyler, Tom R., and Steve Blader. 2000. *Cooperation in groups*. Philadelphia: Psychology Press.Tyler, Tom R., Robert J. Boeckmann, Heather J. Smith, and Yuen J. Huo. 1997. *Social justice in a diverse society*. Boulder, CO: Westview.

Tyler, Tom R., Jonathan D. Casper, and Bonnie Fisher. 1989. Maintaining allegiance toward political authorities. *American Journal of Political Science* 33:629-52.

Tyler, Tom R., and John Darley. 2000. Building a law abiding society: Taking public views about morality and the legitimacy of legal authorities into account when formulating substantive law. *Hofstra Law Review* 28:707-39.

Tyler, Tom R., and Yuen J. Huo. 2002. *Trust in the law*. New York: Russell Sage.

Tyler, Tom R., and Heather J. Smith. 1997. Social justice and social movements. In vol. 2 of *Handbook of social psychology*, 4th ed., edited by Daniel Gilbert, Susan Fiske, and Gardiner Lindzey, 595-629. New York: Addison-Wesley.

Weber, Max. 1968. *Economy and society*. Edited by G. Roth and C. Wittich. New York: Bedminster.

Wissler, Roselle L. 1995. Mediation and adjudication in small claims court. *Law and Society Review* 29:323-58.

Controlling Street-Level Police Discretion

By
STEPHEN D. MASTROFSKI

The Committee to Review Research on Police Policy and Practices' *Fairness and Effectiveness in Policing: The Evidence* provides a review of research on the causes of street-level police behavior, but the report offers little insight into how to control that discretion effectively. This is not due to deficiencies in the report but rather to limitations of the available research. This article discusses four problems with that research: underdeveloped theory, weak research designs, insufficient generalizability of findings, and inattention to the kinds of police discretion that really matter to policy makers, practitioners, and the public. The article gives special attention to the last problem and makes recommendations for improving the quality of research to better inform choices about how to control police street-level discretion.

Keywords: police; discretion; performance evaluation

Any comprehensive assessment of what police accomplish must account for the actions of personnel at the lowest rungs of the organizational ladder—the rank-and-file police officers and civilians in whom most of the organization's resources are invested. Police leaders and other public officials have long been obsessed with exercising a substantial degree of influence, if not control, over how policing is

Stephen D. Mastrofski is a professor of public and international affairs at George Mason University, where he directs the Administration of Justice Program and the Center for Justice Leadership and Management. He received his doctorate in political science from the University of North Carolina at Chapel Hill and has served on the faculty at the Pennsylvania State University and Michigan State University. His research interests include measuring police performance and assessing police reforms. Recent publications include studies of the public's image of the police, police disrespect toward the public, evaluations of community policing and Compstat, and the "romance of police leadership." He served as a member of the Committee to Review Research on Police Policy and Practices, National Academy of Sciences. In 2000, he received the Academy of Criminal Justice Science's O. W. Wilson Award for outstanding contributions to police education, research, and practice.

DOI: 10.1177/0002716203262584

practiced at the street level. Currently, there is great concern about how to eliminate racial bias in police enforcement, how to get officers to engage in more and higher quality community policing and problem solving, and how to get officers to make arrests when the law demands it (drunk driving and domestic violence). But readers of the National Academies' volume on police practices who are looking for ways to control street-level police discretion more effectively will surely be disappointed because the report in general, and chapters 4 and 5 in particular, simply sheds little light on this issue (Committee to Review Research 2003). The authors of the report do not bear the responsibility for this. The fault lies with the body of research available for review, which provides scant insight into the consequences of different methods by which street-level police discretion (hereafter called "police discretion," with "street-level" inferred) might be purposively controlled. The purpose of this article is to outline the major deficiencies of the existing body of research, focusing especially on one, and to suggest ways in which these problems might be overcome.

An Overview of the Problems with Extant Research

Before discussing the challenges confronting us, we need to be clear about some terms, and we need to establish the limits of the domain under consideration. By *discretion*, I mean the leeway that officers enjoy in selecting from more than one choice in carrying out their work. I use *control* in the same way as the report. That is, I mean for it to cover a range of influence over discretion extending from little to absolute. As with the report, my comments will concentrate on the control of patrol officer discretion, where most of the available research is concentrated.

Readers of chapters 4 and 5 will be struck by how inconclusive most of the committee's findings are. By far the most common conclusion is that the committee cannot draw a conclusion, because one or more of the following pertains: there is not enough research on the topic, the available research is not sufficiently rigorous, or the results are too mixed to provide a conclusive pattern. In this section, I identify four reasons for these problems, but in the remainder of the article, I concentrate on the last of them, the irrelevance of many of the measures of discretion that have been used in police research. I argue that attention to this issue is the first order of business for those hoping to develop a body of research that answers the question, "How can we better control the discretion of the police?"

Theory takes a holiday

The philosopher George Santayana (1955) noted, "Theory helps us to bear our ignorance of fact." Theory not only "fills in the blanks" where evidence is lacking, but it also allows us to make sense of those many, often-conflicting bits of evidence that we do possess. Unfortunately, most extant research on police discretion is underdeveloped theoretically or uses theories that are only tangentially useful to those who wish to know how better to control police discretion. Consider, for example, the question of how to avoid undesirable racial discrimination in the exercise of police authority, one of the most discussed police policy questions of our time. The committee's review of more than thirty studies on this topic led it to conclude that the mixed results about the impact of race were due to the contingent nature of effects. Research fails to take into account relevant features of the policy and social environments in which officers operate. I would add that for results to be meaningful for our purpose, the research needs to be framed in theories of *control* of police discretion (Punch 1983).

Such theories must acknowledge that many forces vie for control of officer discretion: not just the formal hierarchy of the police department but also other forces within and outside the organization. Police unions, civil rights organizations, and more recently, the federal justice system have figured prominently in the struggle over what to do about allegations of police racial discrimination, yet studies attempting to assess the influence of the citizen's race on police discretion do not take these important variables into account in explaining their results.

Efforts to exert control can take different forms. For example, some police chiefs may stress the disciplinary consequences of racial discrimination (Mastrofski, Reisig, and McCluskey 2002), while others may emphasize strategies of officer recruitment and training, and others still may structure patrol work (through permanent beat assignments) so that officers foster better relations with neighborhoods, regardless of racial composition. Or, for example, one might hypothesize that the presence of active neighborhood-level organizations that frequently engage the police at the street level would have stronger effects on race-related police practices than would the top-down approach that comes from centralized civilian review boards. The former is largely preventive and the police-citizen interactions are more frequent, varied, and diffuse (i.e., they work through establishing positive relationships), while the latter is corrective and relies upon formal processes to focus in a legalistic way on specific cases, the ultimate mechanisms of control being deterrence, incapacitation, and rehabilitation to prevent racist police practices.

To make sense of the variety of discretion-control mechanisms, we need to enrich our conceptualization of them. The current state of theoretical discussion in studies of police behavior has not advanced much beyond clustering sources of influence into a few categories, such as situational features, officer characteristics, organizational characteristics, and environmental characteristics (Sherman 1980; Riksheim and Chermak 1993). The frequently repeated finding that situational considerations dominate the choices that patrol officers make (Committee to Review Research 2003, 4-9) hardly constitutes a useful insight for policy purposes. It also undoubtedly holds for the choices made by lawyers, health care professionals, educators, social workers, and clergy. Patrol officers are expected to exercise discretion precisely because coping with "situational exigencies" is the raison d'être of the police (Bittner 1970). Barring the replacement of patrol officers with programmed "robocops," the overwhelming influence of situational factors will continue. Shifts or variations in patterns of influence on police discretion (e.g., comparing a change over time from race effects to no-race effects in a jurisdiction) should be the object of explanation sought by researchers, rather than just measuring the relative strength of situational influences versus those associated with officer and organization characteristics.

The police subculture figures largely in discussions of policing, but as the committee indicates, it is seldom treated by researchers in a theoretically interesting way.

Building useful theories of discretion control can draw on a wide range of disciplines and from the literature on police reform itself, some of which sets forth prescriptions on how best to control the police. The process might begin by considering *who* attempts to influence police discretion and then inventorying the mechanisms of influence available. A useful way to frame the field of players comes from Cyert and March (1963, 27-32), who see organizational goal setting and control as worked out through negotiation among competing groups, at least some of whom establish a "dominant coalition." The advantage of this approach is that it does not assume that there is a singular, hierarchically determined leadership that sets goals but that there may be many groups of players within the organization—drawn from middle managers, supervisors, and labor—who seek accommodation of their interests and who may enlist or themselves be influenced by outside players seeking influence over policing. And it allows for the possibility of "organized anarchy," where the distribution of power is in flux or no dominant coalition emerges, creating ambiguity for street-level decision makers, a condition quite common to public organizations such as the police (Cohen, March, and Olsen 1976; Scott 1992, 297). Comprehending the players and the degree of consensus or anarchy relevant to a given type of police discretion is the first step toward creating a realistic framework for modeling the effectiveness of systems intended to control it.

Control systems in police organizations seek to channel efforts toward the accomplishment of goals and interests. Formal organizations establish structures (centralization, hierarchy, rules), incentives and sanctions, supervision, and so on to coordinate and control the activities of the organization's members. This rational approach attempts to manipulate people's behavior by distributing consequences that matter to members of the organization, such as career advancement, recognition, material reward, and status. But no organization is completely successful in this regard, and indeed, police organizations find control of this sort highly problematic because the organizations are limited in their capacity to manipulate what employees really care about, and the systems of control themselves are cumbersome, elaborate, conflicting, and often (as a consequence) only loosely connected to the day-to-day world of the decision makers whose activities they are intended to direct (Crank and Langworthy 1992; Scott 1992, 315; Mastrofski and Ritti 1992). Understandably, once police rookies hit the street, the veterans tell them to "forget what you learned in the academy" and "throw away the rule book" (Rubinstein 1973; Van Maanen 1974). The resulting organizational environment is sometimes called a "punitive bureaucracy," one more effective at extinguishing undesired behavior patterns than promoting desired ones. This proposition has some support in the small body of research reviewed by the committee that shows that formal rules and guidelines and strong disciplinary practices appear to reduce the frequency with which police resort to lethal force or corrupt practices (Committee to Review Research 2003, 157-58, 272-73, 285).

To promote desired behaviors, it has become increasingly popular in police management texts and among reformers to advocate exerting control through legitimacy rather than the raw power to manipulate consequences for the officers. This is sometimes called "transformational leadership," because the officer's compliance derives from a personal transformation rather than from a quid pro quo transaction of compliance in exchange for something of value (Bass 1985). Police managers are encouraged to persuade officers to embrace certain goals and values not because doing so will produce desirable personal consequences, or failing to do so will produce negative ones, but because doing so is simply right and proper or the best way. This is, for example, the assumption of reformers who argue that community policing can be implemented effectively only when officers embrace it as a "philosophy" (Sparrow, Moore, and Kennedy 1990; Trojanowicz and Bucqueroux 1990). This approach and proposals about specific ways for leaders to accomplish it (see, e.g., Peters and Waterman 1982, chap. 9; Sparrow, Moore, and Kennedy 1990, chap. 5) date back at least as far as Selznick (1957), but there is remarkably little empirical research that tests whether and when it is effective in police organizations.

Another organizational element to consider is the police culture, "the shared internalized beliefs and norms that provide meaning and guidance to individual members engaged in collective action" (Scott 1992, 315). The police subculture figures largely in discussions of policing, but as the committee indicates (Committee to Review Research 2003, 130-33), it is seldom treated by researchers in a theoretically interesting way. It is widely regarded as only a defense mechanism of street-level officers coping with pressures from management and environmental threats (e.g., a hostile public)—a monolithic obstacle to management's ability to govern the organization and society's capacity to hold the organization accountable. Interestingly, overwhelming "the police culture" is often the target of bureaucratic approaches to create consequences for the officers, while the transformational leadership approach seeks to shift this culture from hostility to receptiveness (if not enthusiastic embrace) of management's values and goals. But the culture is not assessed as an independent influence on the exercise of discretion. Alternatively, if one begins with the assumption that a police organization culture is an independent *variable* over time and place, not a constant, then rich theoretical possibilities emerge from considering the impact of variation in an organizational culture's strength and complexity—and the impact of various management strategies for control of discretion in different cultural environments. An example of this approach is offered by Klockars et al. (2000), who developed a method to measure the orientation of officers to tolerate abuse of authority and corruption among their colleagues. One might presume that the effects of management interventions to reduce abusive police practices would vary considerably between an organization with a strong cultural predisposition not to tolerate those practices compared with one that was far more tolerant.

The task of empirically sorting out the effects of different modes of discretion control will be challenging for police researchers. Despite claims of organizational revolutions, sea changes, and paradigm shifts, police departments do not produce pure discretion-control systems, and it is certainly a rarity for radical change to occur in a short time period. This means that researchers must deal mostly with hybrid control systems, where one layer of reform is laid atop the structures of other, older reforms. And some control interventions themselves are complex, containing a variety of components. And sometimes even these components conflict, such as when they demand a high degree of individual manager accountability for producing results and for collaboration and teamwork (Willis, Mastrofski, and Weisburd 2003). This makes it important to know how the different components of a control intervention worked (or did not work) together to produce a given result. Compstat in New York City is a good example of this problem. This management accountability program was implemented simultaneously with a so-called broken-windows or zero-tolerance approach to policing neighborhoods, and it is hard to tease out how much each contributed to the increase in the enforcement of minor offenses in the city (Eck and Maguire 2000, 231).

Efforts within the organization to exert control over police discretion do not occur in isolation from larger environmental influences, a point carefully stressed by chapter 5 of the committee's report. A popular conceptualization of environmental influences is that they have their greatest effect on police discretion working through organizational features, such as the goals and desires of the police chief, which in turn affect the policies and structures of the organization and ultimately patterns its officers' practices (Wilson 1968). The report points out a variety of environmental entry points of influence: neighborhood characteristics, city characteristics, the actions of local political officials, appellate court rulings, and so on. However, to advance beyond the mere listing of hypothesized effects of these categories of environmental influence, we need at least two kinds of theoretical developments. First, we need theories that specify the environmental conditions when internal organizational control systems will be more and less successful in shaping officer discretion. For example, is it in fact the case that critical events (e.g., scandals or riots) make it possible to implement formal policies that shape discretion in desired ways, as some have argued for use of lethal force and corruption (Sherman 1978, 1983)? If so, what sort of control systems are most effective, and how long do they retain their effectiveness following the critical event? Second, we need greater specification of the processes through which environmental forces are presumed to shape officer discretion—whether they operate through organization mechanisms or independently. For example, how does a new appellate court ruling about what is permissible in police stop-and-search work its way, if at all, into the daily practices of patrol officers? Some influence may be exerted through department efforts (guidelines and training), and some may come through officers' exposure to the way that members of the local criminal "courtroom workgroup" respond (Eisenstein and Jacob 1977).

Weak internal validity

The report makes clear that most of the research on the causes of police behavior is based on correlational studies of variations in police practice from one encounter, officer, department, or neighborhood to another. The randomized experiments summarized in the report examine the effects *of* the police, not the effects of anything *on* the police. In most of these cases, causal inference is problematic. For example, in studies that show that college-educated officers perform better than those without a college education, we are unable to distinguish the contributions of the actual educational experience in college from the selection effects of getting into college and completing it. This is not just an academic issue, because if there is little "value added" for the quality of police work by a college education, then a tremendous amount of effort is being expended on something that gives poor return for the investment. Without a doubt, the quality of evidence on this and most other issues of discretion control would be enhanced by studies with stronger designs for making causal inferences. While ethics and limited resources preclude many cases from the random assignment required by an experimental design, quasi-experiments and more carefully constructed statistical controls in correlational studies would do a lot to strengthen our confidence in the results of studies assessing the effects of various ways to control police discretion.

Limited external validity

Some very good studies have been conducted that assess the impact of controls on police discretion, but they appear like little islands scattered across a vast, uncharted archipelago of police agencies. And we police researchers, with too much regularity, insist on returning to the same islands time and again to assess the state of police discretion. It is as if we had visited Hawaii and, from our visit, declared that we know the nature of the whole South Pacific. In technical terms, the extant research has a generalizability problem.

One aspect of the generalizability problem is that we do not have a large and diverse storehouse of comparable studies conducted at different times and places so that we can say with confidence just how universal certain findings are. For example, the three largest multijurisdiction, systematic field observations of police patrol (Reiss 1971; Caldwell 1978; Mastrofski et al. 1998) included only twenty-nine different jurisdictions over the period 1966 to 1996, and only one department appeared in more than one study, making it difficult to make meaningful comparisons over time. Even among these studies, which use similar data-collection methods, the sampling plans and data-collection instruments are sufficiently divergent to make comparative secondary research across studies challenging. The Spouse Abuse Replication Project (SARP) was an effort to rectify the generalizability problem following the groundbreaking findings of the Minneapolis domestic violence study (Sherman 1992). SARP brought together research teams in different

---

Researchers might strive harder to work in agencies that are experiencing problems with police discretion.

---

cities, requiring that all maintain certain design and measurement features in common so that cross-site comparisons and secondary research would be possible (Maxwell, Garner, and Fagan 2001). The same practice should be followed in research on the control of police discretion. Funding agencies should promote multisite research that introduces theoretically meaningful variation across sites and that insists upon design and data-collection features that ensure comparability of findings.

The extant research on police discretion is biased in a number of ways regarding the types of agencies that are included. The vast majority of studies focus on relatively large municipal police forces, leaving mostly unexplored small urban departments, sheriff's departments, rural agencies, special police agencies, and large but geographically dispersed state police agencies. There are reasons to expect some different patterns in the exercise of police discretion from the usually studied agencies, thus undoubtedly restricting the possibility of new insights about what influences police discretion under what circumstances. And perhaps most telling, except for the occasional research compelled by legal process, research on police discretion tends to occur at the more progressive agencies that have less discomfort in exposing themselves to scrutiny by outsiders (Fyfe 2002). Departments in crisis and those that perpetually experience problems in the control of police discretion would seem, understandably, less willing to participate in such studies. This may overstate the severity of the problem, however. Of course, it is sometimes the case that departments in crisis are most susceptible to requests to be studied because their leaders, particularly if recently brought in to "clean up the mess," have less to lose and a lot to gain by learning what is happening.

Those who fund studies are often more interested in featuring results in departments thought to lead the field rather than those that are or might be in trouble. Always studying the best or most progressive departments deprives policy makers of useful information on struggling departments where there are much better prospects for improvement, since they are presumably further from the "ceiling."

This is not an easy challenge to overcome, but researchers might strive harder to work in agencies that are experiencing problems with police discretion. Agencies that fund police research and evaluation might do more to offer incentives for agencies experiencing discretion-control problems to obtain quality external evaluations. In some cases, courts and reform political leaders may require or welcome objective research, and in other cases, departments may agree to participate if the agency's identity remains masked in published reports. Some advocate a central government mandate for the collection of sensitive information about how police exercise discretion (Fyfe 2002). And finally, another approach is to avoid stiff departmental resistance by attempting to build professional pressure among police organizations to participate voluntarily in standardized reporting of certain aspects of police discretion, such as use of force.

Irrelevance of measures of police practice

Throughout chapters 4 and 5 of the report, the committee bemoans the lack of good measures of police practice. Much of the committee's concern addresses the tendency of researchers to focus on a very limited range of police discretion—arrest and other forms of enforcement and coercion—while ignoring the many other things that police do (assist, persuade, advise, mediate, mobilize people and organizations, analyze problems, gather and disseminate information; Maguire 2003). This is a legitimate criticism of the extant research, but even if researchers were to study vigorously all of these aspects of police practice, the resulting body of knowledge would be woefully inadequate for our purposes unless those attributes of police practice described features that are worth controlling. For example, the fairly substantial body of research that attempts to illuminate what causes police to make an arrest tells us absolutely nothing about what causes the police to make arrests that we want them to make. To use my own research as an example, colleagues and I have shown that in one department, officers who embraced community policing values were less inclined to arrest suspects than were officers who were less positive about community policing, other things being equal (Mastrofski, Worden, and Snipes 1995). While this certainly tells us something about the impact of community policing on officers' law enforcement tendencies, it does nothing to help the chief of this department decide whether this pattern is a good thing. Unless one takes the mindless position that more (or fewer) arrests are always preferred, one finds that our research, and the literature generally, does not tell us what causes police to make arrests that we want them to make and what causes them to make arrests that we do not want them to make. The same can be said of the practice of field interrogations and other police-initiated stops of citizens, searches, interrogations, and a wide range of physically and verbally coercive methods, all of which are legitimate and useful under some circumstances but not others. And, of course, the same holds for the variety of other seldom-studied practices, such as mediation, that police perform with a high degree of personal discretion.

All this is to say that our measures of police discretion are, by and large, free of standards that would allow us to judge the quality of those choices. Without incorporating such standards into our study of police discretion, we can say little that is helpful to the police, public officials, and the public itself in assessing what is and is not effective in controlling what matters most in the exercise of police discretion. The remainder of this article will elaborate the challenges of defining and measuring those aspects of police discretion that we wish to control and will make some suggestions about how to meet these challenges.

Measuring What Matters in Controlling Police Discretion

A few years ago, the National Institute of Justice and the Office of Community Oriented Policing Services convened a series of meetings of distinguished researchers and scholars, police leaders, and others to revitalize thinking on how to measure police performance. A volume, *Measuring What Matters*, was produced with fifteen essays that offered some interesting observations and provocative proposals about what should be measured and how (Langworthy 1999). Measuring the police capacity to control crime, fear of crime, and stem disorder consumed most of the volume's pages, and the book also gave considerable attention to what police constituencies expected. With one exception, no attention was paid to measuring police discretion and its control. This is a remarkable omission because the public appears to care a great deal about controlling police discretion. Tom Tyler and colleagues have shown in a series of important studies that the public cares a great deal about the processes of policing—at least as much, if not more, than the outcomes those processes produce (e.g., Tyler 2001; Tyler and Huo 2002). That is to say, they care *how* the police exercise their discretion. Police organizations rarely experience crises for failing to control crime; it is failure to control police discretion that most often places the jobs of top leadership in jeopardy (especially abuse of force, corruption, and neglectful service provision). The following section of the article is the beginning of an attempt to fill that lacuna.

Strictly academic research can be satisfied with answering, "What do police do, and what explains variations in what they do?" However, research on control of the police requires answers to a different set of questions: "What do we *want* police to do, and what accounts for variation in how well they do it?" Whereas the first set of questions requires only astute observation (Bittner 1970), the latter set also requires conscious engagement with norms about what police should be accomplishing.

There are two ways to justify norms: (1) because the practice is believed to have inherent value and (2) because the practice is believed instrumental to accomplishing something that has value. An example of the first is the claim that police search-and-seizure practices should conform to constitutional requirements for the protection of civil liberties; in a democracy such as ours, there is inherent value in a police who follow the Constitution. An example of the second is the claim that the more drug dealers who are stopped and searched in areas plagued by street-level drug markets, the greater the disruption of those markets, which ultimately should make the area less attractive to drug dealers, thus decreasing drug crime and improving the quality of life. Obviously, a style of stop-and-search less fettered by legal standards can be more disruptive, but then officers, their superiors, or high-up policy makers must decide how to reconcile the tension between two conflicting values. In recent research, a colleague and I found that in one police department, officers chose to conduct searches that violated the suspect's constitutional rights in three of every ten searches, and that searches to find drugs were the most likely to violate constitutional standards (Gould and Mastrofski forthcoming). Our research was not designed to measure the extent to which these improper searches reduced crime, but we were able to provide a rough indication of the cost to citizens' constitutionally protected liberties. This, at least, provides policy makers with some measure of the civil liberties cost paid to acquire at least the prospect of some (unknown) increment of crime control.

One can readily envision a set of values about some aspects of police authority that might be carefully measured. Suppose that a department placed a high value on its officers' following the law closely in making arrests for felonies and misdemeanors, the classic "legalistic" department (Wilson 1968). That is, the department wants officers in these cases to make an arrest whenever, but only if, the evidentiary requirement of probable cause is satisfied—what is sometimes called a "full enforcement" policy. Under these conditions, the officer can produce three outcomes: an arrest that is justified by the evidence, an arrest that is not justified by the evidence, and a failure to arrest when the evidence justifies it. Field observations of police suggest that under normal operating conditions, police do not come anywhere near full enforcement, even with felonies and serious misdemeanors (e.g., drunk driving) and even when there is a willing complainant present, asking the police to make an arrest (Mastrofski et al. 2000). Rather, they tend to err on the side of underenforcement (Black 1980, 91; Brown 1981; Reiss 1971, 134).

Despite many studies of police arrest, researchers know relatively little about the extent of enforcement "error," its patterns, and the things that influence those patterns. Measuring and explaining both the extent and the nature of the errors of overenforcement and underenforcement in a given sample of police encounters with suspects would be far more useful than simply measuring whether an arrest was made. Indeed, it is selectivity in leniency that doubtlessly most troubles those who charge the police with racial profiling or with neglect of a neighborhood (DiIulio 1993, 3; Kennedy 1997). When such selectivity is hierarchically orchestrated, such as the zero-tolerance policy that seeks maximum enforcement of all laws in certain neighborhoods while others experience far more selective enforcement, antagonistic police-community relations also tend to ensue on a selective basis (Scheingold 1999, 186).

One can also envision an evaluation of police arrests that took into account instrumental expectations, such as reducing the likelihood of future offending. After discussing evidence that violent domestic abusers are affected differently by arrest, depending upon such things as employment status, Sherman (1992, 186) suggested that the most effective domestic violence reduction strategy might be

---

There are two ways to justify norms: (1) because the practice is believed to have inherent value and (2) because the practice is believed instrumental to accomplishing something that has value.

---

returning to officers the discretion to make or not to make these arrests and offering them guidelines based on the latest scientific evidence to make those choices. Assuming that the evidence was sufficiently sound and the results sufficiently compelling to justify such a policy, a conscientious police chief would certainly wish to monitor the extent to which officers were complying with guidelines about the factors to be taken into account—or at least to determine which factors were most influential, so as to monitor for potential abuse of discretion. A system of measuring police discretion that took these factors into account would enable researchers to provide police management with a much better understanding of the extent to which street-level domestic violence enforcement practices were conforming to department expectations, and embedded in the proper evaluation design framework, the impact of training, supervision, and other control efforts could also be assessed.

Of course, legal standards for taking enforcement actions are among the most elaborated, and that is also where empirical research on the consequence of the police action is also most developed. Can we measure the merits of police action in other, less legally structured discretionary domains? The answer, I think, is clearly yes. Let us consider a couple of the more challenging aspects of discretion.

Suppose that a department takes to heart the finding by Tyler and Huo (2002) that when police treat the public with respect and give them a sense that they are trying to act fairly (by, for example, seeking information before acting, giving citizens the opportunity to tell their sides of the story, and explaining to citizens what the officer is doing and why), citizens accord the police greater legitimacy. Inasmuch as legitimacy is a critical prerequisite of effective democratic governance, such a finding indicates that there are profound implications for how police do whatever they do (arrest, search, use force, mediate disputes, or render other assistance). The law does not demand that officers act with a certain style or demeanor, but the community policing movement may have increased among the public the expectation that police will do whatever they do in a fair and respectful manner. Measuring what matters then would require a means to monitor this crucial aspect of police discretion. Most of the research that undergirds this perspective focuses on general descriptions of judgments made by the public rather than on specific police actions or failures to act. For example, surveys ask citizens to judge whether the officer treated them politely, whether the citizen understood why he or she made decisions, and whether he or she was basically honest (Tyler and Huo 2002, 152). Focusing instead on the actions taken by the officers would clearly be more useful to police since they are in direct control of their own actions and not the judgments others make about them. Fortunately, a model for such measures is available in a research report based upon expensive, systematic field observation (McCluskey 2003, 122), but researchers might also obtain this information by debriefing members of the public or officers about their encounters with each other.

Most studies of street-level discretion have examined what officers do once they have been mobilized to engage in a face-to-face encounter with the public. An entire class of police discretion that has only recently been given much attention by researchers is how, when, and where officers choose to mobilize. Most of this effort has focused on racial profiling, but the domain is much broader than that. Let us focus again on one of the strategies that the committee identified as having strong evidence of effectiveness: hot-spots policing (Committee to Review Research 2003, 249). This involves concentrating police surveillance and enforcement efforts at a particular location that is "hot" with undesirable activity (e.g., drug dealing).

Two models exist for hot-spots policing: low discretion and high discretion. The low-discretion model assigns to the supervisory hierarchy the designation of which hot spots require the officers' attention, and it holds them accountable for directed patrol or enforcement efforts in that area. In some instances, the level of discretion afforded the rank and file may still be substantial, with management specifying only that officers log a prescribed amount of time in the hot spot without specifying what they must do there (Sherman and Weisburd 1995, 634). But some management policies are more restrictive, specifying in addition the sort of tactics to be undertaken in the hot spot (Willis, Mastrofski, and Weisburd 2003, 103). Attempts to limit officer discretion in these ways have met with considerable rank-and-file resistance (Buerger, personal communication, 2003; Willis, Mastrofski, and Weisburd 2003). Under the special circumstances of the scrutiny afforded by the use of field observers at the hot spots, researchers have reported a high degree of conformance to experimental protocols for directed patrol of hot spots (Sherman and Weisburd 1995, 638), but the protocols specified only time present and not officer tactics while present. That compliance would be so high without the added scrutiny seems doubtful, especially when large portions of the rank and file object to it. In addition, when a department makes directed patrol a high priority, even some middle managers subvert the system by instructing patrol officers to record all enforcement activities as the consequence of directed patrol, regardless of the situation (Willis, Mastrofski, and Weisburd 2003, 28), thereby communicating a degree of cynicism about directed patrol from the department hierarchy itself. Thus, even in low-discretion programs, implementation compliance is problematic and far from certain.

The high-discretion approach to hot-spots policing approximates problem-oriented policing. Here, officers are given discretion to identify hot spots on their beats, to study the situation, to devise the most effective solution, and to implement it as they think best (Committee to Review Research 2003, 243). The low-discretion model of hot-spots policing is easier to evaluate since management provides more constraints that serve as standards against which to judge an officer's activities (self-reported, based on department records, or independently observed). It is also possible, however, to measure the extent and nature of the high-discretion problem-solving effort. Colleagues and I have measured the quantity of problem-solving effort (in terms of time expended) using systematic field observation (DeJong, Mastrofski, and Parks 2001). The greater challenge is to determine the quality of these efforts. One might attempt to make summary judgments about the thoroughness, thoughtfulness, scientific rigor, and so on that characterize a given problem-solving effort (Braga and Weisburd 2002), but one also might wish to break this down further to determine how much problem-solving time was devoted to identifying the problem, analyzing it, planning an intervention strategy, conducting the strategy, and evaluating it (assuming that one uses the SARA [Scanning, Analysis, Response, and Assessment] model as a standard). As problems become more unusual or obstreperous, managers might well desire officers to spend more time on the early stages of problem analysis and planning. Given the enormous resources given to promoting problem-oriented policing in the last decade, it is disappointing that so little has been done to develop systematic measurement of this new form of discretion.

One cannot overemphasize the importance of doing more to measure the discretion exercised by street-level police officers in deciding when and where to mobilize to do something. A colleague and I found that contrary to the received wisdom (but consistent with a fair amount of empirical research that has been ignored), American police patrol is not overwhelmingly driven by 911 and the calls-for-service apparatus (Mastrofski and Parks 2003). Police officers spend most of their work time free to decide when and where to mobilize and what to do. In two medium-sized urban police departments in the late 1990s, we found that patrol officers typically spent three-fourths of their time engaged in activities that neither a dispatcher nor superior officer instructed them to do. And of that time spent on officer-selected activities, only 15 to 16 percent was spent on face-to-face encounters with the public. General patrol, administrative activities, and personal breaks accounted for the majority of the officer's self-directed time. If many departments take the committee's findings seriously and attempt to move toward more focused strategies of police intervention, they will need to develop much more sophisticated measures of how, where, and when officers are mobilizing at their own discretion—regardless of the scope of discretion they give officers in selecting targets and modes of intervention. If police leaders begin to reorganize their patrol operations around hot-spots-focused strategies, it will be especially important to monitor systematically precisely where officers spend their time doing what to or with whom. Given the pinpoint requirements of hot-spots policing, a block may make all the difference in the effectiveness of the intervention.

If community policing efforts have accomplished anything, they have shown that it is possible to establish a useful give-and-take between police and community that is designed to identify and solve problems.

Thus far, I have argued that it is both paramount and possible to measure aspects of police discretion that really matter to those who want to control it. But the parties wishing to control police discretion are many, and their values and priorities are undoubtedly varied. Consider reactions to the Louima and Diallo use-of-force cases in New York City. At least three distinct perspectives emerged on what matters: police management, police officers and collective bargaining representatives, and spokespersons of minority racial and ethnic groups who felt their group members were at special risk for police abuse of coercive authority. Each group brings a different view of how much discretion the officers should have and how to define well-executed discretion.

How can one proceed to measure what matters when the perspectives differ so strikingly? Answering this question is of course a political enterprise, but it is possible for scientists to both help and benefit by participating. First, police researchers can help to facilitate a dialogue among representatives of the various groups—for the purpose of seeking clarification of differences and establishing what common ground, if any exists. Conducted without care, such sessions can degenerate into mere "gripe sessions," where each group articulates its frustrations with the others, such as the community relations session recounted by Wilson (1983, 108) where a disgruntled citizen asked a beleaguered sergeant, "Why you cats always kicking cats' asses?" Yet if community policing efforts have accomplished anything, they have shown that it is possible to establish a useful give-and-take between police and community that is designed to identify and solve problems, even when the police and communities come together initially without mutual warmth and trust (DuBois and Hartnett 2002; Forman 2003; Lurigio and Skogan 1998). Second, the product of that dialogue can provide a clear topography of differences and common ground in what should be measured in police discretion. And, obviously, researchers can play a central role in designing specific measures and methods that can speak to the full range of perspectives bearing on the control of police discretion. Providing a more diverse and comprehensive set of measures will do more to inform the political and policy dialogue about whether and how to control officer discretion.

Conclusion

Readers of *Fairness and Effectiveness in Policing: The Evidence* will readily observe that the report has a lot to say about the importance of controlling police discretion and little to say about how to do it effectively or wisely. We should not fault the messenger for the message; the committee did the best it could with a body of research that, by and large, has paid relatively little attention to the issue and that has many serious deficiencies, for the purpose of both advancing knowledge and making policy about the control of police discretion. I have outlined problems with the existing literature and suggested some ways to overcome them. The highest priority is developing measures of police discretion that matter to those who exercise it, oversee it, and experience it. But developing theories of discretion control, strengthening research designs to make stronger causal inferences, and expanding the generalizability of findings are also important and certainly familiar challenges to the research community. It is possible to make substantial progress in these areas. Researchers should accept responsibility for attending to this agenda, but realistically, making advances will be significantly expedited if those with the funds to shape the direction of policing research establish the control of street-level police discretion as a very significant priority. For too long, the usual funding sources have been concerned mostly with determining what prevents or reduces crime or related outcomes, such as fear of crime. In the 1990s, the Office of Justice Programs found it sufficiently important to commission a literature review to assess what works and what does not in preventing crime (Sherman et al. 1997). Perhaps before this decade is out, the Office of Justice Programs may find it worthwhile to commission one or more studies to learn how to control police discretion. Any candid police chief will agree that it is at least as challenging to get the "troops" to implement the strategy as it is to select the right strategy. For democratic policing, accountability means little without the capacity to control officer discretion. This could hardly be a more compelling priority than now, a time when American police are being pressured to move onto the new terrain of promoting homeland security and respond to the threat of terrorism.

References

Bass, B. M. 1985. *Leadership and performance beyond expectations*. New York: Free Press.

Bittner, Egon. 1970. *The functions of the police in modern society: A review of background factors, current practices, and possible role models*. Chevy Chase, MD: National Institute of Mental Health.

Black, Donald J. 1980. *The manners and customs of the police*. New York: Academic Press.

Braga, Anthony, and David Weisburd. 2002. Qualitative insights on the problems of place and the development of problem oriented policing interventions. Unpublished manuscript.

Brown, Michael K. 1981. *Working the street: Police discretion and the dilemmas of reform*. New York: Russell Sage.

Caldwell, Eddie. 1978. Patrol observation: The patrol encounter, patrol narrative, and general shift information forms. *Police services study methods report MR-2*. Bloomington, IN: Workshop in Political Theory and Policy Analysis.

Cohen, Michael D., James G. March, and Johan P. Olsen. 1976. People, problems, solutions, and the ambiguity of relevance. In *Ambiguity and choice in organizations*, edited by James G. March and Johan P. Olsen, pp. 24-37. Bergen, Norway: Universitetsforlaget.

Committee to Review Research on Police Policy and Practices. 2003. *Fairness and effectiveness in policing: The evidence*. Washington, DC: The National Academies Press.

Crank, John, and Robert Langworthy. 1992. An institutional perspective of policing. *Journal of Criminal Law and Criminology* 83:338-63.

Cyert, Richard M., and James G. March. 1963. *A behaviorist theory of the firm*. Englewood Cliffs, NJ: Prentice Hall.

DeJong, Christina, Stephen D. Mastrofski, and Roger B. Parks. 2001. Patrol officers and problem solving: An application of expectancy theory. *Justice Quarterly* 18:31-61.

DiIulio, John J., Jr. 1993. Rethinking the criminal justice system: Toward a new paradigm. In *Performance measures for the criminal justice system*, pp. 1-18. Washington, DC: Bureau of Justice Statistics.

DuBois, Jill, and Susan M. Hartnett. 2002. Making the community side of community policing work: What needs to be done. In *Policing and community partnerships*, edited by Dennis J. Stevens, pp. 1-16. New York: Prentice Hall.

Eck, John E., and Edward Maguire. 2000. Have changes in policing reduced violent crime? An assessment of the evidence. In *The crime drop in America*, edited by Alfred Blumstein and Joel Wallman, pp. 207-65. New York: Cambridge University Press.

Eisenstein, James, and Herbert Jacob. 1977. *Felony justice: An organizational analysis of criminal courts*. Boston: Little, Brown.

Forman, James, Jr. 2003. Community policing, social norms, and youth as assets. Unpublished manuscript.

Fyfe, James J. 2002. Too many missing cases: Holes in our knowledge about police use of force. Report prepared for the National Research Council, Committee to Review Research on Police Policy and Practices Data Collection Workshop, Washington, DC.

Gould, Jon B., and Stephen D. Mastrofski. Forthcoming. Suspect searches: Assessing police behavior under the Constitution. *Criminology and Public Policy*.

Kennedy, Randall. 1997. *Race, crime, and the law*. New York: Random House.

Klockars, Carl B., Sanja Kutnjak Ivkovich, William E. Harver, and Maria R. Haberfeld. 2000. *The measurement of police integrity*. Washington, DC: National Institute of Justice.

Langworthy, Robert H. 1999. *Measuring what matters: Proceedings from the Policing Research Institute meetings*. Washington, DC: National Institute of Justice.

Lurigio, Arthur J., and Wesley G. Skogan. 1998. Community policing in Chicago: Bringing officers on board. *Police Quarterly* 1:1-25.

Maguire, Edward. 2003. Measuring the performance of law enforcement agencies: Part 1. *CALEA Update*. Fairfax, VA: Commission on the Accreditation of Law Enforcement Agencies.

Mastrofski, Stephen D., and Roger B. Parks. 2003. The myth of reactive policing. Paper presented at the 13th World Congress of Criminology, Rio de Janeiro, Brazil.

Mastrofski, Stephen D., Roger B. Parks, Albert J. Reiss Jr., Robert E. Worden, Christina DeJong, Jeffrey B. Snipes, and William Terrill. 1998. *Systematic observation of public police: Applying field research methods to policy issues*. Washington, DC: National Institute of Justice.

Mastrofski, S., Michael D. Reisig, and John D. McCluskey. 2002. Police disrespect toward the public: An encounter-based analysis. *Criminology* 40:101-33.

Mastrofski, Stephen D., and R. Richard Ritti. 1992. You can lead a horse to water . . . : A case study of a police department's response to stricter drunk-driving laws. *Justice Quarterly* 9:465-91.

Mastrofski, Stephen D., Jeffrey B. Snipes, Roger B. Parks, and Christopher D. Maxwell. 2000. The helping hand of the law: Police control of citizens on request. *Criminology* 38:307-42.

Mastrofski, Stephen D., Robert E. Worden, and Jeffrey B. Snipes. 1995. Law enforcement in a time of community policing. *Criminology* 33:539-63.

Maxwell, Christopher D., Joel H. Garner, and Jeffrey A. Fagan. 2001. *The effects of arrest on intimate partner violence: New evidence from the Spouse Assault Replication Program*. Washington, DC: National Institute of Justice.

McCluskey, John D. 2003. *Police requests for compliance: Coercive and procedurally just tactics*. New York: LFB Scholarly Series.

Peters, Thomas J., and Robert H. Waterman Jr. 1982. *In search of excellence: Lessons from America's best-run companies*. New York: Warner.

Punch, Maurice, ed. 1983. *Control in the police organization*. Cambridge, MA: MIT Press.

Reiss, Albert J., Jr. 1971. *The police and the public*. New Haven, CT: Yale University Press.

Riksheim, Eric C., and Steven M. Chermak. 1993. Causes of police behavior revisited. *Journal of Criminal Justice* 21:353-82.

Rubinstein, Jonathan. 1973. *City police*. New York: Garrar, Straus and Giroux.

Santayana, George. 1955. *The sense of beauty, being the outlines of aesthetic theory*. New York: Modern Library.

Scheingold, Stuart A. 1999. Constituent expectations of the police and police expectations of constituents. In *Measuring what matters: Proceedings from the Policing Research Institute meetings*, edited by Robert H. Langworthy, pp. 183-92. Washington, DC: National Institute of Justice.

Scott, W. Richard. 1992. *Organizations: Rational, natural, and open systems*. Englewood Cliffs, NJ: Prentice Hall.

Selznick, Philip. 1957. *Leadership in administration*. New York: Harper and Row.

Sherman, Lawrence W. 1978. *Scandal and reform: Controlling police corruption*. Berkeley: University of California Press.

———. 1980. Causes of police behavior: The current state of quantitative research. *Journal of Research in Crime and Delinquency* 17:69-100.

———. 1983. Reducing police gun use: Critical events, administrative policy, and organizational change. In *Control in the police organization*, edited by Maurice Punch, pp. 98-125. Cambridge, MA: MIT Press.

———. 1992. *Policing domestic violence: Experiments and dilemmas*. New York: Free Press.

Sherman, Lawrence W., Denise Gottfredson, Doris MacKenzie, John Eck, Peter Reuter, and Shawn Bushway. 1997. *Preventing crime: What works, what doesn't, what's promising?* Washington, DC: National Institute of Justice.

Sherman, Lawrence W., and David Weisburd. 1995. General deterrent effects of police patrol in crime "hot spots": A randomized, controlled trial. *Justice Quarterly* 12:625-48.

Sparrow, Malcolm K., Mark H. Moore, and David M. Kennedy. 1990. *Beyond 911: A new era for policing*. New York: Basic Books.

Trojanowicz, Robert, and Bonnie Bucqueroux. 1990. *Community policing: A contemporary perspective*. Cincinnati, OH: Anderson.

Tyler, Tom R. 2001. Trust and law-abidingness: A proactive model of social regulation. *Boston University Law Review* 81:361-406.

Tyler, Tom R., and Yuen J. Huo. 2002. *Trust in the law: Encouraging public cooperation with the police and courts*. New York: Russell Sage.

Van Maanen, John. 1974. Working the street: A developmental view of police behavior. In *The potential for reform in criminal justice*, edited by Herbert Jacob. Beverly Hills, CA: Sage.

Willis, James J., Stephen Mastrofski, and David Weisburd. 2003. Compstat and organizational change: Intensive site visits report. *Final Report to the National Institute of Justice*. Washington, DC: Police Foundation.

Wilson, James Q. 1968. *Varieties of police behavior: The management of law and order in eight communities*. Cambridge, MA: Harvard University Press.

———. 1983. *Thinking about crime*. Rev. ed. New York: Vintage.

Environment and Organization: Reviving a Perspective on the Police

Police researchers have largely ignored the role that organizational and environmental factors play in determining how officers behave during interactions with citizens. This has resulted in a body of policing knowledge that contains little information about how and why police practices are affected by features of the agencies officers work for and forces outside police departments. This article points out the consequences of this dearth of knowledge for understanding what the police do and why they do it, reviews the limited literature on organizational and environmental determinants of police activity, and calls for a research program that views interface between police organizations and their environments as a central question.

Keywords: police; environment; organization; ecology

By
DAVID A. KLINGER

In 1967, at the dawn of modern social science research on the police, Albert J. Reiss Jr. and David J. Bordua provided a research framework for the budding field that stressed inquiry into how the organizational properties of law enforcement organizations, the environments in which they are situated, and the interplay between the two shape police practices. Noting that police departments are quintessentially formal organizations that "have as their fundamental task the creation and maintenance of, and their participation in, external relationships" (pp. 25-26), they asserted that research grounded in a sociological perspective that focused on organizational and environmental properties and their interface should yield substantial insights into policing.

Reiss and Bordua (1967) drove home their point about environmental relations by provid-

David A. Klinger is an associate professor of criminology and criminal justice at the University of Missouri–St. Louis. His research interests include the ecology of social control, the use of force by police officers, and risk management in crisis situations. Prior to pursuing an academic career, he worked as a street cop for the Los Angeles and Redmond (WA) police departments.

DOI: 10.1177/0002716203262498

ing a partial list of the sorts of transactions with external entities in which the police in municipal agencies regularly engage:

> directing traffic, investigating complaints, interrogation, arresting suspects, controlling mobs and crowds, urging prosecutors to press or drop charges, testifying in court, participating with (or battling, as the case may be) probation officers in juvenile court, presenting budget requests to the city council, pressing a case with the civil service commission, negotiating with civil rights groups, defense attorneys, reporters, irate citizens, business groups, other city services, and other police systems (p. 26).

Reiss and Bordua go on to note that because many of the police's dealings with other entities are (or at least can be) antagonistic, they are not entirely in control of their interactions with external constituencies. As a consequence of this, police actions can be substantially influenced by the nature of the tasks they are called upon to do in the environment, by the qualities of the external entities with which they must interact, and by the broader social contexts in which these interactions occur.

On the organizational side of the coin, Reiss and Bordua (1967) noted that the police are most fundamentally a bureaucracy with the same properties as any other formal organization and thus readily amenable to organizationally based analysis. Because police organizations are so deeply intertwined with external entities, Reiss and Bordua went on to argue, a thorough understanding of the organizational properties of police departments requires knowledge of how environmental forces penetrate and influence law enforcement agencies. Without such knowledge, organizational accounts of police operations will be incomplete.

Despite their elegant argument and the evidence they brought to bear for their case, inquiry of the sort called for by Reiss and Bordua (1967) did not become a major aspect of the police research program. This is not to say that there is no research on these matters (see, e.g., Crank 1990) but rather that the body of knowledge about how organizational and environmental forces shape American law enforcement practices are not nearly as developed as one might have expected, given the spadework that Reiss and Bordua contributed.

The purposes of this article are threefold: (1) to offer a (partial) explanation for why research that focuses on organization and environment has been limited, (2) to review what we have learned about the police from the research that has considered organizational and environmental properties, and (3) to reassert the value of the sort of research program Reiss and Bordua called for nearly four decades ago. The work begins with a discussion of how the very nature of American policing is an impediment to research on how organizational and environmental forces affect police practices.

Roadblocks to Knowledge

Policing in the United States is a highly fragmented enterprise in terms of both structure and function. American policing consists of a patchwork of about 20,000 distinct organizations spread across federal, state, and local governments. No one knows precisely how many police organizations dot the land, but the most liberal count indicates that there were more than 21,100 federal, state, and local law enforcement agencies in the United States in the late 1990s (Roth et al. 2000), while the U.S. Department of Justice (DOJ) puts the number at 19,160 (Reaves and Goldberg 2000; Reaves and Hart 2000).

Among these various agencies, the lion's share of police departments are arms of municipal governments. DOJ data for 2000 (Reaves and Hickman 2002) show that approximately 13,000 municipal police forces employ at least one full-time law enforcement officer, about half of which employ fewer than ten officers. Among these municipal agencies, "big city" police departments, defined as those with one thousand or more sworn officers, employ a disproportionate share of the law enforcement personnel in the United States. Although the forty-seven big city agencies constitute less than one-tenth of one percent of municipal departments, they employ about a third of all local U.S. law enforcement officers (Hickman and Reaves 2003a).

Local law enforcement is also organized at the county level, primarily around the office of county sheriff.[1] The 2000 DOJ data indicate nearly 175,000 sworn officers are employed by the three thousand or more sheriff's offices throughout the nation (Hickman and Reaves 2003b). One of the central distinctions between sheriff's offices and municipal police departments is that the head of the agency (i.e., the sheriff) is nearly always an elected official, while municipal police chiefs are executive branch employees. At the aggregate level, sheriff's offices tend to be a bit larger than municipal departments with about 80 percent employing 10 or more sworn officers.

State law enforcement agencies fall into several categories. About half of the states maintain a state patrol that is primarily responsible for traffic enforcement. The other half of the states maintain a state police agency with general law enforcement responsibilities. Many states also maintain state-level bureaus of criminal investigation with broad law enforcement responsibilities and/or specialized law enforcement agencies such as wildlife and alcohol enforcement departments. Data indicate that the forty-nine primary state law enforcement agencies[2] together employ more than 56,000 sworn officers, with a high of nearly 6,000 in California and a low of about 150 in Wyoming (Reaves and Hickman 2002).

The picture at the federal level is somewhat muddied by structural changes since the terrorist attacks on September 11, 2001, but data from 2000 show that almost seventy federal law enforcement agencies were spread across the three branches of government, which employed almost 90,000 sworn officers. As is the case with local and state policing, the size of federal law enforcement agencies varies substantially. At the top of the federal heap in 2000 sat the Immigration and Naturalization Service with nearly 18,000 officers. At the bottom was the Inspector General of the U.S. Printing Office, which had 8 sworn officers.

Where police function is concerned, different law enforcement agencies have substantially different responsibilities. Local police have the broadest mandate. Nearly all local agencies provide service, maintain order, and enforce state laws and local ordinances on a day-to-day basis, and most county sheriff's agencies have the additional responsibility of providing security for county courts and of operating county jails. Federal police agencies generally have the most narrowly circumscribed responsibilities, as most of them have mandates to either undertake specific sorts of law enforcement actions under specific circumstances (e.g., the Customs Bureau enforces import and export laws) or police specific Federal Property (e.g., the Supreme Court Police patrol the grounds of the Court). The most visible aspect of state police agencies is the patrol they provide on U.S. roads and highways. But state police agencies do much more than road patrol. Across the nation, state law enforcement officers provide basic police service in many unincorporated areas and small towns that do not have their own police forces, they conduct investigations of major crimes such as homicides, they analyze evidence in their crime labs, and they provide many other sorts of assistance to smaller jurisdictions.

The vast differences in the tasks that police agencies undertake, the nature of the governmental entities to which they are attached, their sizes, and other features of their structure and function make it difficult for researchers to generalize about the American police. Because policing is not a monolithic enterprise, it is simply not possible to develop general propositions about how and why "the police" writ large do anything.

One way for researchers to develop understanding about the American police is to recognize the differentiation and treat various aspects of structural and environmental differentiation as independent variables to model the effects of such factors on police practices (after all, the art of social science rests on comparison). Some research has been done along this line (discussed in the next section), but some notable factors have limited the utility of it. The first is that we lack comprehensive data about many aspects of American police departments. There is no central repository of information about many critical police organizational outputs (such as how many people each agency shoots each year, see below), and the information we have about agency structure and other aspects of police organizations that might predict outputs (or themselves be dependent variables of interest) is limited in two ways. First, the vast majority of police agencies in the nation provide no information of this sort to any national data bank. Second, among the agencies that do provide such data, the list of organizational properties they have reported on is a rather short one where factors of the sort organizational theorists have identified as important go.[3]

The second major impediment applies equally to both the organizational and the environmental components of the issue: the costs associated with conducting many sorts of productive research (e.g., systematic observation) are so high that it limits the number of agencies researchers can study. As a consequence, studies using some of the potentially fruitful research designs have not included a large enough number of agencies to adequately examine the roles that various structural features of police organizations and elements of the environments in which they operate play in determining police practices.

Another strategy researchers might adopt to deal with the differentiation issue is to use it to select for study specific sets of agencies that share similar structural characteristics and carry out similar functions. Researchers (e.g., Reiss 1971; Smith 1984; Klinger 1994) have, for example, conducted several studies of municipal police agencies that share the common tasks of patrol to enforce laws, provide services, and maintain order in local communities and studied specific actions patrol officers in such agencies commonly perform (e.g., write tickets, make arrests). The obvious limitation with this strategy, however, is that it is difficult to generalize from such research, for example, to nonmunicipal agencies that do not provide patrol services. Another, perhaps less obvious, limitation is that it is problematic to generalize to other municipal agencies in different regions of the nation, with different numbers of sworn personnel, with different rank structures, with different population compositions, and so on.

Police agencies are not required to report to anyone the number of people they kill (or wound, for that matter) each year, so no nationwide shooting data are collected regularly.

A pair of cultural obstacles—one in the realm of police work, the other within the social sciences—have also contributed substantially to the lack of research on how organizational and environmental forces shape police practices. Police agencies and the individuals who populate them are notoriously insular, often seeking to limit the access of outsiders to their inner workings (e.g., Crank 1998; Skolnick 1966). As a consequence, many law enforcement agencies have been reluctant to allow researchers to "snoop around," and many police administrators do not wish to provide potentially sensitive data to researchers (see, e.g., Fyfe, Klinger, and Flavin 1997; Fyfe 2002). While this limiting factor is a challenge common to all policing research, its consequences are particularly pernicious where inquiry regarding organizational properties is concerned.

The lack of access to agencies has limited the sorts of places where researchers have been allowed to conduct research. This has created a situation where the information we do have tends to be limited to agencies that are progressive enough to allow researchers on site, which casts further question on the utility of generalizing from the research that has been conducted to American policing as a whole. We simply cannot say whether the way organizational properties are related to police actions in agencies that permit researcher's access are mirrored in agencies that do not. For as Fyfe, Klinger, and Flavin (1997) argue, agencies who would block research might have problems they would rather keep in the dark.

The lack of interest in providing certain sorts of data to researchers compounds the aforementioned impediment of limited national data, further restricting researchers' capacity to conduct thorough research on critical aspects of policing. Fyfe (2002), for example, has noted that there is no central repository for arguably the most important aspect of police behavior in a democratic society—the use of deadly force. Police agencies are not required to report to anyone the number of people they kill (or wound, for that matter) each year, so no nationwide shooting data are collected regularly. And police executives generally show little interest in volunteering these numbers. As a consequence, the information we do have about organizational and environmental (as well as all other) determinants of the use of deadly force is substantially incomplete.[4]

While the consequences of police insularity are notable, it is not entirely clear that a more open posture (which the police have come to adopt in more recent years; Walker and Katz 2002) would have led to substantially greater knowledge about the roles that organizational and environmental forces play in shaping police practices and actions. This is due to the fact that police researchers have simply not shown much interest in pursuing the organizational-environmental research opportunities that have been available over the past four decades. From the beginning, police research has been dominated by micro-level questions about the role that various situational factors, such as the race and social class of citizens, might play in individual police-citizen interactions. In addition, police scholars have devoted hardly any effort to developing theories about how organizational and environmental properties might affect how the police operate as they do.

One major contributor to this state of affairs is that social scientific interest in the police emerged at a time when criminological inquiry was dominated by micro-level research and theory. Social-psychological theories of crime and delinquency that tended to strip individuals from the social contexts in which they were embedded rose to prominence in the 1950s. Criminologists then turned to survey research to investigate these perspectives, which further isolated people from the places they lived, worked, and played. The combination of micro-level theory and survey research continued to dominate the criminological landscape well past the time that policing research took off in the late 1960s and early 1970s.[5]

It was only logical, then, that when social scientists turned their gaze to the police that it focused on micro-level processes and the role that citizens' status characteristics and other features of individual police-citizen encounters played in determining police actions. Mirroring what happened with the rise of survey research to explore the determinants of offending, this orientation gave rise to systematic observation of police-citizen encounters (wherein researchers accompanied officers on patrol and documented how officers and citizens interacted on the streets) as the preferred method of studying the police. The first observational studies (e.g., Black and Reiss 1970; Lundman, Sykes, and Clark 1978) collected almost no data on the contexts in which such encounters occurred, and when a study that did collect such data was launched in the mid-1970s (the Police Services

Study [PSS]), the many publications that flowed from it were dominated by micro-level concerns (see, e.g., Smith and Visher 1981; Visher 1983; Smith and Klein 1983; Smith, Visher, and Davidson 1984; Worden 1989).

It was not until the mid-1980s, when widespread interest in the role that the contexts in which criminal offending and delinquent behavior occur reemerged in criminology, that researchers using the PSS data began to seriously consider how organizational and environmental factors might shape police practices (Smith 1984, 1986). By that time, however, the intellectual inertia of the micro-level orientation of police research was so powerful that it dominated police research then (and still does to this day). Despite the dominance of micro-level concerns and data derived from observational studies designed to investigate such concerns, researchers have produced some notable work on how organizational and environmental considerations shape policing. Our attention shifts now to a discussion of this work, beginning with organizational matters.

Organizational Determinants of Police Action

Organizational theory is thick with ideas about how aspects of formal organizations affect the operations of those organizations and the actions of their members. A short list of such factors would include bureaucratization, task complexity, occupational differentiation, functional differentiation, nature of compliance regimes, span of control, technology, coupling, culture, professionalization, and size (see, e.g., Scott 1998). One of the first notable studies of the police focused on two of these factors as keys to explaining how officers' behavior varies across police departments. In a classic study, Wilson (1968) argued that the degree of professionalization and bureaucratization evident in a department gave rise to a particular organizational ethos that guides the actions of its officers. He labeled agencies that do not display a high degree of professionalism "Watchman" departments and asserted that officers working there tended to adopt a less than vigorous posture toward meeting all the policing needs of the citizenry. Professional departments that are highly bureaucratized he dubbed "Legalistic" and asserted that police work in them was characterized by uniform enforcement of the law. Finally, he called professional agencies that do not display a high degree of bureaucratization "Service" departments and asserted that officers who work there focus their attentions on providing assistance to the community, as opposed to seeking to enforce the law.

One notable attempt to empirically assess Wilson's (1968) contentions came in 1984 when Smith cross-classified sixty police agencies on the degree of professionalism and bureaucratization they displayed and then examined how officers in different quadrants of his two-by-two schema handled encounters with citizens. His analysis disclosed that officers in the different sorts of agencies did indeed police somewhat differently in some ways—among them, that officers in departments classified as highly professional and highly bureaucratized tended to be more likely to arrest under certain circumstances—but that many of the expectations drawn from Wilson's ideas did not pan out.

Since at least the 1930s, some observers of the American police scene have asserted that police in many small communities could better serve their citizenries by consolidating their departments (Walker 1977).[6] To assess the validity of the assertion implicit in the argument that larger agencies do a better job, researchers devoted attention to whether and how departmental size might affect police operations. This research provides no clear picture about the role that size plays, even where one of the most basic questions about policing—how many cops are out on the streets—is concerned.

One study that used data collected in the mid-1970s (Ostrom, Parks, and Whitaker 1978) looked at over one thousand different police agencies from several dozen metropolitan areas that varied in size from just a handful to more than one thousand officers and found that smaller agencies tended to put more officers on the streets per citizen than do larger ones. This occurred not because smaller agencies had a larger number of sworn officers per citizen but rather because smaller agencies were less likely to be highly specialized, thus devoting a larger portion of their personnel assets to patrol, and because supervisory and management personnel in smaller agencies tended to work the streets rather than inside jobs. On the other hand, a follow-up study that also used data from the 1970s focused on larger agencies (i.e., those with well over one hundred officers) and found a positive relationship between the agency size and the officer/citizen patrol ratio (Langworthy 1983). These two findings suggest that the relationship between the agency size and the level of patrol service is not constant across the range of department size. Unfortunately, large-scale follow-ups have not been conducted, so we know not much more than that about how size was related to patrol deployment in the 1970s and virtually nothing about the nature of the relationship between the two factors before or since then.

The literature on how organizational properties affect what officers do when they are working the streets is somewhat better developed. Where size is concerned, work conducted in the 1970s suggests that officers in larger agencies tend to arrest and use force against citizens more frequently than do their peers in smaller agencies (e.g., Mastrofski 1981). The pattern of officers in larger agencies being more active did not extend to all police activities, however, as research also showed that officers in smaller departments tended to more frequently provide assistance to citizens and more thoroughly investigate crimes (e.g., Parks 1979).

These coarse patterns, however, did not hold up across the offense spectrum. Wilson (1968), for example, reported that while agencies serving small middle-class suburbs had higher levels of arrests for peace disturbances than did a large nearby agency, their arrest rates for theft were lower. More recently, research by Mastrofski and Ritti (1996) on drunk driving enforcement patterns in Pennsylvania showed that officers working in extremely small agencies (i.e., those employing five or fewer officers) made about three times as many driving-under-the-influence arrests (per officer) as did their peers in large agencies (i.e., those employing one hundred or more officers).

Both researchers and practitioners have suggested that many structural aspects of police organizations besides size might well affect how officers carry out their duties. In fact, one way that those interested in improving the police have sought to do so is by advocating changes in the ways that police agencies are structured. Those seeking to make the police more efficient, for example, have argued that increasing the occupational and functional complexity of police agencies would allow departments to commit specially trained officers and units to specific problems (e.g., traffic, vice, etc.). In a similar vein, advocates of community policing and similar reforms have called for a reduction of hierarchy in police agencies as a means of giving line officers the power and freedom to deal with the specific needs of the areas and people they serve without getting bogged down by bureaucratic considerations. Unfortunately, the research on these various claims is not sufficient to draw any firm conclusions about how various aspects of organizational structure affect line officers' actions.

Both researchers and practitioners have suggested that many structural aspects of police organizations besides size might well affect how officers carry out their duties.

One example of this lack of evidence concerns the question of how decision making is dispersed in police organizations. The only comparative research on this matter examined how the degree of centralization in police agencies changed over the course of the 1990s, with no attention to how such differentiation affected police activities (Maguire et al. 2003), so we have no large-scale evidence on whether decentralized command structures make for more effective policing.

The evidence is not quite so bleak regarding occupational specialization, as a handful of studies conducted in three police departments have considered whether line officers working specialized assignments act differently than their peers who are police generalists (e.g., Mastrofski, Worden, and Snipes 1993; Novak et al. 1999). These studies found no appreciable differences in the ways that officers assigned to special community police patrols and those assigned to regular patrol exercised their discretionary powers. Because these studies look at just one aspect of specialization (in the patrol ranks) and because they involved a small number of agencies, it is not possible to draw any firm conclusions about either how other sorts of specialization might affect officers' actions in these agencies or how any sort of specialization might operate in the larger world of policing.

Although we are largely in the dark about the extent to which the structure of police organizations affects officers' actions, a good amount of evidence suggests that a wholly different organizational property—rules and regulations—can substantially affect how officers act on the streets, at least in some areas of police work. Police officers have a substantial degree of discretion about how they choose to carry out their duties, but they are by no means wholly unencumbered by the rules of the organizations for which they work. In police work, the most important and far-reaching discretionary choice that officers can make concerns the use of force—especially deadly force—against citizens. In recent decades, police executives have promulgated policies designed to control how and when their officers exercise their coercive powers, especially the power to take life.

Perhaps because the use of deadly force is the ultimate police action, researchers have devoted considerable attention to examining the notion that shooting policies can shape officers' use of their firearms. The first study to empirically assess the possibility was Fyfe's (1979) longitudinal study of firearms discharges among members of the New York City Police Department (NYPD), which found a steep decline in NYPD shootings after the agency implemented a restrictive shooting policy in the early 1970s. Examination of time-series data from several other major cities disclosed similar downward trends following the imposition of restrictive shooting policies (e.g., Fyfe 1988). Estimates of the number of police shootings across the nation show a general downward trend since restrictive shooting policies became widespread in the 1970s (e.g., Geller and Scott 1992). While the previously noted lack of comprehensive data on firearms use makes it difficult to develop a clear picture of the precise relationship between shooting policies and officers' use of their guns, the available evidence indicates that policy directives are a strong determinant of how officers exercise their most serious discretionary power.

Some evidence suggests that policies can also affect how officers exercise their arrest powers. Recent decades have seen a sea change in how the criminal justice system approaches violence that occurs between intimate partners and others with close relational ties, often called "domestic violence" (e.g., Sherman 1992). One aspect of this change has been a move across the nation toward policies that encourage or mandate officers to arrest perpetrators of domestic violence. The available data suggest that police officers have indeed become more likely to arrest domestic batterers since the policy shift began in the 1980s (e.g., Sherman 1992). This trend does not, however, provide clear evidence that the policy shift is the cause of more aggressive policing of domestic violence. This is because researchers have not isolated the effect of arrest policies from the other recent changes in the criminal justice system that might affect officers' actions, most notably, a shift in state legal codes around the nation that were designed to get officers to arrest those who commit domestic assault. With broad changes in both law and policy across the country, it is simply not possible to conclude from nationwide data that shifts in departmental policy have an appreciable effect on officers' actions over and above those wrought by statutory change. In fact, the limited evidence on the point suggests that statutory changes have indeed had an appreciable affect of the degree to which officers use their arrest powers in cases of domestic violence (Chaney and Saltzstein 1998).

Environmental Determinants of Police Action

The notion that changes in criminal statutes can change how officers execute their duties when policing domestic violence incidents highlights the fact that forces external to police agencies hold the potential to influence officers' actions. Consideration of the roles that environmental factors play in police work begins with a discussion of what we know about how other entities within the criminal justice system shape police practices.

The term *criminal justice system* is a catch phrase in popular speech, yet we know very little about how other elements of the criminal justice system influence how police officers do their jobs. For example, virtually no research has been conducted on the relationships between police activity and various corrections system elements (e.g., jails, prisons, and parole departments) or on how police organizations can affect one another.[7]

Concerning the courts, research indicates that they can influence police practices through judicial rulings that delimit the sorts of police actions that are constitutionally permissible. A good deal of the evidence on this point comes from research on police interrogation practices following the U.S. Supreme Court's ruling in *Miranda v. Arizona*, which set a new requirement that officers inform citizens in police custody that they did not have to answer any questions before commencing an interrogation. Numerous studies indicate that it took some time for officers to adjust their interrogation behavior (e.g., Black and Reiss 1967) but that, as time passed, the police generally came to follow the Court's guidelines (e.g., Leo 1996).

Another aspect of the external police environment that has received a fair amount of attention by police researchers is the local political landscape in which police agencies are embedded. In fact, one of the first major studies of variability in police behavior (Wilson 1968) identified the local political culture as a key determinant of how officers act. In short, Wilson (1968) argued that the culture of local politics is expressed through the appointment and control of police chiefs—because the political executives who appoint chiefs can also fire them. More recent research does not offer a great deal of support for the notion that local political leaders have a pronounced effect on police practices. Two case studies, for example, suggest that police departments possess a substantial ability to resist efforts of elected leaders to change their practices (Scheingold 1991; Guyot 1991). And aggregate analyses suggest that hypothetically important status characteristics of local leaders do not affect how officers carry out their duties. Chaney and Saltzstein's (1998) previously mentioned study of how officers deal with domestic violence shows that the presence of a female mayor does not increase the extent to which officers opt to arrest batterers, and Saltzstein (1989) reports that the race of a city's mayor is not related to how officers handle public order matters.[8]

A wholly different sort of question about external influences on police practices concerns the roles that features of the ecological environments in which police operate might play. As previously noted, the hold that social-psychological theories of crime and deviance had on criminology began to visibly ease in the 1980s, and a subsequent smattering of quantitative studies considered the possibility that aspects of the communities that officers patrolled might influence the ways they policed. The first of these studies treated select aspects of neighborhoods (e.g., the poverty level; see Smith and Klein 1983; Smith, Visher, and Davidson 1984) as add-ons in multivariate analyses that focused on the role that situational factors (race, offense type, etc.) played in how officers handled interactions with citizens. Soon after, Smith (1986) presented the first study that placed spatial properties at the center of the analysis of police activities when he published his research on the effects of eleven neighborhood characteristics (e.g., residential stability, crime rate, and racial heterogeneity) on five different sorts of police activities (e.g., arrest and report taking). Among the key findings were the following: police are more likely to stop suspicious people in racially heterogeneous neighborhoods, the odds of arrest were higher for suspects in neighborhoods of lower socioeconomic status, and the odds that officers will take a crime report decreases as neighborhood crime rates increase.

This small group of studies established the viability of the notion that police practices were contingent on the spatial contexts in which they occurred. Despite these findings, researchers paid little immediate attention to the obvious implication that any complete explanation of police behavior must include attention to the social ecology of the communities in which it is embedded. Instead, they continued to focus their research efforts on how situational forces influence police action (e.g., Worden 1989; Klinger 1994, 1996; Lundman 1994). As a consequence, the state of knowledge about the role that community properties play in police practices remained quite rudimentary well into the 1990s.

Hypothesizing that one reason for the lack of interest in community considerations among police researchers was an utter absence of social theory that addressed the ecological basis of police behavior, Klinger (1997) offered a theory that sought to fill this gap. Beginning with the fact that American policing is a territorially organized enterprise wherein officers work specific areas that are delineated by legal and administrative boundaries,[9] he argued that levels of crime and other sorts of deviance in the areas officers patrol are a crucial determinant of how they carry out their duties. In short, he asserted that as levels of deviance increase, officers become more cynical, view victims as less deserving of police protection, come to see more crimes as normal features of the social scene in the areas they patrol, and have fewer resources to deal with any specific incident because higher levels of deviance translate into higher police workloads. As a consequence, officers working patrol areas characterized by higher levels of deviance will adopt a more lenient approach to their jobs, being less likely to vigorously enforce the criminal law, and thus let pass more minor sorts of criminal conduct.

Although this theory is rooted in social ecology, it also has deep roots in an organizational assessment of police work. Klinger (1997) argued that patrol officers were able to police in a fashion that is responsive to community crime levels because police departments are loosely coupled systems in which it is not possible for police managers to constantly monitor the actions of officers on the streets. Moreover, the uncertain nature of the work that officers are called upon to do makes it exceptionally difficult for police managers to control patrol cops' actions via rules and regulations. The organizational tradition is also invoked by the

Virtually no research has been conducted on the relationships between police activity and various corrections system elements or on how police organizations can affect one another.

assumption that street police work is a corporate undertaking in which the individual officers working any given patrol area are not free to police however they see fit. Rather, officers who patrol each specific area constitute work groups that must negotiate a set of norms about how they should police, which they then follow to produce the above-mentioned pattern in which a less vigorous style of police work emerges in areas with higher levels of deviance. Because Klinger's theory identifies specific organizational properties of the police as vital precursors for the hypothesized ecological effects, it is as much an exercise in integrated as in ecological theorizing.

It is by no means, however, the last theoretical word on the interface between police organizations and their environments. In fact, the theory was presented as a first theoretical step to provide a platform upon which additional, more complete, integrated theory of the police could be built. Because it offers a multi-level perspective that traces how macro-level features of police organization and local communities affect the micro-level actions of police officers in individual encounters with citizens, this framework has the capacity to integrate not only the organizational and the environmental perspectives but also the micro and the macro levels of analysis. The remainder of this article is devoted to pointing out some ways in which this theory can be expanded to provide additional understanding of how organizational and environmental forces affect police practices.

Developing the Integrated Perspective

Space constraints preclude a comprehensive consideration of integrative work; therefore, the remaining discussion will be limited in two ways. First, it will adopt the rather prosaic approach of simply identifying variables found in other theoretical and empirical literature as possible determinants of police action that could be added as predictors to those already present in Klinger's schema. Second, it will consider only a small number of variables: one in the realm of organizations and a few that lay outside it.

A key component in Klinger's model is the previously mentioned assertion that police agencies are loosely coupled organizations in which patrol officers are largely free from administrative constraints, an argument drawn from a good deal of other police literature (e.g., Brown 1981; Wilson 1968). It is likely, however, that the degree of coupling varies to some extent across police departments, which suggests that the theory should be expanded to account for this. One place for modification in this connection would be to treat coupling as an endogenous variable, identify factors that explain variation in coupling, and then explain how such variation affects the rules that guide officers' conduct on the streets.

The vast literature on formal organizations identifies several possible determinants of the degree of coupling between elements of organizations. With local police agencies varying in size from less than a handful to more than 30,000 officers, one variable that would likely be an important determinant of coupling is organizational size. As size increases, span of control concerns dictate that organizations put more layers of bureaucracy between line personnel and their executive officers (e.g., Scott 1998). As the number of supervisory and management layers in police departments increases, the ability of the chief to monitor the actions of his or her officers decreases substantially, decoupling the patrol force for the administrative apparatus and providing patrol officers more freedom to create their own rules about how they should carry out their duties. In large agencies, then, the chief must delegate the vast majority of direct oversight to subordinates, who then pass their power down through multiple layers of command. In very small agencies (with fewer than ten officers, let us say), on the other hand, the chief is likely to spend a considerable amount of time in direct contact with his or her subordinates, primarily, in many instances, while patrolling the streets with them (see, e.g., Walker and Katz 2002). Because the chief is actually part of the patrol force in very small departments, he or she actually becomes a member of the patrol work group, thus utterly coupling the administrative and line functions of the agency. In such departments, then, the police chief would have a great deal more power to set and to enforce norms about police practices.[10]

Whatever the degree of coupling in any given department might be, and whoever might be involved in developing the rules that guide officers' actions, it is Klinger's key contention that the social ecology of the communities' officers work drives how they will police. In focusing on levels of deviance, however, this theory does not address the possibility that other community characteristics may play some role in determining police practices. As noted above, the limited quantitative research on the ecology of police behavior suggests that neighborhood-level factors such as socioeconomic status and racial composition can influence officers' actions (e.g., Smith 1986). While it is not clear whether the reported effects are spurious (they may be due to unmeasured variation in individual characteristics, such as socioeconomic status; see Smith 1986, 338), if they are not, they can easily be incorporated into the theory as additional ecological variables that influence the negotiation of patrol-work-group rules.

This theory also has room to incorporate external factors that lay outside the realm of local communities. For example, as previously noted, research suggests that state legislatures and local governing bodies can influence officers' conduct by passing legislation directing particular enforcement practices (e.g., Chaney and Saltzstein 1998). Differences in the legal environments in which police agencies are embedded can be incorporated in the theoretical scheme by including variables that reflect such differences. Differences of other sorts can be similarly incorporated by adding them to the list of macro variables that might ultimately influence police action—factors such as city size, degree of racial inequality, and levels of violence (see, e.g., Jacobs and O'Brien 1998).

Conclusion

Nearly four decades of concerted police research have established that Reiss and Bordua (1967) were correct: both organizational and environmental forces exert effects on police behavior, there is a complex interplay between these forces, and any complete understanding of police action must be based on theory that can account for this conjunction. Because police researchers have paid comparatively little attention to the organizational and environmental sources of police action, however, we have only limited evidence about which aspects of police organizations and their environments actually affect police action and even less evidence about the processes through which they exert their effects. These serious gaps in our understanding of the police present both challenges and opportunities for social scientists. In the theoretical realm, the challenge is to develop more complete integrated models that precisely specify how macro-level organizational and environmental properties exert effects at the micro-level of police interactions with citizens. In the empirical realm, the challenge is to develop and execute research plans that can both inductively inform the development of such theory and deductively test it. The opportunity is that such research holds great promise for increasing our understanding of policing as we move into the twenty-first century. All we need to do is finally to heed Reiss and Bordua's prescient call from the dawn of police research.

Notes

1. Fewer than 100 of the 3,100 or so county law enforcement agencies go by the designation "police department," while the rest are titled "sheriff's office" (or "department") (Reaves and Goldberg 2000).

2. Hawaii has no primary state police agency.

3. See Langworthy's (2002) discussion of the limitations of the Law Enforcement Management and Administrative Statistics data, the primary source for national police organizational data.

4. The FBI annually collects some data on fatal police shootings as part of the Supplemental Homicide Reports (SHR) aspect of their Uniform Crime Reports program. These data are notoriously incomplete, however (see Fyfe, 2002, for a discussion of the limitations of the SHR data). The consequences of the problems with the SHR data for social science research that uses it are discussed below.

5. See, for example, Stark (1987) for a brief discussion of how social-psychology and survey research came to dominate criminology in the second half of the twentieth century and some of the consequences of that phenomenon for the development of knowledge about how social contexts affect criminal offending.

6. On the other hand, counterclaims have shown that breaking up large departments is the way to go because it enhances community control of the police.

7. Some work has examined how specific organizational forms and structures diffuse across police agencies (e.g., Weisburd et al. 2003; Klinger 2003), but this small body of work does not directly address police behavior per se.

8. Jacobs and O'Brien (1998) did report that the presence of a black mayor was related to lower rates of fatal police shootings, but questions about the validity of the FBI Supplemental Homicide Reports data they used (see discussion of deadly force data in note 4 above; Fyfe 2002) cast doubt on this conclusion.

9. City and county lines delimit law enforcement organizational boundaries. Larger police agencies then divide their territories into smaller parcels for groups of officers to patrol (typically called precincts, divisions, or areas). All large agencies (and all but the smallest of the rest) further divide their territories into beats to be patrolled by a single squad car.

10. Another structural feature that one might consider in this connection is structural differentiation (conceived of as the number of specialized units), which, while likely correlated with size, could have independent effects on coupling.

References

Black, Donald, and Albert J. Reiss Jr. 1967. Interrogation and the criminal process. *The Annals of the American Academy of Political and Social Science* 374:47-57.

———. 1970. Police control of juveniles. *American Sociological Review* 35 (1): 63-77.

Brown, Michael K. 1981. *Working the street*. New York: Russell Sage.

Chaney, Carole K., and Grace H. Saltzstein. 1998. Democratic control and bureaucratic responsiveness: The police and domestic violence. *American Journal of Political Science* 42 (3): 745-68.

Crank, John P. 1990. The influence of environmental and organizational factors on police style in urban and rural environments. *Journal of Research in Crime and Delinquency* 27 (2): 166-89.

———. 1998. *Understanding police culture*. Cincinnati, OH: Anderson.

Fyfe, James J. 1979. Administrative interventions on police shooting discretion: An empirical examination. *Journal of Criminal Justice* 7 (4): 309-23.

———. 1988. Police use of deadly force: Research and reform. *Justice Quarterly* 5 (2): 165-205.

———. 2002. Too many missing cases: Holes in our knowledge about police use of force. Special issue, *Justice Research and Policy* 4:87-102.

Fyfe, James J., David Klinger, and Jeanne Flavin. 1997. Differential police treatment of male on female spousal violence. *Criminology* 35 (3): 455-73.

Geller, William A., and Michael Scott. 1992. *Deadly force: What we know.* Washington, DC: Police Executive Research Forum.

Guyot, Dorothy. 1991. *Policing as though people matter.* Philadelphia: Temple University Press.

Hickman, Matthew J., and Brian A. Reaves. 2003a. *Local police departments 2000.* Washington, DC: Bureau of Justice Statistics.

———. 2003b. *Sheriffs' offices 2000*. Washington, DC: Bureau of Justice Statistics.

Jacobs, David, and Robert M. O'Brien. 1998. The determinants of deadly force: A structural analysis of police violence. *American Journal of Sociology* 103 (4): 837-62.

Klinger, David. 1994. Demeanor or crime? Why "hostile" citizens are more likely to be arrested. *Criminology* 32 (3): 475-93.

———. 1996. More on demeanor and arrest in Dade County. *Criminology* 34 (1): 61-79.

———. 1997. Negotiating order in patrol work: An ecological theory of police response to deviance. *Criminology* 35 (2): 277-306.

———. 2003. Spreading diffusion in criminology. *Criminology & Public Policy* 2 (3): 461-68.

Langworthy, Robert H. 1983. *The formal structure of municipal police organizations*. Ph.D. diss., State University of New York, Albany.

———. 2002. LEMAS: A comparative organizational research platform. Special issue, *Justice Research and Policy* 4:21-38.

Leo, Richard A. 1996. The impact of *Miranda* revisited. *The Journal of Criminal Law and Criminology* 86 (3): 259-88.

Lundman, Richard J. 1994. Demeanor or crime? The Midwest city police-citizen encounter study. *Criminology* 32:631-56.

Lundman, Richard J., Richard E. Sykes, and John P. Clark. 1978. Police control of juveniles: A replication. *Journal of Research in Crime and Delinquency* 15 (1): 74-91.

Maguire, Edward R., Yeunhee Shin, Jihong "Solomon" Zhao, and Kimberly D. Hassell. 2003. Structural change in large police agencies during the 1990s. *Policing: An International Journal of Police Strategies and Management* 26 (2): 251-75.

Mastrofski, Stephen D. 1981. *Reforming the police: The impact of patrol assignment patterns on officer behavior in urban residential neighborhoods*. Ph.D. diss., University of North Carolina, Chapel Hill.

Mastrofski, Stephen D., and R. R. Ritti. 1996. Police training and the effects of organization on drunk driving enforcement. *Justice Quarterly* 13 (2): 291-320.

———. 2000. Making sense of community policing: A theory-based analysis. *Police Practice and Research: An International Journal* 1 (2): 183-210.

Mastrofski, Stephen D., Robert E. Worden, and Jeffrey B. Snipes. 1993. Law enforcement in a time of community policing. *Criminology* 33 (4): 539-603.

Novak, Kenneth, Jennifer Hartman, Alexander M. Holsinger, and Michael G. Turner. 1999. The effects of aggressive policing of disorder on serious crime. *Policing: An International Journal of Police Strategies and Management* 22 (2): 171-90.

Ostrom, Elinor, Roger B. Parks, and Gordon P. Whitaker. 1978. Police agency size: Some evidence of its effects. *Policy Studies Journal* 1:34-36.

Parks, Roger B. 1979. Police reorganization. A review of its evaluation. In *How well does it work? Review of* Criminal justice evaluation, 1978. Washington, DC: U.S. Government Printing Office.

Reaves, Brian A., and Andrew L. Goldberg. 2000. *Local police departments 1997*. Washington, DC: Bureau of Justice Statistics.

Reaves, Brian A., and Timothy C. Hart. 2000. *Law enforcement management and administrative statistics, 1999: Data for individual state and local agencies with 100 or more officers*. Washington, DC: Bureau of Justice Statistics.

Reaves, Brian A., and Matthew J. Hickman. 2002. *Census of state and local law enforcement agencies, 2000*. Washington, DC: Bureau of Justice Statistics.

Reiss, Albert J., Jr. 1971. *The police and the public*. New Haven, CT: Yale University Press.

Reiss, Albert J., Jr., and David J. Bordua. 1967. Environment and organization: A perspective on the police. In *The police: Six sociological essays*, edited by David J. Bordua. New York: John Wiley.

Roth, Jeffrey, Joseph F. Ryan, et al. 2000. *National evaluation of the COPS program—Title I of the 1994 Crime Act*. Washington, DC: National Institute of Justice.

Saltzstein, Grace H. 1989. Black mayors and police policies. *The Journal of Politics* 51 (3): 525-44.

Scheingold, Stuart A. 1991. *The politics of street crime: Criminal process and cultural obsession*. Philadelphia: Temple University Press.

Scott, W. Richard. 1998. *Organizations: Rational, natural, and open systems*. 4th ed. Upper Saddle River, NJ: Prentice-Hall.

Sherman, Lawrence W. 1992. *Policing domestic violence: Experiments and dilemmas*. With Janell D. Schmidt and Dennis Rogan. New York: Free Press.

Skolnick, Jerome H. 1966. *Justice without trial: Law enforcement in democratic society*. New York: Wiley.

Smith, Douglas A. 1984. The organizational context of legal control. *Criminology* 22 (1): 19-38.

———. 1986. The neighborhood context of police behavior. In *Communities and crime*, edited by Albert J. Reiss Jr. and Michael Tonry. Chicago: University of Chicago Press.

Smith, Douglas A., and Jody R. Klein. 1983. Police agency characteristics and arrest decisions. In *Evaluating performance in criminal justice agencies*, edited by Gordon P. Whitaker and Charles David Phillips. Beverly Hills, CA: Sage.

Smith, Douglas A., and Christy A. Visher. 1981. Street-level justice: Situational determinants of police arrest decisions. *Social Problems* 29 (2): 167-77.

Smith, Douglas A., Christy A. Visher, and Laura A. Davidson. 1984. Equity and discretionary justice: The influence of race on police arrest decisions. *Journal of Criminal Law and Criminology* 75 (1): 234-49.

Stark, Rodney. 1987. Deviant places: A theory of the ecology of crime. *Criminology* 25 (4): 893-909.

Visher, Christy A. 1983. Gender, police arrest decisions, and notions of chivalry. *Criminology* 21:5-28.

Walker, Samuel. 1977. *A critical history of police reform*. Lexington, MA: Lexington Books.

Walker, Samuel, and Charles M. Katz. 2002. *The police in America: An introduction*. 4th ed. New York: McGraw-Hill.

Weisburd, David, Stephen D. Mastrofski, et al. 2003. Reforming to preserve: Compstat and strategic problem solving in American policing. *Criminology & Public Policy* 2:421-56.

Wilson, James Q. 1968. *Varieties of police behavior: The management of law and order in eight communities*. Cambridge, MA: Harvard University Press.

Worden, Robert E. 1989. Situational and attitudinal explanations of police behavior: A theoretical reappraisal and empirical assessment. *Law & Society Review* 23 (4): 667-711.

Science and Politics in Police Research: Reflections on Their Tangled Relationship

By
SAMUEL WALKER

Police research in the United States has been heavily influenced by external politics. This influence is agenda-setting rather than truth-suppressing. Agenda-setting influence occurs where external political influence causes researchers to undertake research on a subject or subjects they had previously neglected. The influence of politics on research has, in some very important respects, greatly enriched social science research on the police, forcing scholars to confront subjects and methodological issues they had previously neglected. The relationship between police research and the external political environment is extremely complex and is by no means simple or one-directional. There are also some important examples, notably, community policing, of where research findings have influenced the political agenda.

Keywords: police; research; politics; police reform

As a member of the committee that produced the report, reading the final version of *Fairness and Effectiveness in Policing: The Evidence* (Committee to Review Research 2003) and having a chance to see it whole proved to be a curious experience. I take considerable pride in having contributed to what will stand for some time as the definitive review of what we know about policing. I am also proud of the fact that the report elevates concern for fairness to a level coequal with effectiveness in policing. This is a significant and overdue shift in emphasis compared with previous reports that have attempted to provide a comprehensive picture of American policing (President's Commission 1967a, 1967b; National Advisory Commission on Criminal Justice Standards and Goals 1973).

Reading the report, however, brought a nagging sensation that something important is missing from it. I finally concluded that the missing element is the dynamic aspect of police research in the United States. Although chapter 2 pro-

Samuel Walker is Isaacson Professor of Criminal Justice at the University of Nebraska, Omaha. He is the author of eleven books on policing, criminal justice history and policy, and civil liberties.

DOI: 10.1177/0002716203262699

vides a comprehensive review of the nature and development of police research (Committee to Review Research 2003, 20-46), it now strikes me as missing an important aspect of how that research has developed over the years.[1] The driving force behind much police research has been the influence of external politics. The police stand at the center of several issues that touch raw nerves in American politics, most notably, race relations and the tangled relationship between race and crime, and public concern about these issues has greatly influenced police research.

Whether police research is more or less influenced in this regard than, for example, research on public education, family policy, or public welfare is an interesting question that merits examination. It is quite possible that research on all politically sensitive social issues such as crime, education, employment, and others is heavily influenced by the political environment. It is also possible that this is an inevitable feature of social science research and one that sets it apart from research in the natural sciences. These questions, however, go far beyond the scope of this article, which focuses on the nature of political influence on police research.

The relationship between police research and the external political environment is extremely complex and is by no means simple or one-directional. I will argue in this article that while external political factors have heavily influenced police research, it is also true that research findings have shaped the public discourse about policing and the direction of public policy. In addition, and perhaps more controversial, I will argue that the influence of politics on research has, in some very important respects, greatly enriched social science research on the police. I will develop my argument by positing four basic propositions and then illustrating them through discussions of a few selected episodes in the history of police research.

The observations in this article are in part a response to an unjustly neglected article by Lawrence W. Sherman (1974), which raised a number of important issues about the relationship between police research and police reform through the mid-1970s. Unfortunately, Sherman's article provoked no noticeable response, and the issues it raised have not been addressed in the intervening years. As a result, our understanding of the relationship between politics, research, and public policy is not as well developed as it might have been.

The idea that political influence could have a positive effect on police research, or any social science research for that matter, will undoubtedly strike many people as outrageous. The history of research in the entire criminal justice field is filled with stories of improper political influence. Completed studies have been suppressed by their sponsors (Martinson 1974), findings have been subtly or not-so-subtly designed to serve a political agenda or to make them politically palatable (National Institute of Justice 1983; Fyfe 1983), and studies where the researchers have deliberately avoided investigating certain issues or asking certain questions because the results would probably not please the sponsoring agency and/or the agency granting access to the data.[2] Indeed, self-censorship on the part of researchers may actually be a larger problem than overt censorship by public officials. A full-scale review of the various forms of improper political influence over research in criminal justice research would be a valuable and overdue contribution to our understanding of the enterprise of research in this politically volatile field.[3]

The political influence that I discuss in this chapter is of a very different sort. My discussion involves *agenda-setting* influence rather than *truth-suppressing* influence. As the case studies discussed below illustrate, agenda-setting influence occurs where external political influence causes researchers to undertake research on a subject or subjects they had previously neglected, with the result that the agenda of research is significantly altered. Agenda-setting influence in no way distorts truth (although it undoubtedly shapes research in certain directions with undoubted political ramifications), but as I will argue, it has in fact often enriched the study of policing in the United States.

The Argument: Four Propositions

Police research in the United States involves a complex interplay between science and politics. To make sense of this complexity, I posit four general propositions.

> *Proposition 1:* External political factors have had a major impact in shaping the agenda of police research. That is to say, many of the important research questions in policing that have preoccupied social scientists over the past half century have been, in the first instance, prompted by external political concerns.

This model of research is different from what might be considered the model of "normal science" as defined by Kuhn (1962) in his famous and enormously influential book *The Structure of Scientific Revolutions*. In the normal-science model, scientific inquiry is driven by the internal logic of science itself; research raises unanswered questions that stimulate further inquiry. Kuhn (1962, 43-51) further argues that scientific research is guided by a dominant paradigm that defines problems and directs scientific inquiry. A scientific revolution occurs when the prevailing paradigm is replaced by an alternative paradigm that redefines problems and redirects scientific inquiry. In my interpretation of the development of police research, external influences have introduced new topics for research, but only one change in police research in the past sixty years—the American Bar Foundation (ABF) Survey of the 1950s (discussed below)—rises to the level of a genuine paradigm shift (Walker 1992).[4]

> *Proposition 2:* Once a question or set of questions is introduced into police research—for example, the exercise of discretion by patrol officers, alleged racial or ethnic discrimination in traffic enforcement—the process of normal science begins to operate. Research findings raise unresolved issues that stimulate further scientific inquiry that may answer some questions but also generates new unresolved issues and additional inquiry. At this point in the process, the external

political factors, while still present as part of the environment in which research is conducted and disseminated, cease to be a motive force.

Proposition 3: The impact of external political influence on police research has often been extremely beneficial and has enriched it in important ways. External factors have forced researchers to confront important issues they had previously neglected and to wrestle with complex and methodological issues that often have broader application. The most recent and notable example of this impact is the current controversy over racial profiling, which I discuss in the next section.

Proposition 4: In several subtle but nonetheless important ways, police research has influenced the external political environment and played a significant role in shaping public policy. Much police research produces essentially negative findings, in the sense that certain ideas, assumptions, or policy recommendations are not supported by empirical evidence. (Indeed, many readers will be struck by the recurring refrain in *Fairness and Effectiveness* that the evidence on various points is "inconclusive.") The external audience is often highly frustrated by this outcome. It much prefers what might be called positive findings, for example, a finding in the medical arena that a certain treatment has a significant impact in preventing or treating a major illness.[5] As I will argue in detail later, a number of important studies, including the Kansas City Preventive Patrol Experiment (Kelling et al. 1974), undermined conventional assumptions about policing and as a consequence opened the way for creative new thinking about public policy.

Case Study 1: The Racial Profiling Controversy

The current controversy over racial profiling (Harris 2002) is a classic example of the extent to which external political factors have shaped the agenda of police research. This subject serves as a useful starting point for several reasons, even though it is out of chronological sequence with respect to other examples discussed here. The impact of external political factors in this example is both very clear and very strong. In this respect, the case provides a useful illustration of propositions 1, 2, and 3. In addition, the controversy is a matter of immediate concern and will be familiar to virtually all readers of this chapter. Subsequent case studies, on the other hand, involve events in the past with which not all readers will be as familiar. Finally, depending on how the response to the racial profiling controversy develops, it could eventually illustrate proposition 4 as well.

Racial profiling burst onto the national political and legal agenda around 1999, largely as a result of court cases in Maryland and New Jersey alleging systematic racial discrimination in traffic enforcement by state police officers (American Civil Liberties Union [ACLU] 1999). Law professor David Harris (1997) popularized (and possibly coined) the phrase "driving while black," first in a law review article and then in a report published by the ACLU (1999). The phrase—graphic and potent in its imagery—struck a nerve with the public, and with surprising speed, the issue of racial profiling became a national political issue.[6]

In part because of the key evidence introduced in the Maryland and New Jersey cases, civil rights activists made traffic-stop data collection their principal strategy for reforming the police and reducing racial discrimination in traffic enforcement (ACLU 1999). This choice of strategy involved rejecting other possible reform strategies, such as improved police training or administrative rule making (Police Executive Research Forum 2001, 49-114; Cohen, Lennon, and Wasserman 2000; Walker 2001a). The basic assumption underlying the data-collection strategy is that systematic data on traffic enforcement (including traffic stops, searches

Law professor David Harris popularized (and possibly coined) the phrase "driving while black."

of vehicles, and the various outcomes of arrest, citation, or warning) will reveal whether a pattern of illegal discrimination based on race or ethnicity exists. Legislative bills to require data collection by law enforcement agencies were introduced in Congress (U.S. House of Representatives 1999) and a number of states. State laws with varying data-collection requirements have been enacted in an estimated fourteen states.[7] Meanwhile, beginning with the San Diego (CA) Police Department (2000), several hundred law enforcement agencies have undertaken voluntary traffic-stop data collection. Police chiefs undertook these voluntary efforts to be responsive to the minority communities in their jurisdictions (San Jose Police Department 1999; Walker 2001a).

The mandated and voluntary data-collection efforts have already produced a small flood of official traffic-stop data reports and promise to produce still more.[8] The data-collection movement presented police researchers with some formidable challenges, both scientific and ethical.[9] Some researchers have been directly involved in data collection and analysis efforts, including writing official reports (Missouri Attorney General 2002; San Diego Police Department 2002). Meanwhile, many other scholars have been asked to comment publicly on specific traffic-stop data reports or on the issue generally.

Traffic-stop data collection has forced police researchers to confront the basic question of what kind of data are sufficient to prove or disprove that a pattern of illegal racial or ethnic discrimination in enforcement exists. This question was not chosen by the research community but forced on them by the data-collection strategy itself, namely, the civil rights activists' assumption that enforcement data will reveal patterns of discrimination. The debate among researchers quickly narrowed into a consideration of what data could serve as the proper benchmark (or denominator or base rate) against which traffic-stop data can be analyzed (Fridell 2004; General Accounting Office 2000; Home Office 2000; Police Executive Research Forum 2001, 115-44; Walker 2001a). There are also related questions involving exactly what data on traffic stops are necessary and, most important, whether data on individual officers are needed.

In the politically driven rush to collect traffic-stop data, few people paused to reflect on the nature of the data entered in the Maryland and New Jersey cases and on the implications of the methodology used. As developed by John Lamberth (2000), the research design in those cases involved direct observation of driving patterns on the highways in question and collection of data on the racial composition of both the total driving population and those drivers observed to be violating a traffic law. In both cases, the Lamberth-based data were sufficient to persuade the courts that patterns of racial discrimination did exist (Harris 1997, 1999, 2002). It is important to enter the qualification that the evidence was persuasive to courts and, apart from expert witnesses on the other side, not to peers in the scientific community. Without entering the controversy over "junk science" (Huber 1991), it is sufficient to say that courts might not accept as persuasive much of the data that have appeared in official traffic-stop data reports.

The official traffic-stop data reports, however, have used official census data on the resident population as the benchmark or denominator (Missouri Attorney General 2002; San Jose Police Department 1999, 2000). Scholars and other commentators, however, wasted little time pointing out that census data are not a proper benchmark for proving or disproving the existence of a pattern of race discrimination in traffic enforcement. Census data do not represent the at-risk driving population by race or ethnicity, in terms of either the overall driving population or the observed law violators (General Accounting Office 2000; Home Office 2000; Walker 2001a). Thus, while virtually every official report has found racial disparities in persons stopped, relative to the resident population, none has been able to make a persuasive case that a pattern of racial or ethnic discrimination exists. In fact, it is questionable whether such data would be persuasive to a court of law, much less a peer-reviewed journal.

The racial profiling controversy has enormously enriched police research in several ways. First, it has forced police researchers to study traffic enforcement, a subject they had virtually ignored for decades. The one major previous study of the subject was John Gardiner's (1969) book. The implications of this neglect of traffic enforcement were heightened by release of the Bureau of Justice Studies (Langan et al. 2001; Schmitt, Langan, and Durose 2002) study of police-citizen contacts (itself a product of the external political forces), which found that half (52 percent) of all citizen contacts with the police occur in traffic stops.

Second, the debate over the proper benchmark or denominator has been intellectually extremely rich. It spawned a flurry of special conferences and sessions at regular scholarly meetings including three at the Northwestern University's Center for Public Safety, one at Harvard University Law School, regular sessions at the annual meetings of the American Society of Criminology, and most recently, a conference at Northeastern University that brought together most of the major researchers involved in the subject (Northeastern University forthcoming). The Police Executive Research Forum, in the process of developing two reports on the subject (Police Executive Research Forum 2001; Fridell 2004), has held several meetings bringing together academics and law enforcement officials. The International Association of Chiefs of Police held two national meetings and issued a formal policy statement (International Association of Chiefs of Police 2000).

Scholars and law enforcement agencies have wrestled with a number of alternatives to the basic census data on residential populations. In perhaps the first such effort, Harris (1999) attempted to develop estimates of licensed drivers by race. The San Jose Police Department (1999, 2000) offered an interpretation using a combination of official crime data by police district and police officer deployment patterns by district. Other efforts have sought to use traffic-accident data as a surrogate measure of the driving population by race. Walker (2001a, 2003) has proposed an internal benchmarking approach that compares officers with peer officers. In addition, the debate has prompted scholars to develop explicit theories that would explain racial profiling (Engel, Calnon, and Bernard 2002). A comprehensive discussion of alternative benchmarks is forthcoming from the Police Executive Research Forum (Fridell 2004).

In sum, the advent of the racial profiling controversy illustrates propositions 1, 2, and 3. It was forced on the research community by external political factors and has greatly enriched research on the police. Scholars have been forced to direct their attention to an important but neglected aspect of police-citizen interactions and have been forced to address difficult methodological issues related not just to the study of traffic enforcement but, far more important, to the larger issue of racial and ethnic discrimination.

While it is a bit premature to predict how events will unfold, the current research activity on racial profiling ultimately may illustrate proposition 4. It is entirely possible that the criticisms of census-population-based data-collection efforts may eventually convince policy makers that alternative approaches to addressing the problem of alleged racial profiling are appropriate.[10]

Case Study 2: The ABF Survey and the Creation of the Modern Paradigm

Sustained social science research on the police began with the ABF Study of the mid-1950s.[11] The operative word here is *sustained*. Westley's (1970) study of the police subculture in the Gary, Indiana, police department, which is generally recognized as the first academic study of the American police (Sherman 1974), was essentially stillborn. Although rich in provocative insights (even though one of the most important findings rested on two interview questions involving thirteen and fifteen officers, respectively!) (Westley 1970, 113-14), it stimulated no immediate research and was rediscovered only in the 1960s as a consequence of the police-community relations crisis.[12] Research interest in policing began to develop largely as an outgrowth of research on juvenile delinquency, one of the major concerns of criminology in the 1950s, and the impact of police actions on juveniles. Westley's study, in fact, is one of the few major police studies that would fit the model of normal science as defined by Kuhn (1962). It originated out of an ongoing body of research, in this case the sociology of occupations, and sought to extend that field of inquiry to a previously neglected occupation.

The ABF Survey originated outside the academic community for reasons related to political and legal concerns (Walker 1992). Leaders in the legal community became convinced in the early 1950s that a "crisis" in the administration of criminal justice existed. In light of the great crime increase and police-community relations crisis that began in the 1960s, their notion of a crisis seems almost laughable today. Nonetheless, their real concern that something was wrong prompted them to act. With funding from the Ford Foundation, the ABF undertook field studies of criminal justice agencies in three Midwestern communities as a pilot project that would set the stage for a more comprehensive study. The field studies involved the collection of qualitative data through direct observation of officials at work in law enforcement, prosecution, and the courts. These field studies represented the first systematic study of routine police work.

The field observations stunned the members of the research team with respect to their richness and complexity and soon forced a complete revision of the project.[13] Plans for further research were cancelled, and the pilot project became the final project. In a very Kuhnian (1962) sense, the observations shattered the paradigm of criminal justice under which they were working and prompted the development of a new one. A summer seminar with a number of scholars was organized to discuss and try to make sense of the observations (Walker 1992). This seminar led not just to a series of publications that were enormously influential on subsequent research (Goldstein 1977; LaFave 1965; Newman 1966) but to a new paradigm for criminal justice research.

With respect to the police, the new (and still prevailing) paradigm holds that the police are called upon to respond to a wide range of social problems, only some of which involve law enforcement in the strictest sense; that the police exercise very broad discretion in handling these matters; that this discretion is (or was at the time) almost entirely unguided; that the exercise of discretion reflects a variety of situational, personal, and bureaucratic influences, with arrest and prosecution being only one goal; and finally, that much police behavior is of questionable legality (Walker 1992).[14]

In part because of its association with the University of Wisconsin Law School, where that perspective had taken root, the ABF findings emerged within the framework of the "law-in-action" perspective. This perspective shaped not only the publications that emerged directly from the survey but also several other extremely important studies. These include Skolnick's (1965) classic study *Justice without*

Trial, arguably the second major study of the police after Westley (1970), and Reiss's initial explorations of the mobilization of law (Reiss 1971, x). (It is important to be sensitive to the contingency of historical events. There was nothing inevitable about how the ABF Survey developed. Under different influences, it could have taken a very different direction, with an unknowable impact on the development of police research.)

The paradigm that emerged from the ABF findings has guided the research that is summarized in *Fairness and Effectiveness in Policing* (Committee to Review Research 2003). Indeed, it is difficult to imagine the present field of police studies without ultimate reference to the ABF Survey. In this respect, the story of the ABF Survey illustrates propositions 1, 2, and 3. The survey, which was prompted by forces external to the research community, redefined the research agenda in policing (proposition 1). Once that occurred, the process of normal science took hold and much of the subsequent has been driven by the internal logic of scientific

Research interest in policing began to develop largely as an outgrowth of research on juvenile delinquency, one of the major concerns of criminology in the 1950s.

inquiry (proposition 2). All told, this process has enormously enriched research on the police, forcing scholars to address both substantive and methodological issues of major importance (proposition 3).

One intriguing question is why social scientists had ignored the police prior to the ABF Survey. Why was Westley's (1970) earlier study stillborn? Why did the process of normal science not take hold, despite the important questions his study identified and the obvious limitations of his methodology? To be sure, there was some nascent interest in policing as a consequence of research on juvenile delinquency during the 1950s, but this was largely an adjunct of the criminologists primary concerns about juveniles. These questions, however, are beyond the scope of this article and would require some review of and reflection on the sociology and political science professions and their respective priorities in the 1950s.[15]

Another profound impact of the survey was not on police research, broadly defined, but on the specific issue of the police role. This impact can be traced in the work of Herman Goldstein, who began his career in policing as one of the ABF Survey field researchers. Goldstein played a major role in disseminating the idea that the police role involves not narrowly focused crime fighting but a far broader and more complex role as peacekeepers and problem solvers who are asked to respond to an infinite range of social problems (Goldstein 1977). He advanced this view in chapter 2 of the President's Crime Commission *Task Force Report: The Police* (President's Commission 1967b, 13-41) and the American Bar Association's *Standards for the Urban Police Function* (1980, 1-1.1) and then in his book *Policing a Free Society* (Goldstein 1977). The basic insight about the complexity of the police role moved from an exciting new finding in the late 1950s to the conventional wisdom a decade later. Goldstein pressed forward on the implications of this point, and his thinking ultimately led to the idea of problem-oriented policing, which along with community-oriented policing is the most important new idea in policing (Goldstein 1979, 1990).

The line of thinking that flows through Goldstein from the original ABF Survey to problem-oriented policing illustrates our proposition 4 regarding the impact of research on public policy. Evidence emerging from research called into question the prevailing assumptions about the role of a major social institution and set in motion thinking that eventually led to a reconceptualization of that role. This development, however, is only one part of the larger story involving the development of community policing that is discussed in the next section.

Case Study 3: The Origins of Community Policing and Problem-Oriented Policing

Our third case study, which illustrates proposition 4, involves the development of community policing (Greene 2000), which, along with its first cousin problem-oriented policing (Goldstein 1979), is arguably the most important development in policing in the past quarter century (Bayley 1994).

Often described by its advocates as representing a "new era" in policing, community policing rejects the professional model that dominated policing since the early 1900s (Kelling and Moore 1988). The community policing idea had its origins in a twofold crisis of legitimacy for the police. On one hand, there was a loss of public confidence in the ability of the police to control crime. At the same time, the police faced continuing problems with respect to racial and ethnic minority communities. Although there were only occasional civil disturbances after 1968, virtually every police department faced allegations of race discrimination, involving unjustified use of deadly force, excessive physical force, failure to provide adequate police services, and employment discrimination. The two prongs of the crisis of legitimacy coalesced in the politics of "law and order," with some Americans demanding more aggressive anticrime activities (and with fewer procedural restraints on police actions) and with others demanding greater restraints on the police to reduce discrimination and police misconduct (Walker 1998).

The crisis of legitimacy led to a major rethinking of the police role and took the form of what we know as community policing. For the purposes of this article, the important point is that the specific content of community policing was heavily shaped by the accumulated research on policing. The influential research findings were both negative and positive in nature: negative in the sense of undermining basic assumptions at the core of the professional model of policing, and positive in the sense of pointing in new directions for police policy.

Three studies with negative findings were particularly influential in shaping thinking about the police. The Kansas City Preventive Patrol Experiment found that changes in the level of routine patrol had little impact on crime (Kelling et al. 1974). Studies also found that decreasing police response time produced no benefits in terms of either more arrests or greater citizen satisfaction (Kansas City Police Department 1977; Spelman and Brown 1981). Finally, the RAND study of criminal investigations found that traditional investigation activities were highly unproductive, that the most powerful determinate of solving crimes were factors associated with the crimes themselves (and independent of police effort), and that the prospects for increasing clearance rates were very dim (Greenwood, Petersilia, and Chaiken 1977). These studies had a devastating impact in undermining the basic assumptions surrounding the professional model of policing. Particularly important was the impact of the Kansas City patrol study in undermining assumptions about the role of routine patrol that had guided police thinking since the days of Robert Peel.

At the same time, the development of the community policing idea was influenced by certain intriguing findings from other studies. The most important of these findings involved the heavy influence of citizens over police work. Citizen requests for service through the 911 system were found to be a major determinant of routine police work (Reiss 1971). Citizen preferences were found to be an important factor in influencing arrest discretion (Black 1980). Eye witnesses identification, from either victims or observers, were the critical factors in solving crimes (Greenwood, Petersilia, and Chaiken 1977). Finally, and particularly intriguing, the Newark Foot Patrol Study (Police Foundation 1981) found that while increased foot patrol did not reduce crime, it did decrease citizen fear of crime and improve public perceptions of the police.

These findings coalesced into a more general insight that the police do not function as independent professionals who bring to bear their special skills on problems. Rather, the police are heavily dependent on citizens for the problems they face, how they respond to those problems, and the success of some of their most important functions. This insight eventually formed the core component of community policing: that to be successful, policing needs to be community oriented and that police departments need to develop the appropriate organizational and programmatic strategies to enhance their relations with communities and their residents. (Again, it is important to be sensitive to the contingency of historical events. The crisis of legitimacy that struck policing in the 1970s could have led in a very different intellectual and policy direction.)

The development of the community policing idea, in short, illustrates proposition 4. Insights from an established body of police research played an important role in shaping the development of public policy and, in this case, a complete reorientation of the role of a major social institution. To be sure, the demand for a redirection of policing was primarily a product of external political forces, but research findings played an important role in demolishing the assumptions of the traditional model of policing and developing an alternative model. This is no small accomplishment and one in which the police research community can legitimately take pride. When skeptics ask what useful purpose is served by the investment in social science research on the police, the case of community policing provides an eloquent reply.

Notes on Other Chapters in the History of Police Research

Space does not permit a full discussion of all of the relevant cases involving the interplay of external politics and police research. Nonetheless, several additional examples deserve brief discussion because they amplify aspects of our four propositions.

Race relations and the police

It almost goes without saying that the ongoing problem of relations between the police and racial or ethnic minority communities has been a major influence on police research. The police-community relations crisis of the 1960s had an enormous impact on police research at the time, defining issues for research and directly spawning innumerable studies. Indeed, this crisis led to the rediscovery and eventual publication of Westley's (1970) pioneering but neglected study of the police subculture. It is safe to say that the focus on fairness and legitimacy in the National Academy of Sciences report is a product of this influence. The racial profiling controversy and its impact on police research represents the latest chapter in this story. These events illustrate our proposition 1.

At the same time, in an illustration of proposition 4, it should be noted that the police research community has had some impact on public policy with respect to questioning the effectiveness of many and perhaps even most of the programs designed to improve police-community relations. As the police-community relations crisis of the 1960s unfolded, civil rights leaders and their political allies advanced three major reform proposals: employing more African American police officers, creating special police-community relations units, and establishing external civilian review boards (National Advisory Commission on Civil Disorders 1968; Walker 1998).

As the *Fairness and Effectiveness* report makes clear, there is no strong support for any of these propositions. Most notably, there is no convincing evidence that increasing the number of racial or ethnic minority officers—in and of itself—improves police-community relations. (Improving police-community relations is a different goal than complying with equal employment opportunity laws).[16] Nor is there any research demonstrating the effectiveness of special police-community relations units (U.S. Department of Justice 1973). Nor have there been any studies even investigating whether external civilian review boards do a better job of either investigating citizen complaints or reducing officer misconduct (Walker 2001b).

In sum, the police research community has responded to external concerns about the crisis in police-community relations, and there is substantial research documenting the nature and depth of that crisis. Research has also played some role in not confirming the effectiveness of some of the most popular reform ideas.

The police and domestic violence

The case of research on police response to domestic violence is particularly complex. The impact of external political factors, in this case the women's movement, has been very strong. There was little interest in the issue prior to the 1970s. The first published study of police response to domestic violence was Raymond Parnas's (1967) article, which was based on the ABF field studies. Morton Bard's (1970) crisis-intervention experiment was one of the most highly publicized reforms of the late 1960s and early 1970s and reflected the 1960s popularity of reducing the formal role of the criminal justice system.

Research on police response to domestic violence took a dramatic new direction in the late 1970s and early 1980s, largely as a result of the women's movement. The women's movement not only defined domestic violence as a major social problem but also effected a 180 degree reversal in the thinking about the appropriate police response. The movement identified police failure to arrest as a major contributing factor to repeat violence. (The extent to which studies such as Black, 1980, contributed to this is not clear.) Litigation and advocacy soon led to the popularity of mandatory arrest, or arrest preferred, as the preferred policy goal (Loving 1980; Sherman 1992). These events established the context for the Minneapolis Domestic Violence Experiment designed to test the deterrent effect of arrest for domestic violence (Sherman and Berk 1984).

The saga of the Minneapolis experiment is well known. The study found a deterrent effect for arrest (Sherman and Berk 1984). The highly publicized findings are believed to have contributed to the spread of mandatory-arrest or arrest-preferred policies (Sherman and Cohn 1989). Replications of the Minneapolis experiment produced very mixed findings, however. For this and other reasons, many people in the domestic violence reform movement have serious questions about the wisdom of mandatory arrest or are now opposed to it completely (Sherman 1992, 124-53).

For our purposes, the domestic violence issue contains two important points. First, the impact of external politics in the form of the women's movement on both policy and research agenda seems quite strong. Second, the impact of research on policy is far more complex and particularly intriguing. The impact of the Minneapolis experiment sparked a serious debate among scholars about the wisdom of basing social policy on a single study. Some critics argued that this is a very unsound way to develop social policy and argued that scholars should exhibit greater humility with regard to the policy implications of their research (Lempert 1984, 1989; Meeker and Binder 1990; Sherman and Cohn 1989).

This case of the impact of research on policy is more complex. There is good reason to argue—consistent with our first proposition here—that the emergence of mandatory-arrest policies (and statutes) was a response to political forces that were at work before the Minneapolis experiment and would have continued to influence policy even if the experiment had never been conducted. The published study added a nice scientific gloss to a political agenda but was not itself a crucial factor in policy making. The doubts about the deterrent effect of arrest that have been raised by the later studies have not notably affected public policy. Arrest-preferred policies appear to have remained in place across the country. A possible interpretation is that the political audience that eagerly received the initial Minneapolis experiment findings has been disinterested in contrary findings.

Discussion

In his review of the relationship between police research and police reform, Sherman (1974) argued that there should be a fruitful partnership between the two domains. He was careful to emphasize that each domain has its own responsibilities the other should respect and that social science research would betray its mission if it were wholly subservient to the interests of practitioners. The best result, he argued, would be a process in which researchers would address issues raised by police practitioners and police practitioners would value and use the fruits of scientific research.

Looking back over the intervening quarter of a century since Sherman's article, during which there has been a veritable explosion of research on the police (as the *Fairness and Effectiveness* report makes clear), I would argue that in some complex and imperfect way, Sherman's model has been achieved. The essence of proposition 1 is that police researchers have responded to issues raised by the external environment. And as proposition 4 asserts, the external world has, in some important respects, responded to the findings of police research. What Sherman did not anticipate in his article, however, is the beneficial impact of politically driven research issues on the research enterprise that I have defined in terms of proposition 3.

One important distinction between Sherman's article and my analysis needs to be made. When he talked about "police reform," he referred to people who were directly active as police administrators and others with some close relationship with them. My analysis broadens the picture to take into account the much larger political environment, which includes both elected officials and, particularly important, political activists who help to shape the political agenda. I would argue that the police administrators that Sherman cites are as affected by major developments in the political realm as are police researchers.

What, then, is the larger meaning of the analysis contained in the four propositions offered here? I think several observations can be made.

The first observation is that external political influence in shaping the agenda of police research is not only pervasive but probably inevitable, given the salience of policing and the volatile relationship between crime and race in American society. The intriguing question is whether policing (and criminal justice generally) is a special case in this regard. As I suggested at the outset, it is entirely possible that research on all politically sensitive issues is similarly influenced. These issues include, most notably, public education, employment and income, social welfare programs, and health care. In this regard, we should probably accept the fact that social science research will probably proceed in a very different way than does research in the natural sciences. I could be wrong on this and readily concede that I

The women's movement not only defined domestic violence as a major social problem but also effected a 180 degree reversal in the thinking about the appropriate police response.

know little about the enterprise of natural science research. Several years ago, I read and enjoyed Richard Rhodes's (1986) prizewinning book *The Making of the Atomic Bomb*. One point that comes through most strongly in that book is the extent to which science has been mobilized to serve military ends. This is not to say that political considerations (war being politics by other means) shaped the agenda of research in physics, but it would be difficult to ignore the enormous influence of government funding in the sciences. A thorough review may find that perhaps the worlds of social science and natural science are not completely different with respect to agenda setting.

A second observation involves the different forms of politically driven agenda setting in police research. We should distinguish between two very different forms. The racial profiling controversy represents one form, where controversies in the streets or the courts thrust an issue onto the national political agenda and then onto the research agenda. A second form involves a conscious effort to promote certain policies by a presidential administration through the use of federal research funds. The Clinton administration (1993-2001), for example, made an enormous investment in police research as part of its effort to promote community policing. Other administrations, both past and current, use federal funds in a similar manner. Lyndon Johnson used both the Crime Commission and the Office of Law Enforcement Assistance to further criminal justice programs consistent with the larger assumptions of liberal social policy (Walker 1998). Ronald Reagan pursued different criminal justice policies. These efforts represent the legitimate prerogative of government officials to shape the direction of social policies they were elected to implement. We might disagree with the policy orientations of the Reagan or Clinton administrations, but I do not think we can question their right in a democratic society to advance their policies.

A third observation, involving proposition 4, is that despite the heavy influence of external politics on the research agenda, the case of community policing seems to indicate that research can shape public policy. This is a matter of considerable significance, particularly for all those involved in producing *Fairness of Effectiveness in Policing: The Evidence*. The underlying assumption of the report, and of the National Academy of Sciences itself, is not only that scientific research should guide public policy but that it can do so. One of the common refrains among social scientists (and among many critics of higher education) is that published studies remain buried in obscure academic journals with no readership—much less impact—beyond professional peers. My discussion related to proposition 4 suggests that in certain circumstances, some of the best scientific research in policing has had some notable effect on the external world and on public policy.

Concluding Thoughts

The relationship between police research and the external political environment has been extremely complex. In this article, I have attempted to sketch the main themes. While the word *politics* generally has a negative connotation, one of my main arguments has been that with respect to agenda setting, political influence on police research has often been highly beneficial. At the same time, research findings have had an important influence on the external world and on public policy. This is no small achievement.

This article has raised a number of important questions that merit further inquiry. Particularly important is the question of whether the agenda of police research is more heavily influenced by external political considerations than is the research agenda in other politically sensitive fields such as public education or social welfare. The impact of government policies (and war in particular) on research in the natural sciences is another intriguing question. Finally, the entire relationship between research and public policy and the larger political environment merits a far more detailed discussion than has been possible here.

Notes

1. As a member of the committee, I have to accept my own responsibility for whatever I now find missing or inadequate in the final report.

2. The highly influential Harvard Executive Sessions on Policing, which played a major role in advancing the idea of community policing, managed to avoid almost any mention of police misuse of force, corruption,

or racism. This neglect finally prompted two participants to write an additional paper raising these issues (Williams and Murphy 1990). This author has always speculated that the omission was due to the fact that these topics were unpalatable to Attorney General Edwin Meese whose agency not only funded the project but actively participated in the sessions.

3. A related issue involves the actions by the current Bush administration in controlling the dissemination of research findings to advance specific policies. Some previously available reports have been removed from agency Web sites, while in other agencies, all research reports are now reviewed by politically appointed agency officials.

4. Even a study as important as the Kansas City Preventive Patrol Experiment (Kelling et al. 1974) would not qualify as effecting a paradigm shift, because the findings discredited prevailing assumptions about patrol but did not question its central role in policing.

5. Examples are listed by Sherman (1992, 55) in his discussion of controlled experiments on police response to domestic violence.

6. Harris (personal communication, 2003) recalls first hearing the phrase from a law client and possibly seeing it in an article by Henry Louis Gates in *The New Yorker* magazine. In any event, his journal article (Harris 1997) undoubtedly deserves credit for popularizing it among social scientists.

7. The most current data, including legislation and reports, are at http://www.racialprofilinganalysis.neu.edu.

8. There are now more reports than need be cited here. The most current source for these reports, together with other relevant materials, is the Web site maintained by Northeastern University: http://www.racialprofilinganalysis.neu.edu.

9. Space does not permit a full discussion of the ethical issues raised by data collection. In brief, however, the key issue is whether a social scientist should participate in a study where he or she believes the nature of the data cannot answer the question under investigation (e.g., the methods used in a study are not capable of determining whether a pattern of discrimination in traffic enforcement exists).

10. This author is not a disinterested party in this process, having published criticisms of the use of census data and advocated the internal benchmarking alternative (Walker 2001a, 2003).

11. The National Research Council report tends to underplay the influence of the American Bar Foundation (ABF) Survey and trace the beginnings of sustained research with the President's Commission (1967a, 1967b) in the mid-1960s.

12. To be sure, there were some studies, notably, the neglected and virtually forgotten Kephart (1957). But they do not represent the kind of sustained field of study that we associate with normal science (Kuhn 1962).

13. The original field reports and the commentaries on them by Frank Remington are fascinating to read. The original materials are available at the University of Wisconsin Law School Library.

14. With respect to the entire criminal justice system, the new paradigm may be summarized as follows: the administration of justice can be conceptualized as a system, involving a series of discretionary decisions, influenced by a variety of situational and organizational factors that only partly represent strict matters of law.

15. Donald Newman, who was only later brought in to write the book on plea bargaining based on the ABF field research, provided a telling anecdote. He wrote his sociology dissertation on plea bargaining at the University of Wisconsin. In later years, he recalled members of the sociology department, including some members of his committee, asking, "But is this Sociology?" Many sociologists now believe that the field ignored criminal justice in those years because of its association with police training and lacked sufficient theoretical rigor.

16. Similarly, there is no evidence to support early assumptions that female officers would be more effective than male officers because, as women, they would be less likely to use force and be more skilled at negotiating conflicts.

References

American Bar Association. 1980. *Standards for criminal justice. The urban police function*. 2nd ed. Boston: Little, Brown

American Civil Liberties Union. 1999. *Driving while black*. New York: Author.

Bard, M. 1970. *Training police as specialists in family crisis intervention*. Washington, DC: U.S. Department of Justice.

Bayley, D. 1994. *Police for the future*. New York: Oxford University Press.

Black, D. 1980. *The manners and customs of the police*. New York: Academic Press.

Cohen, J. D., J. Lennon, and R. Wasserman. 2000. *Eliminating racial profiling: A third way approach*. Washington, DC: Progressive Policy Institute.

Committee to Review Research on Police Policy and Practices. 2003. *Fairness and effectiveness in policing: The evidence*. Washington, DC: National Research Council.

Engel, R. S., J. M. Calnon, and T. J. Bernard. 2002. Theory and racial profiling: Shortcomings and future directions in research. *Justice Quarterly* 19 (June): 249-73.

Fridell, L. 2004. *By the numbers: A guide for analyzing race data from vehicle stops*. Washington, DC: Police Executive Research Forum.

Fyfe, J. J. 1983. The NIJ Study of the exclusionary rule. *Criminal Law Bulletin* 19 (May-June): 253-60.

Gardiner, J. 1969. *Traffic and the police: Variations in law enforcement policy*. Cambridge, MA: Harvard University Press.

General Accounting Office. 2000. *Racial profiling: Limited data available on motor stops*. Washington DC: Author.

Goldstein, H. 1977. *Policing a free society*. Cambridge, MA: Ballinger.

———. 1979. Improving policing: A problem-oriented approach. *Crime and Delinquency* 25 (April): 236-58.

———. 1990. *Problem-oriented policing*. New York: McGraw-Hill.

Greene, J. R. 2000. Community policing in America: Changing the nature, structure, and function of the police. In *Criminal justice 2000*. Washington, DC: National Institute of Justice.

Greenwood, P. W., J. Petersilia, and J. Chaiken. 1977. *The criminal investigation process*. Lexington, MA: Lexington Books.

Harris, D. 1997. Driving while black and all other traffic offenses: The Supreme Court and pretextual traffic stops. *Journal of Criminal Law and Criminology* 87 (2): 544-82.

———. 1999. The stories, the statistics, and the law: Why "driving while black" matters. *Minnesota Law Review* 84 (December): 265-326.

———. 2002. *Profiles in injustice*. New York: New Press.

Home Office. 2000. *Profiling populations available for stops and searches*. London: Author.

Huber, P. W. 1991. *Galileos's revenge: Junk science in the courtroom*. New York: Basic Books.

International Association of Chiefs of Police. 2000. *Policies help gain public trust: Racial profiling*. Gaithersburg, MD: Author.

Kansas City Police Department. 1977. *Response time analysis*. Kansas City, MO: Author.

Kelling, G. L., and M. Moore. 1988. From political to reform to community: The evolving strategy of police. In *Community policing: Rhetoric or reality?* edited by J. R. Greene and S. Matrofski. New York: Praeger.

Kelling, G. L., A. M. Pate, D. Dieckman, and C. Brown. 1974. *The Kansas City Preventive Patrol Experiment*. Washington, DC: Police Foundation.

Kephart, W. 1957. *Racial factors and urban law enforcement*. Philadelphia: University of Pennsylvania Press.

Kuhn, T. 1962. *The structure of scientific revolutions*. Chicago: University of Chicago Press.

LaFave, W. 1965. *Arrest*. Boston: Little, Brown.

Lamberth, J. 2000. *Statistical report*. New York: American Civil Liberties Union.

Langan, P. L., L. A. Greenfield, S. K. Smith, M. R. Durose, and D. J. Levin. 2001. *Contacts between police and the public*. Washington, DC: Bureau of Justice Statistics. NCJ 184957.

Lempert, R. 1984. From the editor. *Law and Society Review* 18 (4): 505-13.

———. 1989. Humility as a virtue: On the publicization of policy-relevant research. *Law and Society Review* 23 (1): 145-61.

Loving, N. 1980. *Spouse abuse and wife beating*. Washington, DC: Police Foundation.

Martinson, R. 1974. What works? *Public Interest* 35 (Spring): 22-54.

Meeker, J. W., and A. Binder. 1990. Experiments as reforms: The impact of the "Minneapolis experiment" on police policy. *Journal of Police Science and Administration* 17 (2): 147-53.

Missouri Attorney General. 2002. *Annual report on Missouri traffic stops*. Jefferson City, MO: Attorney General's Office.

National Advisory Commission on Civil Disorders. 1968. *Report*. New York: Bantam.
National Advisory Commission on Criminal Justice Standards and Goals. 1973. *Police*. Washington, DC: Government Printing Office.
National Institute of Justice. 1983. *The effects of the exclusionary rule: A study in California*. Washington, DC: U.S. Department of Justice
Newman, D. 1966. *Conviction*. Boston: Little, Brown.
Northeastern University. Forthcoming. Report of the 2003 Conference of Racial Profiling.
Parnas, R. 1967. The police response to the domestic disturbance. *Wisconsin Law Review* 31:914-60.
Police Executive Research Forum. 2001. *Racially biased policing: A principled response*. Washington, DC: Author.
Police Foundation. 1981. *The Newark foot patrol experiment*. Washington, DC: Author.
President's Commission on Law Enforcement and Administration of Justice. 1967a. *The challenge of crime in a free society*. Washington, DC: Government Printing Office.
———. 1967b. *Task force report: The police*. Washington, DC: Government Printing Office.
Reiss, A. J. 1971. *The police and the public*. New Haven, CT: Yale University Press.
Rhodes, R. 1986. *The making of the atomic bomb*. New York: Simon and Schuster.
San Diego Police Department. 2000. *Vehicle stop study mid-year report*. San Diego, CA: Author.
———. 2002. *Vehicle stop study: Year end report, 2001*. San Diego, CA: Author.
San Jose Police Department. 1999. *Vehicle stop demographic study: First report*. San Jose, CA: Author.
———. 2000. *Vehicle stop demographic study: Second report. San Jose, CA: Author.*
Schmitt, E. L., P. A. Langan, and M. R. Durose. 2002. *Characteristics of drivers stopped by the police*. Washington, DC: Bureau of Justice Statistics. NCJ 19148.
Sherman, L. W. 1974. Sociology and the social reform of the American police, 1950-1973. *Journal of Police Science and Administration* 2 (2): 255-62.
———. 1992. *Policing domestic violence*. New York: Free Press.
Sherman, L. W., and R. A. Berk. 1984. The specific deterrent effect of arrest for domestic assault. *American Sociological Review* 49 (2): 261-72.
Sherman, L. W., and E. G. Cohn. 1989. The impact of research on legal policy: The Minneapolis domestic violence experiment. *Law and Society Review* 23 (1): 117-44.
Skolnick, J. 1965. *Justice without Trial*. New York: John Wiley.
Spelman, W., and D. Brown. 1981. *Calling the police*. Washington, DC: Police Executive Research Forum.
U.S. Department of Justice. 1973. *Improving police/community relations*. Washington, DC: Government Printing Office.
U.S. House of Representatives. 1999. H.R. 1443. *Traffic Stops Statistics Study Act of 1999*.
Walker, S. 1992. Origins of the contemporary criminal justice paradigm: The American Bar Foundation Survey, 1953-1969. *Justice Quarterly* 9 (March): 47-76.
———. 1998. *Popular justice: A history of American criminal justice*. 2nd ed. New York: Oxford University Press.
———. 2001a. Searching for the denominator problems with police traffic stop data and an early warning system solution. *Justice Research and Policy* 3 (Spring): 63-95.
———. 2001b. *Police accountability: The role of citizen oversight*. Belmont, CA: Wadsworth.
———. 2003. *Internal benchmarking for traffic stop data: An early intervention system approach*. Omaha: University of Nebraska at Omaha. http://www.policeaccountability.org/racialprof.html.
Westley, W. 1970. *Violence and the police*. Cambridge, MA: MIT Press.
Williams, H., and P. V. Murphy. 1990. The evolving strategy of police: A minority view. *Perspectives on Policing* 13 (January): 1-15.

Research and Policing: The Infrastructure and Political Economy of Federal Funding

By
LAWRENCE W. SHERMAN

Despite major progress in social science helping police to prevent crime, federal funding for police research is at its lowest level in thirty-five years. Only a major restructuring of the political economy of criminology seems likely to revive research with and for the police. For about $1 per American per year, federal funding for "Centers for Crime Prevention" could be established in all sixty-seven cities of more than 250,000 people and in each of the twenty states with no cities that large. By creating much stronger grassroots engagement in research, both the consumption and the production of social science could be greatly strengthened to improve the effectiveness and fairness of police practice.

Keywords: police; criminology; federal research funding

In the wake of the most massive drop in crime in American history, science remains puzzled about why it happened. The modesty of science leads it away from at least one reasonably plausible explanation: that science itself had something to do with it—and perhaps a lot. Of all the changes that occurred in police practices from 1980, when homicide rates peaked, to 2001, when they bottomed out, one of the most dramatic was massive growth of knowledge about the causes and prevention of crime (Ruth and Reitz 2003). Science arguably learned more about crime in those two decades than in the preceding two centuries of criminology. While we have no serious assessment of the extent to which police put that knowledge into practice, there are many indications that police practices are more science based than ever (Blumstein and Petersilia 1995). Yet unless the *infrastructure* of production and consumption of science

Lawrence W. Sherman is Director of the Jerry Lee Center of Criminology and Greenfield Professor of Human Relations at the University of Pennsylvania, where he is also Chair of the Department of Criminology. He is currently collaborating with the Metropolitan Police of London, the Australian Federal Police, and other police agencies in England and the United States on randomized field experiments in police practices.

DOI: 10.1177/0002716204263969

for police work is substantially revised, we face a rapid decline in the growth of that science and an attendant loss of any continuing public benefits from applying that science.

In the wake of the massive 2004 budget cuts in social science research funding at the National Institute of Justice (NIJ) (Butterfield 2004), science remains puzzled about why it happened. The self-absorption of science leads it away from at least one plausible explanation: that science itself had something to do with it—perhaps a lot. Of all the changes that occurred from the early 1970s, when federal funding for such science was at its peak levels, to 2003, one of the most dramatic changes was the *declining involvement of police practitioners* in the conduct of science. Police chiefs and officers are now less engaged in scientific evaluations of their own practices than at any other time in the past four decades. While we have no serious assessment of the extent to which crime-prevention professionals have ever supported federal science funding for their work, there are indications that their support is lower than ever. Unless the *political economy* of consumers and producers of science for policing is substantially revised, it is unlikely that police culture will ever create the level of support for science that is needed to maintain, let alone increase, its federal funding.

This article examines the history of national science policy on policing, focusing on its infrastructure, its products, and its customers. The thesis of the article is that the political economy of science policy has divorced scientific products from their intended customers, in ways that make consumers less likely to "purchase" products they urgently need. This divorce makes it less likely that good science will either be created or applied to improve practice. Supporting that claim requires a brief review of (1) the history of science policy on police issues, of (2) applications of the products of science by communities and police agencies, and of (3) the engagement of police professionals and community leaders in both research and practice. These reviews suggest (4) a modest proposal for making America a safer and fairer nation by building more and better partnerships between scientists and crime responders.

Infrastructure and political economy

The infrastructure for those partnerships would be a network of "Centers for Crime Prevention" in every city with more than 250,000 people and at least one in the largest city of every state. These eighty-seven centers would be funded and coordinated by the National Institutes of Justice, a federal umbrella agency covering separate research and development institutes for distinct consumer groups for science. Modeled on the structure of the National Institutes of Health (NIH), the proposed Institutes of Justice would replace the current NIJ with a more self-sustaining economy of science products and customers. The result could be a more rapid accumulation and synthesis of knowledge about preventing crime: what works, what doesn't, and what's promising (Sherman et al. 1997, 2002). Equally important, building that infrastructure would radically alter the political economy of science for policing, with consumers gaining a much more direct stake in the products of science. That, in turn, could help stabilize the highly erratic fluctuations in federal funding of science on crime and thereby improve the science.

Agriculture, Medicine, and Education

The importance of infrastructure and political economy in evaluation research for crime prevention emerges more clearly in relation to counterfactuals. Three similar fields of endeavor address highly variable populations with decentralized decision making: agriculture, medicine, and education. In each of those fields, federal science policy has attempted to make major contributions. In two of those fields, the infrastructure of science policy appears to have been successful. In the third—education—federal science policy has been far less successful.

Understanding, or at least considering, the record of these other areas of science policy provides an appropriate context for reviewing evaluation policy for police practices. In agriculture, a federal agency was established to guide research policy and to insure that both basic and applied research were closely connected to practice. While farmers generally did not become scientists themselves, they were closely linked to scientists at the grassroots level. In medicine, federal policy supported the creation of a culture of science among practitioners themselves, with practitioner prestige tied to success in publication and original discovery or invention. Education is a sharp contrast to both agriculture and medicine: educators became neither partners with scientists nor took up the scientific method themselves. In the absence of federal policy fostering the integration of research and practice in education, research has had less impact on elementary and secondary teaching than on agriculture and medicine. All three institutions provide examples of structures for combining research and practice, fostered to a greater or lesser extent by federal policy.

Agricultural experiment stations and extension agents

The Morrill Act of 1862 established federal support for what became seventy-two "Land Grant" colleges for the "Benefit of Agriculture and the Mechanic Arts" (U.S. Statutes at Large 12 [1862]: 503). This law was enhanced by the Hatch Experiment Station Act of 1887, providing annual federal funding for agricultural research through the U.S. Department of Agriculture (USDA). These experimental stations, operated by the Land Grant colleges, conducted basic and applied research on food production. They also created a new form of "cooperative education" in the form of "extension agents" who worked for the colleges with ongoing—virtually permanent—support from USDA funds. By 1918, federal funding was greatly expanded for these extension agents to advise farmers on the most effective means of producing food. This advice was based largely on scientific research and was provided largely in face-to-face consultations on each farm in each county. By 1935, Congress responded to the "Dust Bowl" disaster by further expanding extension agents in the Bankhead-Jones Act. With the growth and application of agricultural science, American farming helped defy predictions that the world would not be able to feed a growing population (Crichton 2004).

Teaching hospitals and NIH

The federal role in medical research followed the lead of private foundations concerned about the lack of science in medical practice. This concern was crystallized by the Carnegie Foundation's 1910 report on *Medical Education in the United States and Canada*, by Abraham Flexner. The Flexner report documented many failings of medical education, including the absence of scientific research as a basis for evaluating the medical practices being taught to younger doctors by older doctors. Flexner later became a foundation executive who helped make university-based medical schools the predominant vehicle for medical education by the mid-twentieth century (Cheit 1975). These schools all developed "teaching hospitals" in which clinical practice, research, and physician training were all integrated in one place (Bliss 1999). These hospitals institutionalized the values and ethos of science, growing from small studies of patient outcomes to a vast literature of research results (Millenson 1997). The growth of this research was made possible by the expansion of the NIH grants budget from $4 million in 1947 to $100 million in 1957 and from $1 billion in 1974 (NIH 2003) to a proposed $27 billion for fiscal year 2004. While much of this research has initially had limited influence on medical practice, the growth of the "evidence-based medicine" movement over the past decade has led to increased concordance between medical research and practice (Chalmers 2003).

Laboratory schools and federal education policy

The history of federal policy for education research resembles its counterpart in policing far more than it resembles the history of agriculture or medicine. While federal funding for educational research began during the Civil War, it amounted to little until the "Sputnik" crisis in education policy of the 1950s (Vinovskis 2002). The pioneers of educational research in "laboratory schools" developed an analogue to teaching hospitals, in which teaching practices and learning could be studied as they were performed. Unlike teaching hospitals, laboratory schools were not as dominated by scientific principles and failed to develop an accumulation of rigorous research findings. When the lack of educational research led a blue-ribbon panel to propose the creation of major research and development centers, the Congress enacted the proposal in Title IV of the Elementary and Secondary Education Act of 1965. Research funding grew from $3 million in 1960 to $100 million in 1967. Yet the R&D centers failed to generate rigorous research, focusing on regional issues rather than on evaluations of teaching methods. This left a thin legacy of useful knowledge (Boruch and Cordray 1980) by the time such funding was attacked as wasteful and almost eliminated in the early 1980s. By the late 1980s, interest in program evaluation was revived; by 2002, the No Child Left Behind Act required that schools employ rigorously evaluated teaching methods; and by 2003, the new Institute for Education Sciences displayed a renewed commitment to rigorous evaluations. But given the great cultural obstacles to rigorous evaluations of teaching methods (Cook and Payne 2002), the accumulated body of reliable evidence on what works in education still remains thin (Boruch, De Moya, and Snyder 2002). Absent federal requirements to create or develop public schools that would function like teaching hospitals or agricultural research stations, federal funding for educational research has so far created relatively few collaborations between researchers and practitioners jointly examining operating practices in the classrooms.

Each of these three examples illustrates different models of political economy in relation to infrastructure. Consumers and producers of science in agriculture are partners; in medicine, they are one and the same (with patients increasingly entering the consumer market); in education, there is little consumption or production, despite public demand for both. To be sure, each case is characterized by its own, different, social, political, professional, and scientific culture. But taken together, these case studies suggest that the political economy and infrastructure of federally funded research programs play a vital role in the sustained success and support for science.

Federal Science Policy on Policing

The history of federal science policy on police, and on crime issues generally, has three distinct eras. The first era was 1920 to 1967, during which federal science policy was to produce commission reports and descriptive crime statistics. The second era was 1968 to 1980, when the Congress focused federal science policy on program evaluations to be conducted in each state and to be supported by a National Institute of Law Enforcement and Criminal Justice (NILECJ). The third era was 1980 to the present, when the NIJ (and to a much lesser extent, the Office of Juvenile Justice and Delinquency Prevention) became the central focus of science policy for crime prevention. The third era was shaped heavily by the recommendations of the National Research Council (NRC) (White and Krislov 1977; Blumstein et al. 1978; Martin, Sechrest, and Redner 1981), the role of which merits special consideration in reviewing this history.

Blue-ribbon commissions: 1920 to 1967

The first era began after World War I, when public concern about organized crime in the Prohibition era led President Herbert Hoover to appoint the first national blue-ribbon crime commission, the National Commission on Law Observance and Enforcement (known as the Wickersham Commission). By 1931, the commission produced fourteen separate reports on subjects ranging from police brutality to crime statistics. These reports were produced by a diverse group of academics, criminal justice leaders, and social reformers, some of whom helped author an *Annals* volume on "police and the crime problem" (Sellin 1929). The overall direction of these reports has been described as "groping toward an information-based approach to crime response" (Ruth and Reitz 2003, 47). They identified large gaps in knowledge and policy proposals for filling the gaps. Published at the time the Depression crashed down on the nation, the Wickersham proposals went largely unheeded for thirty-five years—until the rapid increase in crime during the 1960s.

[Agricultural, medical, and educational] institutions provide examples of structures for combining research and practice, fostered to a greater or lesser extent by federal policy.

In that context, President Johnson appointed a second national panel, the National Commission on Law Enforcement and Administration of Justice. This commission's 1967 report placed even greater emphasis on the need for science to guide policing. This time, the recommendations were translated into legislation, funding, and the creation of new federal agencies and programs in the Omnibus Crime Control and Safe Streets Act of 1968. While most of those programs, and most of the funding, have focused on goals other than science, the research and statistics produced under this act arguably constitute its most substantial and enduring product. The fact that more was not accomplished with that funding can be traced directly to the infrastructure of science policy that the Congress created.

State-level evaluations and the Law Enforcement Assistance Administration (LEAA): 1968 to 1980

The 1968 Act created the LEAA, one of the first "new federalism" programs that let state and local governments decide (within certain limits) how to spend federal money for solving a designated problem. The congressional intent was to link that discretion to strong requirements for impact evaluations that produced demonstrable results of the federal spending. A contemporary study of the program and its congressional oversight concluded that "LEAA was probably the most evaluation-conscious of all the social programs initiated in the 1960s and 1970s . . . [envisioning] the states as 'laboratories' . . . to stimulate experimentation with innovative ideas" (Feeley and Sarat 1980, 130-31). The agencies responsible for these evaluations were the state planning agencies (SPAs), which the federal law required states to create to receive federal crime prevention funding. Yet these SPAs—and the 450 autonomous local-level "regional planning units" (RPUs)—were never given the authority to compel local police to participate in evaluations as a condition for receiving federal funds. Neither did they receive the funding needed to conduct scientifically adequate assessments of program impact nor the multiyear time frame needed to design, implement, and assess program effects (Feeley and Sarat 1980, 116-30). These agencies found the obstacles to evaluation so discouraging that the NILECJ was unable to give away $2 million of supplemental funds for evaluations in the mid-1970s, when only 12 of 500 eligible units even applied for the money (Rubinstein 1977a).

The result of a fairly massive investment in state-centered evaluations was virtually nothing of any lasting scientific value. That was the judgment of two General Accounting Office reports in the 1970s, which concluded that the 30,000 LEAA grants per year were not subjected to outcome evaluations as the Congress intended (cited in White and Krislov 1977). That was also the judgment of the University of Maryland group that reviewed state and local evaluations two decades later (Sherman et al. 1997). The description of this work offered by Feeley and Sarat (1980, 130) remained accurate two decades later:

> The vast majority of the so-called evaluation reports we reviewed did not adopt an experimental or quasi-experimental design. Instead, most of them went to great lengths to catalogue long lists of activities, for example, the numbers of people . . . graduated from programs, counselor/client ratios, etc. Such material is only descriptive; it shows that the projects are busy, and it ignores the question of effectiveness. In effect such reports serve as compliance documents for the SPAs which are under pressure from LEAA to "produce" evaluations.

The role of the LEAA's NILECJ was intended to support state and local evaluations with training and technical assistance in evaluation methods. But with high turnover of state and local evaluation staff, such technical assistance had little value. Feeley and Sarat (1980, 129) found a high level of expertise in evaluation methods among the evaluation staff of the SPAs and RPUs. What was lacking was a viable infrastructure in which to conduct scientifically adequate tests of hypotheses. This led the state and local scientists to give up on science.

Perhaps it was no coincidence that the LEAA was eliminated (in name) and restructured (in fact) in the early 1980s. The SPAs survived, although the RPUs did not, depriving most big cities of their only attempts to coordinate the operations of their criminal justice agencies. The drug wars of the late 1980s brought larger scale federal assistance back into the budget with the Byrne Memorial Grants program, which also required, fruitlessly, that all grants be evaluated. But when the LEAA was abolished, the center of gravity for federal science policy on crime shifted from the grass roots to Washington, and the NILECJ was renamed the NIJ.

NIJ: 1981 to 2003

The third era of federal science policy on policing placed primary responsibility at the federal level, in the NIJ. This era was heavily shaped by NRC reports published by the National Academy of Sciences. These reports focused mainly on research methods and strategies and, to a lesser extent, on the infrastructure of grant awards (especially peer review). The reports, however, never addressed the infrastructure of evaluation research, especially the key issue of partnerships between scientists and service providers. The reports were a model of clarity about the kind of science needed to advance knowledge. The shape of the forest needed to produce those trees, however, was not articulated.

The first NRC report was an evaluation of the NILECJ, which criticized its congressionally mandated emphasis on program evaluation (White and Krislov 1977, 94-95). On the basis of the report's recommendation for an investment in basic, peer-reviewed research on crime control theory, the NILECJ created a program to do just that. Even before the name change became official, the new NIJ's Crime Control Theory Program solicited proposals for basic research on the effects of criminal sanctions and policing on crime, as well as natural variation in criminal careers. The "open-window" research solicitations cited as their basis the 1977 NRC report, as well as the subsequent blueprints in the NRC's reports on deterrence research (Blumstein et al. 1978), and correctional program evaluations (Martin, Sechrest, and Redner 1981). With some of the nation's leading criminologists on the peer-review panel, the program funded randomized experiments and quasi-experiments on the effects of police practices, building on the preceding decade of Police Foundation reports (see http://www.policefoundation.org).

By scientific standards, the Crime Control Theory Program was a major success. The list of highly cited scientific publications resulting from this program and its successors is extensive, including work by Weisburd, Eck, Greene, Skogan, Dunford, Sampson and Cohen, Sherman and Berk, and others. The substance of this work later formed substantial parts of future National Academy of Science reports on violence (Reiss and Roth 1993), criminal careers (Blumstein et al. 1986), family violence (Chalk and King 1998), and policing (Committee to Review Research 2003).

On the research methods front, the Crime Control Theory Program also responded to NRC recommendations to employ more randomized field experiments. Falsifying the frequent claims that controlled field experiments in crime and justice are too difficult or expensive to be used to answer key questions of theory or policy, the Crime Control Theory Program became the focus for a major emphasis on controlled experiments from 1982 to 1994 (Garner and Visher 2001), which had also been recommended by the NRC. In an unpublished workshop report in 1981, James Q. Wilson had recommended such a focus, which was strongly endorsed by the renamed NIJ's first director. The program also led to the federal government's first program of replication of a randomized, controlled police experiment: the Spouse Assault Replication Program (SARP), in which six independent investigators attempted to replicate the findings of the 1984 Minneapolis Domestic Violence Arrest Experiment (Sherman and Berk 1984). The program also funded a replication, with a revised design, of the Kansas City Preventive Patrol Experiment, showing that concentrations of police patrols at high-crime hot spots had demonstrable benefits in reducing crime.

The experimental arm of the Crime Control Theory Program constituted only a small portion of its budget, yet it constituted most of the research that engaged police professionals in doing science. Each of the controlled experiments involved extensive negotiations between researchers and local officials. In several cases, the city councils of major cities actually voted to approve the random assignment of arrest or patrol locations for the explicit purpose of accomplishing scientific research. The NIJ reinforced this engagement with national conferences designed solely to brief police leaders on research results. The high visibility and positive

The experimental arm of the Crime Control Theory Program constituted only a small portion of its budget, yet it constituted most of the research that engaged police professionals in doing science.

feedback from these efforts provided the model for a more radical step in federal science policy. This step engaged professionals in the conduct of science more intensely than ever before.

This radical outgrowth of the NRC-recommended Crime Control Theory Program came during the drug policy focus of the late 1980s: the Drug Markets Analysis Program (DMAP). The program's solicitation in 1989 required that a police agency and a research organization enter into a partnership agreement to design and evaluate police strategies for dealing with illegal drug markets. These agreements were to be supported with substantial NIJ investments but under the close supervision of a national advisory panel of a Yale criminologist (Albert J. Reiss Jr.), a former police chief (Al Andrews of Peoria), and a respected statistician (Kinley Larntz). Funding was conditional on step-by-step success at achieving specific milestones: computerized mapping of drug-market activities, operational plans for policing those drug markets, and research designs for evaluating the effects of those efforts. Funding was also split evenly between research teams and police agencies, rather than being allocated primarily to operations.

The NIJ's DMAP experience was a success on two criteria. One was that substantial numbers of highly cited publications were produced by the program, thus contributing to a permanent and cumulative body of scientific knowledge. The other was that DMAP engaged police leadership in doing science. Police chiefs defined the conduct of experiments as part of their profession and visibly enjoyed discussions about research methodology. In the history of criminology, no other program may have so closely approximated the scientist-practitioner model employed in medicine or the direct application of local research results found in agriculture.

Even as this model was succeeding, however, it was abandoned by a new administration at the NIJ in the mid-1990s. Despite its success, DMAP had consumed major portions of the NIJ budget with only four cities and four research organizations. To engage far more cities in NIJ-supported research, the DMAP model was replaced with the Locally Initiated Research Program (LIRP) that created research partnerships in forty-one police agencies, with a very different infrastructure. That infrastructure might, in theory, have returned even more research engagement and results. Instead, the LIRP produced neither research publications nor substantial engagement of professional leaders in research (McEwen 1999). The most likely explanation for the difference in results was the difference in infrastructure and the corollary limitations on the political economy. Consider the differences:

- All DMAP projects were closely supervised by independent peer-review panels; LIRP grants were not.
- DMAP funding levels were in the millions in each site; LIRP grants averaged $75,000 each.
- DMAP projects supported substantial portions of research scientist time, as well as police operational time; LIRP projects did not.
- DMAP projects were major enough to require the sustained attention of police chiefs in the research design process; LIRP grants seemed to attract little chief executive attention.

The results of this change in program structure were clear. After a period of high publication yield and rapid accumulation of rigorous research under the previous programs, the new model saw a rapid decline in both indicators. The number of randomized trials funded by the NIJ dropped to the lowest point in two decades (Garner and Visher 2001), while less than half of all grants for police research produced publications by 2002. The LIRP constituted only 23 percent of grant awards and 11 percent of funding awarded, although the low prevalence of publication and randomized trials across all police research grants was similar.[1]

A different view of the LIRP is that it was more like the USDA extension-agent model than like a teaching-hospital model. McEwen (1999) reports that the tasks performed under these grants ranged widely, from designing databases for record keeping to installing mapping programs. These face-to-face "technology transfers" from researchers to police practitioners seem very similar to the strategy for communicating agricultural research to farm operators and perhaps should be evaluated in relation to that objective. High levels of interpersonal trust between police and researchers were found to be a necessary condition of the success of the LIRP grants in accomplishing even minimal objectives. Such trust is exactly what the extension agents in over 3,000 counties have established over a century of communication, with long-term congressional commitment to funding their work. Whether seen as a teaching hospital or an extension agent, the connection of research to practice under the LIRP was hampered by the same obstacle that saw even the SARP and DMAP ultimately lose so much of the working relationships they had built: the lack of long-term funding for successful partnerships. But before considering the problem of long-term capacity for producing research, we should first consider NIJ's success in applying research, much of which may have come from LIRP itself.

Applying Science to Practice

Much of what federally funded research produced in the 1980s was put to work in the 1990s. Whether this research changed practice in ways that help explain the crime drop may never be known. But the dismal account of practitioner resistance to evaluation knowledge in the 1970s (Feeley and Sarat 1980) was no longer valid by the 1990s, when a new generation of better-educated crime policy leaders increasingly turned to research for ideas and solutions to problems. Los Angeles Police Chief William Bratton, for example, wrote in his memoir after serving as New York City police commissioner about how he had incorporated research into police practice (Bratton 1998, 85-86). He dates this change to the 1980s, which he described as

> an interesting period in policing because the big-city chiefs opened up their doors to the research community. PERF [The Police Executive Research Forum, a group of big-city police chiefs] . . . let these social scientists, who ten years earlier they would have locked up for demonstrating outside the Chicago [Democratic Party] convention, into their station houses to interview prisoners and rifle their files. As a result, the field of policing included a generation of social scientists many of whom probably never thought they would get involved in this world. And, in an extremely conservative and intentionally isolated profession, the idea of the professionally informed and educated police chief began to emerge. (Bratton 1998, 138)

The findings of the Kansas City Preventive Patrol Experiment, the Newark Foot Patrol Experiment, the Minneapolis Domestic Violence Experiment, the Jersey City Drug Markets Experiment, and many other tests of police practice became widely known among police executives and their top managers. So, too, did the results of basic research, such as the discovery of hot spots of crime where crime was highly concentrated and where police patrol time could be focused. New theories of police work were also transplanted from universities to police agencies, such as University of Wisconsin Professor Herman Goldstein's (1990) theory of problem-oriented policing and the "broken-windows" theory developed by Harvard's James Q. Wilson and George Kelling (1982).

Police research became front-page news and sparked enormous interest in its potential application. When the *New York Times* reported on page 1 (Butterfield 1994) that a police patrol experiment (in hot spots) had reduced gun violence in one part of Kansas City by almost 50 percent, police agencies in over two hundred cities contacted the study's senior author to obtain copies of the research report.[2]

How much of this field research led directly to changes in police practice is hard to estimate since little work has been done to survey practices before and after research findings were published. One systematic panel study of domestic violence policies, however, suggests that rapid changes did occur in a short period during which an experiment in police response to domestic violence was widely reported (Sherman and Cohn 1989). Eck and Maguire (2000, 246-47) conclude that the research-based strategies of problem-oriented policing and retail-level drug enforcement were implemented nationwide and that it is possible that directed patrol in crime hot spots was implemented as well; less evidence is available on some other possibilities, such as directed patrol against guns.

Stability of funding could have the long-term effect of creating new career paths for police officers, drawing them from clinical work into advanced research training and activity.

There is no doubt that research had little direct impact on most police agencies, which are found in smaller communities with little crime. But since most police officers work in the cities over 100,000 where most of America's serious crime is reported, it is only necessary for the largest 1 percent of American police agencies to apply research findings for that application to have—at least potentially—a very powerful effect. As of 2000, for example, half of the homicides in the United States were found in fewer than one hundred of the largest cities, in a nation with over 14,000 police agencies (FBI 2001). The founding of the Police Executive Research Forum as an organization limited to police leaders of big cities was intended by its founder, former Police Foundation President Patrick V. Murphy, to make the most out of that concentration and to apply research most intensely where it could do the most good.[3] This focus was enhanced for a decade by the Harvard Executive Session on Policing at the Kennedy School of Government (Bratton 1998, 138).

The creation of these institutions reflected the common hypothesis in the application of science to practice that there is a technology transfer of information from producer to consumer. Whether by publications, conferences, or "telephone trees" (Weiss 1992), this model presumes demand and supply. Someone seeks information, and someone else supplies it. Demand for information may depend on many factors, but production itself is not generally associated with the creation of demand. Public pressures for solving crime problems, newspaper publicity about police failures to meet expectations, notorious incidents that create negative publicity, or just a demand by police executives for better performance are seen as the kinds of factors influencing demand for research that can be applied to practice.

An alternative hypothesis is that the production of research feeds demand by the producers themselves. The more research people do, the more interested they may become in research done by others. Under this hypothesis, it is possible that the rising application of research in big-city police agencies was not only due to better technology transfer. It may have also been prompted by the increasing involvement of more police, and especially more police chiefs, in doing their own research.

Engaging Police as Social Scientists

At its height, the NIJ era managed to prompt extremely intensive concentrations of research activity in a small number of big-city police agencies. Minneapolis, under Chief Anthony Bouza; Newark, under Police Director Hubert Williams; Houston, under Chief (later Mayor) Lee P. Brown; and other cities can be cited as examples. Perhaps the most powerful example, however, is one that spanned the appointment and retirement of eight different police chiefs.

From 1971 to 1995, the Kansas City (MO) Police Department (KCPD) conducted or partnered in over ten million dollars worth of federally funded and foundation-supported research. A generation of police officers was hired, trained, and retired in the context of research as a major and highly valued activity of their agency. Spanning the administrations of 10 chiefs of police, the continuity of engagement with research was supported by an enthusiastic group of patrol officers and middle managers. While the culture of the department was certainly not changed to the degree that hospital culture was by the advent of science in medicine, the interest in research rose substantially from headquarters to patrol cars.

Starting with a series of Police Foundation grants in the early 1970s and ending with the Weed and Seed Evaluation published in 1995, the KCPD became the model of a "research police department" (Sherman 1979). From the Kansas City Preventive Patrol Experiment (finding that variation in dosage of random patrols had little measurable impact on crime), to the response time study (showing that how quickly police respond to 911 calls has little effect on the likelihood of arresting offenders), to the evaluation of restricting shootings by police that was cited by the U.S. Supreme Court in *Tennessee v. Garner* (1985) as a basis for restricting police shootings across the nation, to the random assignment of raids of crack houses (showing they reduced crime for only twelve days), to the evaluation of patrols against illegal gun carrying (showing they cut gun crime over several years), the KCPD produced a record of research that would rival that of most university social science departments.[4] The citation counts of these studies reflected how influential they were in social science journals, while discussions in police forums reflected their potential influence on police practice.

It is hard to account for this level of sustained engagement in research over time. One factor could be the unique independence of Missouri's two largest police agencies (St. Louis and Kansas City), which alone in the nation are controlled by the state governor, who appoints a board of police commissioners in each city. The fact that St. Louis has not achieved this record of research suggests that this factor alone cannot account for it. Nor can the fact that there is no police union in Kansas City, since many research projects have been conducted in cities that have powerful police unions.

What may have occurred in Kansas City is that a critical mass of research funding at an early stage somehow took root and grew a police culture that was extremely hospitable to research and researchers. The very large sums of Ford Foundation funding spent on research included (in very small part) many luncheon and dinner meetings between police and researchers. These meals, unknown in normal police work, communicated the message that research was important. They also communicated the message that the police who were invited to participate in research were important. Those officers were often flown to other cities to observe police practices or attend conferences. They saw their names in print on publications and footnoted in scholarly articles. With the exception of high levels of compensation, they received both the extrinsic and, ultimately, the intrinsic rewards of research that are so commonly found in medicine.

What they lacked, ultimately, was a career path that could lead from police work into research as a primary activity. Funded from grant to grant, research in Kansas City never developed a cadre of police officers with graduate degrees or advanced statistical training. At best, they were college graduates who were assigned to research for a year or two, then reassigned back to "real" police work. The blending of research and "clinical" practice found in a teaching hospital was never an option, given the lack of an infrastructure to support it.

Central to such an infrastructure would have been the expectation of long-term, if not endless, sources of research funds. It was never reasonable to expect such a stream of funding, since the erratic nature of federal and foundation funds repeatedly showed that grants would not last. Dry spells of years between large sums of money led financial managers to demand strict controls on who would be hired for which jobs, in order to limit the financial exposure of the tax-funded police budget. No civil service or classified positions in research were developed, because they were defined as inappropriate for support by tax dollars. Police budgets are always heavily constrained toward "getting police back on the streets" and cutting the number of "desk jobs." When a police budget consumes close to 30 percent of municipal tax dollars, as it did in Kansas City, it is hard to justify spending more for research or less for patrol.

One way to overcome these barriers would be the creation of a long-term and stable source of research funding in departments like Kansas City's. That stability of funding could have the long-term effect of creating new career paths for police officers, drawing them from clinical work into advanced research training and activity. It could also build a culture of police operations in which the demand for better and more research could become part and parcel of accomplishing the core police mission. Research could become as central to policing as it is to medicine but only if police leaders themselves insist upon it. Placing a critical mass of research activity within large police departments could prime the pump for consumer demand for more social science. Police chiefs who see the benefits of research for public safety could then be moved to advocate more forcefully both for stability of research funding and for the use of research as the standard of evidence for making police policy.

Only the federal government, however, could reasonably sustain such funding across large-city police agencies. As the bipartisan U.S. Attorney General's Task Force on Violent Crime (1981, p. 73) observed,

> We are in unanimous agreement that the Federal Government has a unique responsibility to conduct research on criminal justice issues, to develop creative programs based on research findings, to test and evaluate these programs rigorously, and to demonstrate them in several jurisdictions with varying characteristics to be sure that the programs would be successful if implemented in other jurisdictions. . . . [The Justice Department does] not have the funds needed to support the substantial testing, demonstration, and independent evaluation we believe are necessary. The Attorney General should insure that adequate funds are available.

Two decades later, there is less funding available (in constant dollars) to accomplish this mission than at any point since the creation of the federal role in 1968. The federal infrastructure of centralized funding for all criminal justice needs has failed to create a political economy of consumer demand for such social science research. If Congress were to cut the budget for cancer research, a large industry of health care providers would rise up in protest, backed by organizations representing cancer patients. But when Congress cut the budget for police research in 2004, barely a whimper was heard.

The fact that the word *police* appeared nowhere in that budget may explain much about that budgetary decision. Had there been a separate budget for a "National Institute of Police," there may well have been a clearer identification of the police community with the fate of that federal budget. Had there been a separate budget for a "National Institute of Prosecution," there may have been consumer demand by prosecutors, and so on. The umbrella character of research for *justice* may be too broad to engender a political economy of consumer demand for research, just as the word *health* is too broad for any of the specific missions of the NIH. The political economy of consumer demand for health research may thrive at the NIH precisely because that demand is disaggregated and focused on specific issues with which people strongly identify. To create some stability of police research funding, as well as a culture of research in policing, a similar kind of disaggregation may be necessary.

Merely granting an identity to federal research relevant to each of these social science consumer groups, however, would not be enough to show that there is a product worthy of their attention. Despite three decades of achievements (as well as an expected rate of failures) of the NIJ, the lack of engagement in research at the grassroots level suggests a need for more intensive pump priming. That is just what could be accomplished by a linkage of new, consumer-specific institutes (or "divisions") of the National Institute(s) of Justice with ongoing field research operations spread across the nation.

A Proposal: Local NIJ Centers for Crime Prevention

The Kansas City example suggests what could happen with a long-term commitment of research funding to large-city police departments. At the relatively modest but stable level of $1 million per year, such departments could enter into long-term relationships with major universities and research organizations (Figure 1). Those partnerships could be supplemented by a small amount of matching funds provided by the police department, in the form of salaries or information technology for support of data collection and analysis. These functions would be doubly useful for operational management as well as research and hence politically acceptable for funding from local tax dollars.

As of 2004, sixty-seven cities in the United States have a population of more than 250,000. Twenty states have no cities over 250,000. To ensure that every state would participate in a national program of research police departments, the largest city in each state could be included in such a program even with a population under 250,000. This would create a national network of eighty-seven research centers, at the relatively modest sum of $87 million. While this is only slightly more than the $50 million cost of one annual survey of self-reported drug use funded by the NIH National Institute of Drug Abuse, it would be a 1,400 percent increase over the $6 million allocated for discretionary social science research for NIJ in fiscal year 2004 (Butterfield 2004). Yet the returns on the investment in terms of useful results could be far greater.

What would the centers do?

These NIJ Centers for Crime Prevention would operate in conjunction with faculty or researchers from a university or research organization, selected and reviewed on a four-year cycle by NIJ peer-review processes. Each center would be a resource for evidence about the local crime and justice issues, as well as a link to national and international knowledge. Each center's first task would be to merge data systems from across the criminal justice system as the basis for diagnosing local crime problems and testing new solutions, locally applied. The centers could develop ongoing discussions, or even COMPSTAT-style reviews (see Bratton 1998), on a monthly basis that would bring together all local criminal justice officials. While these officials rarely meet in most cities, holding such meetings would

FIGURE 1
PROPOSED STRUCTURE OF A NATIONAL INSTITUTES OF JUSTICE

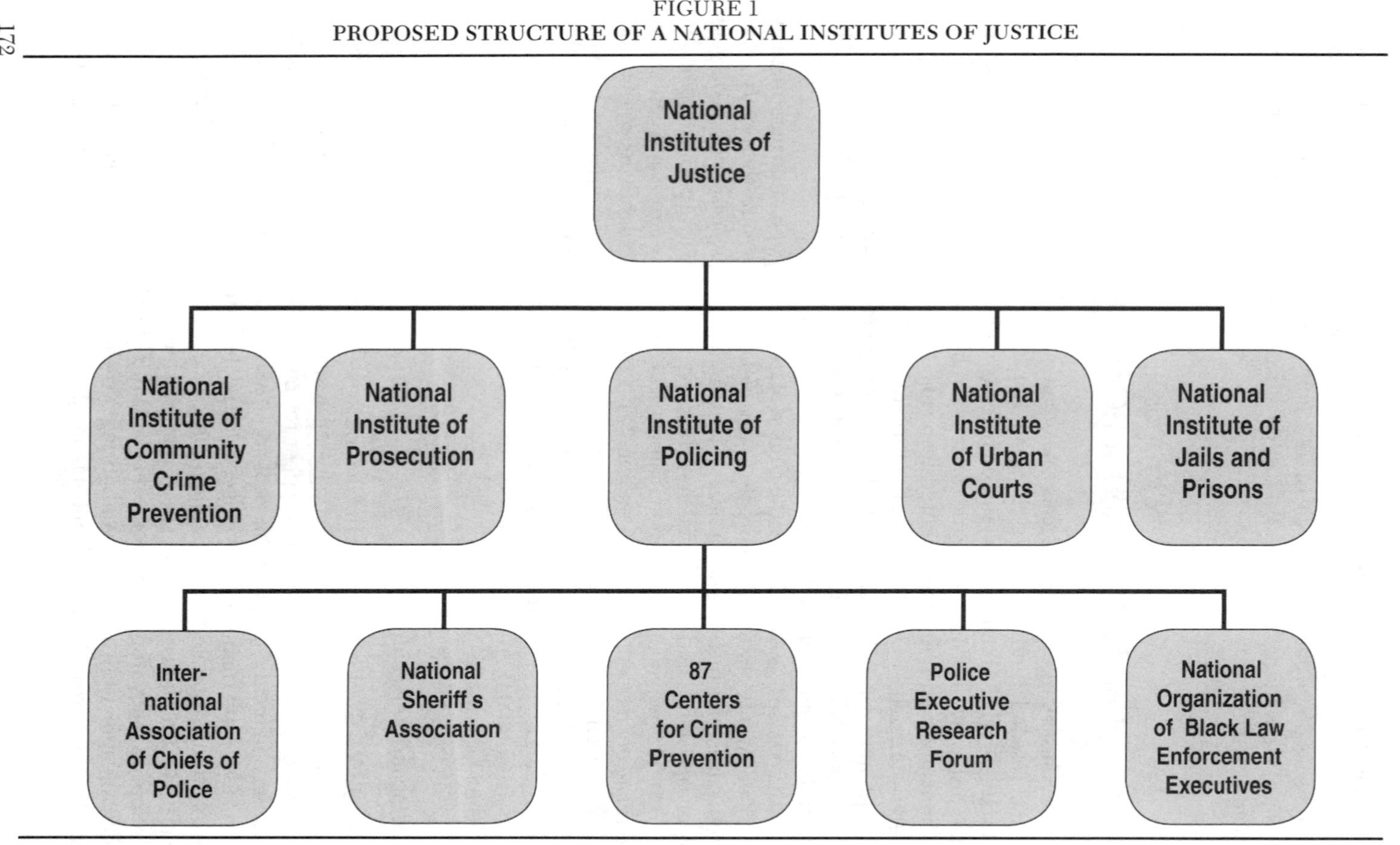

provide a key platform for the NIJ center to engage key local leaders in research. Each center would be governed by an advisory board consisting of the heads of relevant criminal justice agencies, including the state corrections and parole executives, as well as an NIJ official.

In addition to generating evidence about local crime, arrest, prosecution, conviction, sentencing, and recidivism patterns, the centers could participate in nationally generated controlled tests of new programs. With the relevant national associations of police, prosecution, judicial, and correctional practitioners funded to promote communications across the eighty-seven centers, the centers would break the isolation still found in so many cities and create nationally accessible knowledge for all. Multisite randomized trials using standard protocols, and even random assignment of cities to different treatment (program) conditions, would all become possible with such a structure.

Creating the infrastructure

The imminent, if routine, expiration of statutory authority for the U.S. Department of Justice (DOJ) creates an opportunity for reconstructing the political economy of police research, along with the rest of federal support for the social science of crime and its prevention. Embedded in the legislation "reauthorizing" the DOJ is likely to be some language on the NIJ. In that language, this plan could be enacted with three key steps: overall funding levels, allocation by research-consumer institution, and engagement of national organizations representing research-consumer groups.

Funding

While the sum of $1 million per city has the appeal of simplicity, there is an established custom in the Congress of basing block grant funding on the size of state populations. While it may be more important from the standpoint of crime to base funding on the population size of big cities (since they have most of the serious crime), that would also collide with established consensus in Congress. Thus, the use of the $1 million figure as a minimum (starting point) funding level for each center could be grafted onto a figure of approximately $1 per year per person in each state for research on crime in the state.

This figure of almost $300 million per year would be distributed on a statewide population basis to the big cities (over 250,000) in each state—on top of the base sum of $1 million per city over 250,000. This would clearly hurt big cities in states like Ohio that have many cities of that size. It would help big cities in states like Illinois that have only one city that large. Like the logic of each state's having two senators, there is a legacy of compromises built into our federal system that must be reckoned with. Tampering with those compromises could doom an already ambitious plan.

Distribution by consumer group

The logic of the consumer engagement with research would need to be structured into each of the eighty-seven Centers for Crime Prevention. While each center would encompass research on all local crime prevention functions—from schools and prenatal care to jails and state prisons—the funding for each function would probably mean the most to practitioners if they knew it was a fixed earmark for their own function. That earmark could be expressed in percentage terms, based on the percentage of state and local funding of all criminal justice functions devoted to that function, such as the police (as measured annually by the Bureau of Justice Statistics), and be made standard across the nation by an act of Congress (thereby avoiding endless local disputes). Each center would be budgeted for fixed proportions of its total funding to be dedicated to community crime prevention, police, prosecution, urban courts, jails, prisons, and probation and parole for both juvenile and adult offenders. Funding might also be added for crime victims or for innovative practices like restorative justice.

National associations

Because national associations tend to have easier access to Congress than do local criminal justice organizations, the political economy of crime prevention research would be strengthened by including the national associations in the infrastructure. They could play a key role in organizing conferences, hotlines and help desks, Web sites, cross-city tours of innovative programs, and other forms of communication. They could also help to promote the progress of the social sciences by articulating what their membership has learned and gained from such research.

Their main job would be to ensure that successes and key discoveries are quickly transmitted around the United States, so that research reports never gather dust on a shelf. The funding of these functions would be fixed on the same proportionate basis as the funding levels within the state centers. The base amount to be allocated could be fixed as an additional 10 percent over and above total state-center spending. In relation to a National Institute of Policing, the relevant organizations would include the Police Executive Research Forum, the International Association of Chiefs of Police (most of whose members are U.S. chiefs in small towns and cities), the National Sheriff's Association, and the National Organization of Black Law Enforcement Executives.

Benefits

Regardless of whether the NIJ is reconfigured in this way, the proposal could be made just for police. A National Institute on Policing could be established to foster the production and application of police research using just this structure, with great benefits for police and communities. The dedication of resources for creating and disseminating knowledge could address issues of police misconduct and discrimination, as well as issues of police effectiveness and efficiency. With online access to better information about policing, all citizens would be better informed about the issues. This, in turn, could foster better deliberative democracy about the kind of police we all want and what it takes to achieve our goals.

Costs to social science?

One issue of political economy for criminology is whether funds committed to police research would reduce available funding for basic research on crime patterns and criminal careers. To the extent that a program of centers housed in research police departments could foster far more basic research on crime, this might suggest a benefit rather than a cost. Once a program of research police

---

In addition to generating evidence about local crime, arrest, prosecution, conviction, sentencing, and recidivism patterns, the centers could participate in nationally generated controlled tests of new programs.

---

departments is established, it would be possible to imagine many more "basic" investigations of offending patterns using such rigorous methods as longitudinal cohort analysis, cooffending patterns, criminal networks, geographic patterns in offending behavior, repeat victimization studies, systematic observation, and ethnography. There is every scientific and practical reason why research conducted in police agencies should include such basic investigations rather than stifle them.

Without such a program, however, it has proven extremely difficult for basic research to be done in collaboration with police agencies. One major police agency, for example, requires tens of thousands of dollars in fees to perform criminal history checks for criminological researchers following a sample of schoolchildren over their life courses. This practice is justified by inadequate local funding for information technology. Under a program of research police departments, the agency would receive core funding for such a purpose, and researchers would be able to pursue such inquiries at minimal additional cost in federal research grants. This would allow an even wider range of research methods to be used, by both basic and applied research, to address a broad range of questions affecting crime and justice.

How the funding of basic research on crime would fare at a national level would nonetheless remain a concern. The pessimistic assessment would be that basic research funding would lose out. The optimistic assessment would be that social science research has been cut so far back that this plan could only improve the prospects for basic research. Moreover, the need for a basic research arm of NIJ could become even clearer if applied research were decentralized so radically as this proposal envisions. And in the end, if police leaders and practitioners become engaged as both consumers and producers of social science research, their demand for all kinds of research may grow accordingly. That, at least, is the hypothesis that this proposal would test.

Notes

1. The prevalence of publications and controlled trials cannot be systematically compared across all federal grants, in part because of the general absence of performance measurement systems for federal research agencies. Other performance indicators, such as direct influence of research findings on practice and the impact of improved practice on public safety, would clearly be preferable. Any review of models for federal policy about police research is necessarily constrained by limited information.

2. Personal experience of this author regarding Sherman, Shaw, and Rogan (1995).

3. Patrick V. Murphy, personal communication, November 1979.

4. These and other studies are reviewed in Sherman, Gottfredson, MacKenzie, Eck, Reuter, and Bushway (1997) .

References

Bliss, Michael. 1999. *William Osler: A life in medicine*. Oxford: Oxford University Press.

Blumstein, Alfred, Jacqueline Cohen, and Daniel S. Nagin, eds. 1978. *Deterrence and incapacitation*. Washington, DC: National Academy of Sciences.

Blumstein, Alfred, Jacqueline Cohen, Jeffrey A. Roth, and Christy Visher. 1986. *Criminal careers and "career criminals."* Washington, DC: National Academy of Sciences.

Blumstein, Alfred, and Joan Petersilia. 1995. Investing in criminal justice research. In *Crime*, edited by James Q. Wilson and Joan Petersilia. San Francisco: ICS Press.

Boruch, Robert, and David Cordray. 1980. An appraisal of educational program evaluations: Federal, state, and local agencies. Final report submitted to the U.S. Department of Education, Contract 300-79-0467.

Boruch, Robert, Dorothy De Moya, and Brooke Snyder. 2002. The importance of randomized field trials in education and related areas. In *Evidence matters: Randomized trials in education research*, edited by Frederick Mosteller and Robert Boruch. Washington, DC: Brookings Institution.

Bratton, William. 1998. *Turnaround: How America's top cop reversed the crime epidemic*. With Peter Knobler. New York: Random House.

Butterfield, Fox. 1994. Novel way to stop gunmen: Just take away their guns. *New York Times*, November 20, A1.

———. 2004. Justice Dept. ends testing of criminals for drug use. *New York Times*, January 28.

Chalk, Rosemary, and Patricia A. King, eds. 1998. *Violence in families: Assessing prevention and treatment programs*. Washington, DC: National Academy Press.

Chalmers, Iain. 2003. Trying to do more good than harm in policy and practice: The role of rigorous, transparent, up-to-date, replicable evaluations. *The Annals of the American Academy of Political and Social Science* 589:22-40.

Cheit, Earl. 1975. *The useful arts and the liberal tradition*. New York: McGraw-Hill.

Committee to Review Research on Police Policy and Practices. 2003. *Fairness and effectiveness in policing: The evidence*. Washington, DC: National Academies Press.

Cook, Thomas D., and Monique Payne. 2002. Objecting to the objections to using random assignment in educational research. In *Evidence matters: Randomized trials in education research*, edited by Frederick Mosteller and Robert Boruch. Washington, DC: Brookings Institution.

Crichton, Michael. 2004. Aliens cause global warming. Lecture delivered at California Institute of Technology, January.

Eck, John E., and Edward Maguire. 2000. Have changes in policing reduced violent crime: An assessment of the evidence. In *The crime drop in America*, edited by Alfred Blumstein and Joel Wallman, 207-65. New York: Cambridge University Press.

Federal Bureau of Investigation (FBI). 2001. *Crime in America, 2000: The Uniform Crime reports*. Washington, DC: Author.

Feeley, Malcolm, and Austin Sarat. 1980. *The policy dilemma: Federal crime policy and the Law Enforcement Assistance Administration, 1968-78*. Minneapolis: University of Minnesota Press.

Garner, Joel, and Christy Visher. 2001. Paper presented to the American Society of Criminology, Atlanta, GA.

Goldstein, Herman. 1990. *Problem-oriented policing*. New York: McGraw-Hill.

Martin, Susan, Lee Sechrest, and Robin Redner, eds. 1981. *New directions in the rehabilitation of criminal offenders*. Washington, DC: National Academy Press.

McEwen, Tom. 1999. NIJ's locally initiated research partnerships in policing: Factors that add up to success. *National Institute of Justice Journal* 128 (January): 2-10.

Millenson, Michael. 1997. *Demanding medical excellence: Doctors and accountability in the information age*. Chicago: University of Chicago Press.

National Institutes of Health (NIH). 2003. *Fiscal year 2004 budget*. Washington, DC: Author. Retrieved from http://www.nih.gov/news/NIH-Record/03_04_2003/story01.htm/.

Reiss, Albert J., Jr., and Jeffrey A. Roth, eds. 1993. *Understanding and preventing violence*. Washington, DC: National Academy of Sciences.

Rubinstein, Juanita L. 1977a. Case study: Office of evaluation. In *Understanding crime: An evaluation of the National Institute of Law Enforcement and Criminal Justice*, edited by Susan O. White and Samuel Krislov. Washington, DC: National Academy of Sciences.

———. 1977b. Case study: Impact cities. In *Understanding crime: An evaluation of the National Institute of Law Enforcement and Criminal Justice*, edited by Susan O. White and Samuel Krislov. Washington, DC: National Academy of Sciences.

Ruth, Henry, and Kevin Reitz. 2003. *The challenge of crime: Rethinking our response*. Cambridge, MA: Harvard University Press.

Sellin, Thorsten, ed. 1929. Police and the crime problem. *The Annals of the American Academy of Political and Social Science* 146.

Sherman, Lawrence. 1979. The case for the research police department. *Police Magazine* 2 (6): 58-59.

———. 1992. *Policing domestic violence: Experiments and dilemmas*. New York: Free Press.

Sherman, Lawrence, and Richard A. Berk. 1984. The specific deterrent effects of arrest for domestic assault: A field experiment. *American Sociological Review* 49:261-72.

Sherman, Lawrence, and Ellen G. Cohn. 1989. The impact of research on legal policy: The Minneapolis Domestic Violence Experiment. *Law and Society Review* 23:117-44.

Sherman, Lawrence, David P. Farrington, Brandon C. Welsh, and Doris Layton MAcKenzie, eds. 2002. *Evidence-based crime prevention*. London: Routledge.

Sherman, Lawrence, Denise Gottfredson, Doris MacKenzie, John Eck, Peter Reuter, and Shawn D. Bushway. 1997. *Preventing crime: What works? What doesn't? What's promising?* Washington, DC: U.S. Department of Justice.

Sherman, Lawrence, James Shaw, and Dennis Rogan. 1995. *The Kansas City Gun Experiment: Research in brief. Washington, DC: National Institute of Justice.*

U.S. Attorney General. 1981. *Attorney General's Task Force on Violent Crime: Report*. Washington, DC: Department of Justice.

Vinovskis, Maris A. 2002. Missing in practice? Development and evaluation at the U.S. Department of Education. In *Evidence matters: Randomized trials in education research*, edited by Frederick Mosteller and Robert Boruch. Washington, DC: Brookings Institution.

Weiss, Alexander. 1992. The innovation process in public organizations: Patterns of diffusion and adoption in American policing. Ph.D. diss., Northwestern University.

White, Susan O., and Samuel Krislov. 1977. *Understanding crime: An evaluation of the National Institute of Law Enforcement and Criminal Justice*. Washington, DC: National Academy of Sciences.

Wilson, James Q., and George L. Kelling. 1982. Broken windows: The police and neighborhood safety. *Atlantic Monthly*, March, pp. 29-38. http://www.theatlantic.com/politics/crime/windows.htm.

BOOK REVIEW ESSAY

Police Research and the Humanities

By
DAVID THACHER

Steven Maynard-Moody and Michael Musheno. 2003. *Cops, Teachers, Counselors: Stories from the Front Lines of Public Service*. Ann Arbor: University of Michigan Press. 221 pp. ISBN 0-472-06832-6.

Marilynn S. Johnson. 2003. *Street Justice: A History of Police Violence in New York City*. Boston: Beacon. 365 pp. ISBN 0-8070-5022-9.

Tom R. Tyler and Yuen J. Huo. 2002. *Trust in the Law: Encouraging Public Cooperation with the Police and Courts*. New York: Russell Sage. 248 pp. ISBN 0-87154-889-5.

The National Research Council's report on police practices offers a comprehensive review of what scientific research has taught us about policing. In the aftermath of its release, it is worth asking what contributions other varieties of scholarship can make to knowledge about the police. This essay discusses the role of humanistic inquiry.

The humanities produce a different kind of knowledge than the sciences. Where the sciences search for causal laws that govern the social and physical world, the humanities search for interpretive understanding (Weber's *verstehen*). The different ways the two enter-

David Thacher is an assistant professor of public policy and urban planning at the University of Michigan. His work examines how empirical research can help us think more clearly about values in public policy—both in general and in the specific areas of criminal justice, public management, and urban planning. Recent publications include "Interorganizational Partnerships as Inchoate Hierarchies: A Case Study of the Community Security Initiative," Administration And Society *(2004, vol. 36, no. 1); "The Casuistical Turn in Planning Ethics: Lessons from Law and Medicine,"* The Journal of Planning Education and Research *(2004, vol. 23, no. 3); and "Conflicting Values in Community Policing,"* Law and Society Review *(2001, vol. 35, no. 4).*

NOTE: For helpful comments and discussion, I would like to thank Bob Axelrod, Tony Chen, Matt Connelly, Steve Garcia, and Mark Moore.

DOI: 10.1177/0002716203262690

prises use the word *because* can serve to illustrate this contrast. Where science uses the *because* of causal explanation, the humanities use the *because* of motivation and justification; thus, when humanistic study concludes that someone acted because of some consideration, it does not generally mean that a sociological or psychological law made it inevitable but instead (to simplify only a little) that she felt she had a compelling reason to act as she did (Berlin 1960, 20-21). In pursuit of this kind of understanding, the humanities rely on the interpretive methods of narrative and textual analysis, historical reconstruction, and normative critique—methods affiliated loosely, but hardly exclusively, with literary studies, history and classics, and philosophy, respectively. By offering images of the nature and origins of human ideals and motivations, the humanities contribute to society's understanding of itself, clarifying the values and worldview to which our culture, our communities, and our institutions are committed (Callahan 1985). In that sense, normative inquiry is central to humanistic study. Where the sciences focus on means, the humanities tend to emphasize ends.

Scholarship about policing cannot dispense with this kind of inquiry. Historical and narrative studies of policing help to identify the nature and origins of the ideals that shape policing practice, and normative analysis helps to critique and clarify those ideals to make them the best they can be (Thacher 2001). Both kinds of scholarship have direct implications for police reform because they help identify its proper goals. In policing as elsewhere, policy and practice sometimes fail not because they lack the technology to achieve agreed-upon ends efficiently but because they pursue an incomplete or inadequate conception of what the ends themselves should be. At its best, humanistic inquiry makes us aware of this kind of confusion and identifies avenues for escaping it (Thacher 2003). Humanistic study also supports the scientific enterprise, helping it to focus explanatory energy on issues that matter to society. When social scientists ignore this connection, their research loses its vitality and purpose; eventually, it descends into irrelevance or fades away altogether (Zald 1991).

In various ways, by both their acts and their omissions, the three valuable books under review here illustrate these important contributions that humanistic study can make to police research. The first book, Steven Maynard-Moody and Michael Musheno's *Cops, Teachers, Counselors*, is a fine example of the narrative approach to humanistic inquiry. The book's most striking feature is its method. The authors present 36 of the 157 stories they collected from police officers, teachers, and vocational rehabilitation counselors during three years of fieldwork with five organizations. Told in the first person by the workers themselves, these stories offer a fascinating window into bureaucratic decision making. Maynard-Moody and Musheno recognize that these stories are not "representative" of everyday work in any statistical sense; they asked their respondents to tell them stories "about how or when your own beliefs about fairness or unfairness help you make decisions" (p. 170), so the narratives cluster around moments of crisis and tension. But that feature makes them ideal for the authors' purpose, which is to examine the role that moral and cultural judgment plays in decision making by street-level workers.

The authors describe their theme in terms of two contrasting narratives about street-level bureaucracy. On one hand, they describe a "state-agent" narrative that dominates current thinking about public administration—one that "portrays a democratic state as an edifice built on law and predictable procedures that insure that like cases will be treated alike" (p. 4). In their stories, however, they find this narrative coexisting uneasily with a contrasting one—a "citizen-agent" narrative "that is muted in existing scholarship yet prevalent in the stories told to us by street-level workers" (p. 9), one in which "attention to moral beliefs and identities [is] part of the everyday decision making of street-level workers" (p. 5). To make their case, the authors show convincingly in story after story how moral judgment informs street-level decision making, and they show how good practice is always about going beyond the rules. Indeed, one overriding theme in the book is that following the rules is rarely enough to get much done; for example, vocational rehabilitation workers go "by the book" only for clients they want to get rid of, using something like the "work to rule" strategy pioneered by blue-collar workers who knew that rigid adherence to the company rulebook would bring real work to a standstill.

Where science uses the because *of causal explanation, the humanities use the* because *of motivation and justification.*

As that comparison to a well-known bureaucratic phenomenon suggests, however, it is necessary to go beyond the authors' critique of the state-agent narrative to fully grasp the book's contribution. Maynard-Moody and Musheno want to distinguish moral and cultural judgment from rule following, but recent discussions in law, philosophy, and social science about the complexity of rules have made such distinctions difficult to sustain. Put bluntly, the legal-bureaucratic order already is a moral order, for it regularly confronts hard cases that require normative judgment (Dworkin 1977; Nonet and Selznick 1978). Maynard-Moody and Musheno mention a version of this idea in a footnote (pp. 194-95), but they do not incorporate it into their theoretical framework. As a result, they sometimes get sidetracked by interesting but well-traveled findings. For example, although the authors put the point eloquently, students of policing will not be surprised to hear that "legal and bureaucratic . . . justifications often appear as a rubber band stretched around moral decision making, binding but not determining the decisions" (p. 88); James Q. Wilson, among others, noted this aspect of police decision making thirty-five years ago.

The authors identify a more significant contrast between their findings and conventional views when they observe that "the citizen-agent narrative draws attention to workers' constant focus on who citizens are as much as what they do" (p. 13); they reiterate the point later by saying the workers make decisions "based on perceived character, not on acts" (p. 156). These passages are important and somewhat at odds with the book's opening contrast between the state-agent and the citizen-agent narratives: they draw a distinction not between rules and morality but between different *kinds* of moral judgment. Maynard-Moody and Musheno do not mention it, but this distinction is central to moral theory. While most contemporary moral philosophers think ethical judgment should focus on the attributes of *acts* (most prominently, on their consequences or their intrinsic rightness), the so-called virtue ethicists think it should focus on the attributes of a person's *character*—the motivations and enduring dispositions that influence her actions.

The prominent role that character judgments play in the book's stories is important because it flies in the face of most modern conceptions of public administration. Whether they emphasize morality or law, contemporary students of government generally think government should attend to what citizens do, not who they are. The most thought-provoking, even jarring observation in *Cops, Teachers, Counselors* is that some of the most important decisions street-level bureaucrats make rest on judgments about people's character rather than their actions. To be sure, as Maynard-Moody and Musheno acknowledge, character and identity are not all that matter in these stories. In some cases, the workers make decisions based on pragmatic considerations that have little to do with character, and in others, surface judgments about character might admit to alternative interpretations. Policing scholars, in particular, may be inclined to think that when cops give "worthy" people a break, they are really making consequentialist judgments that such people are good risks. But the book offers several stories that argue against this interpretation, notably, the stories about vocational rehabilitation workers who invest a lot of energy in worthy clients even when they are not likely to succeed (p. 105).

Regardless of its generality, the role that character judgments play in these stories has important implications for our understanding of the modern state. The apparatus of modern government is organized around the idea that street-level workers should judge citizens' actions and (in the case of service provision) their needs; the training, advice, and rules that structure street-level work are all directed toward that understanding. But all this is simply orthogonal to the kinds of street-level decision making this book reveals. As a result, when the workers do judge character, they do it blindly. That, at least, is the sense I get from the central third section of *Cops, Teachers, Counselors*, which describes how workers distinguish the worthy from the unworthy. The most troubling pattern appears in stories where the workers judge people by asking, "is this person like me?" Thus, a pregnant, alcoholic prostitute gets particularly harsh treatment from an officer whose own pregnant wife "didn't touch a single sip of alcohol, didn't take any medications or anything, just because she didn't want any possible thing wrong with the baby" (p. 78), and a hearing-impaired vocational rehab counselor chastises a deaf client because the client does not take the same "tough it up" approach toward his disability as she does (p. 82). As Maynard-Moody and Musheno note, such judgments often take too little account of the differences in life circumstances between the workers and their clients.

One natural reaction to all this is to want to stamp such judgments out—to ask how police departments, schools, and rehabilitation agencies can focus workers' attention firmly on actions and needs, not on character and identity. There is undoubtedly merit in that reaction and reasons to follow up on it. At the same time, I think *Cops, Teachers, Counselors* makes it clear how quixotic such an effort will be. Aside from the fact that it is not clear how government could do more to redirect street-level workers' attention than it already does, I get the sense that some of the stories could not be told another way: they would be awkward and strained—bad stories and indeed bad ways to respond to people—if we tried universally to replace the plot lines about character with plot lines about actions.

A more important reaction may be to ask whether and how it is possible to help street-level workers make better judgments about character—an effort that would take guidance, one hopes, from the philosophical discussions of virtue ethics that have tried to clarify the rationale and proper forms of this kind of moral judgment. To that end, *Cops, Teachers, Counselors* offers a useful, if brief, summary of the considerations that drive street-level judgments about character (pp. 101-4), and it briefly considers whether the workers' judgments are defensible in its conclusion (though without considering the literature about virtue ethics). Still, the book might pursue this line of inquiry further. In places, the authors suggest that their task is description and interpretation rather than normative assessment, but no study of moral decision making can remain morally neutral: such studies unavoidably rely on assumptions about what is going to count as a moral judgment and what kinds of considerations moral decision making must address—for example, when interviewers decide what questions they will ask and what kinds of clarification and elaboration they will request from their storytellers. Regardless, at the end of *Cops, Teachers, Counselors*, one cannot help but wonder, are the workers' judgments irretrievably confused, or is it possible to identify some defensible rationale beneath them, even if the workers sometimes fail to do it justice? To answer such questions, it may be necessary to rely on approaches to narrative analysis that can delve beneath the surface of the storyteller's own perspective (e.g., Feldman and Sköldberg 2002) and perhaps go beyond the book's first-person narrative approach altogether. (As the authors recognize, the workers' stories are often "flattering self-portraits" [p. 157], so it can be difficult to evaluate the judgments they make in them without the perspectives of others.) It will also be necessary to address recent debates about virtue ethics in moral philosophy, where critics have drawn on the findings of social psychology to suggest that the whole notion of "character" is problematic—that the demands of situations shape human action more than any persistent internal dispositions. That critique seems very relevant to the moral judgments on display in this book; as I have already noted, those judgments often fail to recognize the importance of situational pressures. If any virtue ethics is going to vindicate street-level judgment, it will need to integrate judgments about character with recognition of the contextual influences that shape human action so powerfully (Harman 2001).

In the meantime, *Cops, Teachers, Counselors* has immediate implications for policing. One important (though often underappreciated) theme in recent police literature holds that patrol officers must place behavior in its context to make defensible decisions about what should be done. Where the most sophisticated discussions of this point emphasize how time, place, and situation give meaning to behavior (esp. Kelling 1999), *Cops, Teachers, Counselors* suggests that police often place a person's behavior in the context of his character as well. That finding raises important questions about whether and how police departments ought to try to shape these judgments. The book also suggests how organizational design may facilitate more informed judgments about character. By asking officers to "get to know their beat" and giving them long-term assignments to a single neighborhood, community policing increases the likelihood that they will become familiar with the people they interact with and thereby provides them with historical perspective that gives context to particular actions. Finally, echoing Muir's (1977) classic study of policing, the authors argue convincingly for the value of storytelling at work as a way of "heightening moral sensitivity and deepening moral understanding" (p. 160). They go on to suggest that vocational rehabilitation agencies offer lessons for policing in this regard because their organizational routines make regular space for storytelling at work. These are only the most obvious of the many stimulating issues this book raises.

Where *Cops, Teachers, Counselors* investigates police practice using a brand of narrative analysis reminiscent of literary studies, Marilynn Johnson's *Street Justice* turns to history, examining police violence in New York City and efforts to control it over the past 150 years. Johnson aims to understand the sociopolitical, economic, and ideological forces that have shaped public understanding of police violence. By searching broadly for the intellectual currents that inform views about the use of force by police, Johnson is able to construct a richer and more complex view of the problem of excessive force in policing than previous studies have offered. Based on this analysis, Johnson finds that the forms and targets of police violence in New York City have changed substantially over time—brutality is not the "timeless, static phenomenon" some observers impressed by recurrent scandals have assumed (p. 2)—but change has not followed an orderly linear progression toward less violence. For example, while interrogations and crowd control have clearly become less violent over the past 150 years, efforts to control "street justice" of the sort dispensed to Abner Louima have had more ambiguous results, and new (often covert) forms of excessive force have appeared in the meantime. Thus, reform has proceeded in fits and starts, as progress on one front gives way to backlash and unintended consequences on others. Current understandings of police violence and strategies for controlling it have emerged out of this unruly history, influenced along the way by broad sociopolitical and intellectual currents having to do with race, international relations, and federalism as much as the specific concerns of criminal justice policy familiar to policing scholars.

One overriding theme of the book is that national and even international forces powerfully shaped local responses to police violence in New York City. As Johnson notes, this perspective has been missing from most studies of urban police, which have mainly focused on the local scene. In an especially compelling chapter focused on the 1930s and 1940s, Johnson shows how World War II and the build up to it shaped organizing efforts against police brutality. Initially, the depression's economic impact made many blacks more open to radical entreaties, and communist organizers discovered the power of the brutality issue as an organizing tactic. Eventually, an unexpected alliance emerged between far-left political groups like the Communist Party and racial organizations like the NAACP, which worked together closely to represent individual brutality victims and press for policy change. (Although the point is more significant for historians than policing scholars, *Street Justice* makes an important contribution by shedding new light on the scope and nature of this alliance; the relationship between communists and civil rights activists is a controversial issue in civil rights history for obvious reasons, and Johnson offers new evidence about this relationship in the area of antibrutality organizing.) As the war approached, much of this activism focused on police mistreatment of black military personnel. As civil rights activists targeted employment discrimination in the defense industry, they found patriotic black servicemen to be sympathetic victims, so they often focused reform efforts on their plights; eventually, activists brought the same strategy to the fight against police abuse. Moreover, military and civilian police had killed black soldiers in several Southern states, and activists drew on the powerful symbolism of these tragedies to frame local cases of police violence against black military officers, comparing New York cops to racist Southern police. Organizers also took advantage of the era's antifascist rhetoric—for example, by calling New York City Police Department officers accused of brutality the "Harlem Gestapo." These invocations of black patriotism, Nazi oppression, and the growing national concern about racism were highly effective, helping to secure federal attention to local police abuses and pave the way for due process reforms in the 1960s. In that way, national and international currents had a major influence on local debates about police violence in New York City. After the war, those same currents undermined many of the reformers' achievements. Police used anticommunist rhetoric to discredit antibrutality activists just as the activists had used antifascist rhetoric to advance their cause. Eventually, the red scare strained relations between civil rights groups and class-oriented radicals, and it poisoned some of the antibrutality rhetoric and tactics that had once been so effective. For example, the NAACP largely turned away from mass protest because of its association with communism, returning to the lower-key litigation strategies it had used in the 1910s.

Although *Street Justice* makes these contributions and more, it neglects some topics that would be of interest to policing scholars. As Carl Klockars (1996, 12) has argued, today, the most pressing issue in the control of excessive force is not outright brutality but the infinitely more common yet less dramatic problem of *unnecessary* force. Because *Street Justice* focuses mostly on dramatic incidents, it has less to say about how and why the use of force has evolved in this middle range of force—the range between necessary force and outrageous brutality. In that sense, the book tends to be a history of the cause célèbre rather than the everyday experience of the use of force. Relatedly, the discussions of reform efforts generally emphasize the processes for investigating complaints and disciplining officers—the control mechanisms most obviously relevant for shocking incidents—rather than organizational policies designed to influence the everyday use of force, such as those governing when and how it is permissible to use different types of weapons. (There are, however, welcome exceptions, notably, the very informative discussions of how police commissioners at various times have revised the officially sanctioned tactics for mass-action policing.) These emphases may partly result from Johnson's sources: finding that archival information from the New York City Police Department was scarce and usually inaccessible, she leaned heavily on newspaper accounts and the files of police critics, and as a result, the book tends to focus on the kinds of acute incidents that capture media attention. But in some places, it appears that Johnson might have pressed harder on the sources she does have (such as commission reports) to describe how police and their critics thought about the distinction between necessary and excessive force. For example, at one point, Johnson tells us that the American Civil Liberties Union proposed "explicit guidelines for the permissible use of force and weapons" (p. 176) but does not report what the guidelines were or what ideas informed them.[1]

Gaps like this suggest that the book's neglect of the everyday use of force results from concept as well as method. A history of excessive force aims to discover what *excessive force* has meant over the years, and how and why our understanding of that concept has changed, by consulting the historical record. But that task cannot be wholly empirical; the researcher needs to come into the study with a tentative sense of what kinds of things the label *excessive force* covers (though a sense that is obviously open to revision if the research findings warrant it) to know what is worth pressing the historical record for. Regrettably, *Street Justice* never offers the kind of detailed analysis of the concept of excessive force that would be needed to guide this investigation. The book says relatively little about the specific conditions under which force is or has been thought to be justified, and it often treats police justifications for the use of force as rationalizations or as pandering to worries about public safety without examining the merits of the relevant arguments in detail. The trouble is that in one of the book's few deliberate attempts to extract "lessons" from history, Johnson herself indicates how important this issue is, showing that many reform efforts have faltered because they could not articulate how police could remain effective once they reduced the use of force. But that conclusion is just another way of saying that the hardest questions a successful reform movement must answer are about how to draw the line between necessary and unnecessary force, not how gratuitous brutality should be handled (at least not since the early twentieth century, when police still argued openly that brutality was an essential crime-fighting tool). It would be immensely interesting to learn more about how reformers and police have drawn this line and what broader ideals have shaped their thinking. While *Street Justice* does offer some analysis of this issue (notably, the discussion of mass-action policing already mentioned), a systematic history of it remains to be written.

What, then, is *Street Justice*'s main contribution to contemporary knowledge about policing? Ideally, one hopes historical study will clarify the roots of current assumptions and ideas so that we can understand better why we think the way we do—a kind of self-understanding that is a necessary first step in reflecting on whether we should continue to think that way (Williams 2000). Robert Fogelson's *Big City Police* (1977), which showed clearly how contemporary debates about police reform still bore the imprint of assumptions developed in the progressive era, is an outstanding example of that kind of contribution. *Street Justice* does not unfold in quite that way. Johnson identifies many important social forces that shaped public discourse about police brutality in the late nineteenth century and

---

One important . . . theme in recent police literature holds that patrol officers must place behavior in its context to make defensible decisions about what should be done.

---

several eras since, but the relationship between contemporary understandings and those earlier eras appears to be more complex than any "legacy-of-the-progressives" story can capture. The book does make clear, however, that the concerns we bring to the problem of excessive force are the product of wider intellectual currents in our and our predecessors' historical moments, including broad national and international currents that have been neglected in most policing scholarship, so they cannot be reduced to any simple notion of efficient administration or compliance with the law.

Where the two books discussed so far illustrate the forms humanistic inquiry can take and the nature of its contributions, Tom Tyler and Yuen Huo's *Trust in the Law* illustrates what that approach might offer to scientific research in policing. This valuable book, firmly in the scientific model, continues Tyler's research into the way ethical judgments shape people's relationships with the law. *Trust in the Law* focuses mainly on the factors that lead people to accept legal authority when they come into contact with it. In both their regulatory role and their role-providing services, legal institutions cannot always give people what they want or what they think they deserve. What leads people to defer to the law when it disappoints them in these ways? Based on survey research about Californians' recent experiences with the police and courts, Tyler and Huo defend a simple and apparently powerful answer: people will defer to a legal institution if they trust its motives and view its procedures as fair (and also when they have more general confidence in their community and its legal institutions—something police and judges can help to cultivate by consistently behaving in fair and trustworthy ways).

Tyler and Huo draw out several intriguing implications of this finding. One of the most engaging sections of the book uses the model it has developed to explain why minorities have more negative views about the police and courts than whites do. Tyler and Huo show that minority discontent does not result from greater unhappiness with the outcomes of their interactions with police and judges but with the way they feel they were treated in the process—a finding that raises important questions for observational studies of race and policing, where research has typically focused on the outcomes of police encounters rather than their process (e.g., Committee to Review Research 2003, 123-4). In a thoughtful discussion of policy implications, Tyler and Huo argue for a "process-based model" of policing that emphasizes respect and fair dealing to gain cooperation rather than the deterrence-based "command-and-control" model they say dominates current thinking. As the authors note, this conclusion offers a hopeful view of police reform in which effective policing need not lean heavily on coercion. (This, incidentally, is exactly the kind of message that Johnson indicates has historically been most successful at reducing the use of force.) Tyler and Huo use their considerable survey evidence to make a plausible empirical case for all of these conclusions, and the case is helped by Tyler's long-term commitment to a remarkably focused research program. In places where the California data support but do not quite prove pieces of the book's argument, the authors ably mobilize past studies to bolster their interpretation.

If there is one place where the book would benefit most from further analysis, it lies in the leap between concept and reality, or the way Tyler and Huo operationalize the sophisticated ideas they develop. There are places where this link might be pursued further within the format of the survey research approach *Trust in the Law* relies on. The authors regularly offer fascinating and subtle conceptual analyses that lesser theorists would not be able to pull off but then jump immediately and without much explanation into the list of survey questions used to measure each concept, justifying their choices only indirectly with a lone alpha statistic (usually high, admittedly). For example, the discussion of instrumental trust versus motive-based trust (pp. 59 ff.) successfully defends a very subtle but important theoretical distinction, but it then jumps jarringly and with little explanation into a list of odd-sounding survey items ("the officer behaved as expected"; "the officer behaved predictably") designed to capture instrumental trust as distinct from motive-based trust. If I were on the responding end of this telephone survey, I think I would just be confused by the questions; no wonder the responses to them explain so little in Tyler and Huo's models. Why were these questions rather than others chosen? Have they been used in other studies? Did people seem to understand them in pretest debriefings? This step is of course crucial in psychometric research—it is essential that we believe the survey questions really capture the conceptual distinctions Tyler and Huo hope to adjudicate—and to my mind, the book could attend to it more extensively. A related gap shows up in the book's path analyses, where latent variables are not clearly distinguished from the survey questions that instrument them. Finally, Tyler and Huo never explain what exactly went into their "objective" measure of outcome favorability, so it is hard to know what their claim that procedures matter more than outcomes really means. (In particular, how is it possible that "among people who said that they had been arrested, we found that the outcome was favorable 52 percent of the time," as the authors state on p. 38? Do they really mean that *arrest* can count as a favorable outcome?)

More precise survey questions (and especially more thorough explanations of the rationale behind them) might reduce some of these ambiguities, but surveys like all methodological tools have their limits. Everett Hughes captured those limits well in these pages many years ago, when he said that "in giving everyone an equal chance to speak, they give no one a chance to speak out with his own voice" (Hughes 1959, 46). Tyler and Huo hope to shed light on very complex attitudes and perceptions, like perceptions of "procedural fairness," "outcome fairness," and "acceptance" of legal authority. In the most behavioral parts of their survey, they ask respondents to describe how police and judges treated them and made decisions ("he/she made decisions based on the facts," "he/she treated me with dignity and respect," etc.; p. 82), but even here, the survey questions do not ask about truly objective behaviors—there is no way they could, for reasons I will return to—so their concept of legal behavior has some of the same haziness as the attitudinal concepts it explains. All of this is appropriate: just because something is indistinct does not mean it is not important. But it does present problems for standardized measurement through surveys. To know what people experienced and how they felt about that experience, it can be very helpful to let them speak out in their own voices, at least in cases where the contours of the experience are fuzzy and the attitudes it inspires are complex.

For that reason, it is easy to see how the kind of narrative analysis that Maynard-Moody and Musheno used in *Cops, Teachers, Counselors* could cast useful light on the ideas in *Trust in the Law*. Such methods trade breadth of representation for depth in understanding—that is the corollary of Hughes's aphorism—but the greatest gaps in knowledge sometimes lie in the second area rather than the first. In any case, Tyler and Huo, who clearly read widely from many research disciplines and styles, recognize this link themselves: to corroborate their findings that perceptions of fairness and dignified treatment matter, they repeatedly mention Elijah Anderson's ethnographic accounts of the important role that respect plays in the lives of young inner-city men, and they also usefully connect their conclusions to those William Muir drew in his qualitative study of police practice. Perhaps one of the most promising ways to flesh out the procedural-justice argument further is to carry this connection to narrative and ethnographic work forward more systematically. This is not, of course, a criticism of a book that simply did not set out to do that; instead, it is a matter for future research (though I can imagine devoting a chapter of *Trust in the Law* to first-person accounts—say, a narrative analysis of stories that a subsample of the survey respondents tell about their encounters with the law—since that would give more depth and realism to the concepts and measures that Tyler and Huo use).

As with the other two books, what is needed is not just description, but description informed by normative theory, and this normative connection is something that *Trust in the Law* as a piece of survey research might already engage more than it does. Many of the book's concepts are explicitly normative ("procedural justice," "outcome justice"), and others ("trustworthy," "dignified," "informed decision making") are what philosophers call "thick ethical concepts"—concepts like "courage" that have both descriptive and evaluative dimensions that cannot be disentangled (Putnam 2002, 91). I do not have the space to say much about what normative analysis can contribute to empirical studies of such things (q.v. Miller 1999, 43-51; Swift 1999),[2] but it is enough to point out that if Tyler and Huo want to claim that their research truly says something about these value-laden concepts, they need to engage philosophical analyses of their meanings more than they do. (The authors briefly mention John Rawls and David Miller in a footnote but do not use their concepts extensively, and the authors neglect philosophers like Robert Nozick, whose procedural theory of justice might be more relevant for their purposes.) There are ways to retreat from this demand—the authors might say they just want to identify antecedents of cooperation, and whether finicky philosophers are willing to agree that those antecedents have anything to do with procedural justice is beside the point (Swift 1999, 346)—but that retreat is not very attractive in this case. When Tyler and Huo conclude that people cooperate when police treat them fairly and act on trustworthy motives, they give some normative imprimatur to the behaviors in question. Because of that, they need to have good normative reasons for saying that the police actions that lead people to cooperate really are fair and trustworthy. *Trust in the Law* sidesteps this issue by leaving most decisions about what counts as "fair" and "dignified" to the survey respondents. The trouble is that respondents may have unjustified, overly demanding views about what fair and dignified treatment involves; it remains possible that police have to be downright indulgent, not just fair, to get cooperation. The opposite possibility may be even more disturbing: the respondents may be tricked by the illusion of fairness, something Tyler worried about briefly in an earlier book (Tyler 1990, 111) but does not mention here. In both cases, the book's happy marriage between cooperation and justice comes apart, and we have to face hard choices to decide whether the reforms it proposes are desirable. Survey questions informed and justified by explicit normative theory would help to investigate these possibilities (Miller 1999, 43-51).

Having suggested how this study, like any good study, might be extended, I should return to the more immediate point: *Trust in the Law* is a stimulating and important book that makes a strong case for a fundamental change in the way we think about criminal justice. Having invited us to look beyond raw deterrence to take account of the moral judgments that shape people's behavior, Tyler and Huo will hardly be taken aback if we accept that invitation wholeheartedly—if we are inspired to ask further questions about the content of those judgments and the moral logic that informs them. To answer those questions, like so many other pressing questions about policing, scholarship needs to take guidance from the humanities as well as the sciences.

Notes

1. Moreover, other parts of Johnson's analysis suggest that even newspaper accounts sometimes delve deeper than the dramatic incidents emphasized in most of the book. The first chapter of *Street Justice* includes an intriguing systematic study of some 270 allegations of police brutality reported in the *New York Times* from 1864 to 1895, giving the best picture we are likely to get of the forms police brutality took and the nature of its victims during that period.

2. The point digresses from this essay's theme, but it is important to mention that the contribution also runs in the other direction: philosophers should take much more note of empirical studies like *Trust in the Law* than they do. As Tyler and Huo note, most political philosophers have emphasized distributive justice rather than procedural justice, but the survey findings suggest that in some contexts, people care far more about procedures than outcomes (subject to some qualifications I make below). If this outlook is as widespread as *Trust in the Law* suggests, and if rests on clear thinking, it should have major implications for the theory of justice in philosophy (Miller 1999, 54-59).

References

Berlin, Isaiah. 1960. History and theory. *History and Theory* 1:1-31.

Callahan, Daniel. 1985. The humanities and public policy. In *Applying the humanities*, edited by Daniel Callahan, Arthur Caplan, and Bruce Jennings. New York: Plenum.

Committee to Review Research on Police Policy and Practices. 2003. *Fairness and effectiveness in policing: The evidence*. Washington, DC: National Academies Press.

Dworkin, Ronald. 1977. *Taking rights seriously*. Cambridge, MA: Harvard University Press.

Feldman, Martha, and Kaj Sköldberg. 2002. Stories and the rhetoric of contrariety. *Culture and Organization* 8:275-92.

Fogelson, Robert. 1977. *Big city police*. Cambridge, MA: Harvard University Press.

Harman, Gilbert. 2001. Virtue ethics without character traits. In *Fact and value*, edited by Alex Byrne, Robert Stalnaker, and Ralph Wedgwood, 117-27. Cambridge, MA: MIT Press.

Hughes, Everett. 1959. Prestige. *The Annals of the American Academy of Political and Social Sciences* 325:45-9.

Kelling, George. 1999. "Broken windows" and police discretion. In *National Institute of Justice research report*. Washington, DC: Government Printing Office.

Klockars, Carl. 1996. A theory of excessive force and its control. In *Police violence*, William A. Geller and Hans Toch, 1-19. New Haven, CT: Yale University Press.

Miller, David. 1999. *Principles of social justice*. Cambridge, MA: Harvard University Press.

Muir, William Ker. 1977. *Police: Streetcorner politicians*. Chicago: University of Chicago Press.

Nonet, Philippe, and Philip Selznick. 1978. *Law and society in transition*. New York: Octagon.

Putnam, Hilary. 2002. *The collapse of the fact/value dichotomy*. Cambridge, MA: Harvard University Press.

Swift, Adam. 1999. Public opinion and political philosophy. *Ethical Theory and Moral Practice* 2:337-63.

Thacher, David. 2001. Policing is not a treatment. *Journal of Research in Crime and Delinquency* 38:387-415.

———. 2003. Value rationality in policy analysis. Unpublished manuscript, University of Michigan

Tyler, Tom. 1990. *Why people obey the law*. New Haven, CT: Yale University Press.

Williams, Bernard. 2000. Philosophy as a humanistic discipline. *Philosophy* 75:477-96.

Zald, Mayer. 1991. Sociology as a discipline: Quasi-science, quasi-humanities. *American Sociologist* 22:165-87.

QUICK READ SYNOPSIS

To Better Serve and Protect: Improving Police Practices

Special Editor: WESLEY G. SKOGAN
Northwestern University

Volume 593, May 2004

Prepared by Herb Fayer (Consultant)
and Robert Pearson (Executive Editor)

Trends in the Policing Industry

Edward R. Maguire, George Mason University,
and William R. King, Bowling Green State University

Background

There are three general areas in which transformations occur in police organizations.

- Goals: potential transformations include changes in the domain of police relative to other providers of security services, responses to terrorism, increasing levels of militarization, a shift toward police as information brokers, increasing involvement in mentoring children, and increased community involvement.
- Boundaries (the things that distinguish the group from outsiders and members from nonmembers): potential transformations include overall growth, employing more civilians and granting them new responsibilities, and increasing the diversity in the race, gender, and education of the workforce.
    - Boundaries also change when organizations the police deal with expand or contract or when the police agency's organizational boundaries change due to consolidations, closing units or opening new ones, new partnerships, and the involvement of the federal government.
- Activity systems (the means by which members accomplish work): potential transformations occur in administrative apparatuses, technological innovation, and organizational behavior.

Research

The police research industry is not currently organized or equipped to systematically detect and monitor trends in policing.

- There is a lack of focus by those who carry out and fund police research on the development of a systematic, cohesive, empirically defensible, longitudinal data-collection strategy at the organization or industry level.
- We are unable to measure, detect, or explain major changes in policing with any scientific confidence.
- The volume of research on police organizations is miniscule compared with that on officers, work, and effectiveness.
- Some of the long-term trends are so abstract or subtle that they defy most of our present techniques for detecting them.
- Sometimes the nature of change is long periods of constancy interrupted by short periods of rapid change, which are almost invisible to short-term investigations or cross sectional research designs.

Recommendations

The overwhelming recommendation is that the police research industry needs to improve its ability to detect, measure, and monitor trends in policing.

- Police researchers, think tanks, and those who organize and fund police research need to implement changes designed to ensure the systematic collection and analysis of longitudinal data useful for understanding long-term trends.
- Where there are good data already collected, they need to be systematically assembled and analyzed. For instance, the FBI's Police Employees data, which are maintained in separate cross sections, need to be combined to conduct longitudinal analyses. This and other data sets need to be made more readily available and in a more analyzable format.
- Existing data collections can be improved and better managed to ensure data integrity.
- There is a need to collect historical data from select police agencies to understand how police agencies change or resist change.
- There is a need for repeated national surveys of random samples of police officers and citizens to detect industry-level trends.

Agencies to Involve

Four agencies are well positioned to implement solutions to the above problems: the FBI, the Bureau of Justice Statistics (BJS), the National Institute of Justice (NIJ), and the Inter-University Consortium for Political and Social Research (ICPSR).

- BJS and NIJ could provide funding incentives to encourage researchers to pool multiwave surveys for studying change and then make the data available to others through ICPSR.
- BJS and NIJ could also provide incentives to create or assemble historical/longitudinal data sets of police agencies.
- ICPSR could host a summer session on using longitudinal data to draw inferences about trends in the policing industry.
- The FBI and BJS could institute fellowships for scholars to work alongside agency data-collection staff and statisticians for short periods to make the data collections better for researchers.
- An advisory board should be created to make recommendations to BJS staff on revisions to the instruments, sampling procedures, and basic research decisions in their Law Enforcement Management and Administrative Statistics data series.

NOTE: This investment in larger-scale longitudinal research will pay many scholarly dividends, while making police research more relevant to the policing industry.

What Can Police Do to Reduce Crime, Disorder, and Fear?

David Weisburd, The University of Maryland, and John E. Eck, University of Cincinnati

Background

The standard model of policing is based on two assumptions:

- Police agencies using the standard model will often measure success in terms of whether a certain number of patrol cars are on the street at certain times. An unfocused "one size fits all" approach to crime prevention can be effective (for example, random patrol across all parts of a jurisdiction).
- Other agencies use response time to citizen calls as a measure. The primary tools of the police are found in their law enforcement powers.

NOTE: The standard model can lead police to become more concerned with how services are allocated than whether they have an impact on public safety.

- These agencies generally employ a limited range of approaches. The threat of arrest and punishment are the core of crime prevention. Despite the continued reliance of many police agencies on the standard model of policing, little evidence exists that it is effective in controlling crime and disorder or reducing fear.
- There are five broad strategies that have been the focus of standard model research: increasing the agency size, random patrols, rapid response, generalized investigations of crime, and generally applied intensive enforcement and arrest policies.

Innovations

Recent innovations in policing have tended to expand beyond the standard model with three dominant trends.

Community policing:

- Studies do not support the view that community meetings, neighborhood watch, storefront offices, or newsletters reduce crime.
- It does reduce community perceptions of disorder and reduce fear.
- Door-to-door visits do reduce crime and disorder.
- Officer demeanor has a positive effect on compliance.

NOTE: There is no research agenda yet that shows strong confidence in the effectiveness of community policing. Community policing may be described as an overall approach that tries to expand the tool box of policing to include the resources of the community.

- Overall, the evidence does not provide strong support for the position that community policing approaches impact strongly on crime or disorder.
- Stronger support is found for the ability of community policing tactics to reduce fear of crime.

Hot-spots policing:

- Policing that is focused on hot spots can reduce crime and disorder.
- Displacement of crime to other areas does not occur.

NOTE: The research evidence is strongest in hot-spots policing. Hot spots policing involves an increase in the level of focus, but often restricts the tools of the police to law enforcement.

- There is strong experimental evidence that policing that is focused on hot spots can reduce crime and disorder.
- Displacement of crime to other areas is generally not reported.

- However, "diffusion of crime control benefits" to areas not directly targeted has been identified in many studies.

Problem-oriented policing:

- Problem solving appears to add to the positive effects of hot-spots policing.

NOTE: The research available suggests that this area can be effective and should be expanded. Problem-oriented policing when properly implemented increases the focus of police efforts and expands the tools of policing much beyond traditional law enforcement approaches.

- There is a growing body of research evidence that problem-oriented policing is an effective approach for reducing crime, disorder and fear.

Conclusion

Knowledge of many of the core practices of American policing remains uncertain.

- Police research must become more systematic and more experimental if it is to provide solid answers to important questions of practice and policy.

Lawful Policing

Wesley G. Skogan, Northwestern University,
and Tracey L. Meares, University of Chicago

Background

People expect the police to enforce laws in order to promote safety; to reduce crime, victimization, and fear; and to redress wrongs, but no one believes that the police should have unlimited power to do it.

- Exercise of police power is largely at the discretion of the police officers.
- Everything about policing makes this exercise of discretion hard to monitor and control.
- We know little about what police do in the field.
- Police are expected to use good judgment rather than enforce the letter of the law.
- Because police work is outside of the public eye, they have opportunities to engage in corrupt activities.
- Police tend to obey the law, and it appears their honesty has gotten better over time, but there is still the need to control police lawlessness, and research is needed to learn the implications of police policies aimed at controlling lawlessness.

Areas of Research

This article reviews what is known about police lawlessness in several key areas.

- Interrogations: In this area are Miranda rights and confession policies, and studies show that these restrictions on police reduce the number of confessions only about 4 to 16 percent and that other evidence is usually available, and the impact on policing is much lower than these percentages suggest.
- Searches and seizures: The exclusion rule puts pressure on police to limit how they collect evidence because a case can be thrown out when evidence is improperly obtained.
  - Police skirt these rules when they can in the interest of deterring crime by jailing the truly guilty.
  - Lost convictions are infrequent due to improper police activities.

- Excessive and lethal force: Police are now limited in when they can use force and are fearful of civil suits based on deadly or excessive use of force.
- Corruption: Corruption is hard to control and hard to study. Some questions are as follows:
  - Is corruption organized or freelance?
  - Is it widespread or only in pockets?
  - Is it linked to political corruption or just in police ranks?
  - What seems to lead to corruption? Prohibition was one of the greater corrupting factors as is drug and prostitution enforcement where opportunity for corruption is everywhere.
- Racial profiling: The problem here is intertwined with the fact that police have a great deal of discretion in performing their job.
  - It is not surprising that their judgments are influenced by racial, gender, or ethnic stereotypes.
  - Because there is no accepted definition of racial profiling, it is hard to determine the extent of it in practice.
  - More studies are needed in this area.

Police Reform

The road to police reform is largely an internal one, featuring training, supervision, internal inspections, performance measures, and policy making.
- To date, there has been little research on the effectiveness of the above managerial strategies to secure officer compliance with policies.
- In addition to internal processes, there is the effect of political and organizational pressures to "get tough" on crime.
- In reaction to the perceived inability of departments to manage themselves, external pressure can be mounted in an attempt to rein in police.
  - Prosecutors can bring charges against individual officers.
  - Civil rights suits can also be brought.
  - Department of Justice investigations can have a great effect on practices and policies.
  - Citizen-complaint review agencies provide another form of external control of police.

Enhancing Police Legitimacy

Tom R. Tyler, New York University

Background

The police must rely upon widespread, voluntary, law-abiding behavior to allow them to concentrate on unlawful people and dangerous situations.
- In addition, the public supports the police by helping to identify criminals and by reporting crimes.
- The public joins with the police in informal efforts to combat crime and address community problems such as with "neighborhood watch."
- Public cooperation is only loosely linked to perceptions about how good the police are at their job and to views about whether cooperation helps catch criminals.

Encouraging Cooperation

How can the police encourage cooperation and support? People have internalized values upon which the police might draw for support.

- A key value that people hold is their widespread support for the legitimacy of the police—the belief that the police are entitled to call upon the public to follow the law and help to combat crime.
- People feel responsible for following the directives of legitimate authorities—it is not just power that makes people obey. In such a law-abiding society, only minimal resources are then needed to maintain social order.
- Such voluntary deference is more reliable than instrumentally motivated compliance, and it does not vary as a function of the situation involved.

Legitimacy-Based Policing

Legitimacy-based policing has clear advantages for the police and the community. It produces self-regulatory behavior.

- Currently, there is a low level of confidence in the police and the courts.
- There is also a racial gap with whites expressing higher confidence than African Americans or Hispanics.
- These negative views undermine the possibility of legitimacy-based policing.

Enhancing Legitimacy

It is important to try to understand how the police shape public views about their legitimacy.

- Effectiveness and procedural justice are the keys.
- Citizens who receive respectful treatment are almost twice as likely to comply than those receiving disrespect.
- If the police demonstrate their commitment to making an informed decision by seeking input and factual information, then citizens are more than twice as likely to comply.
- The impact of procedural fairness and effectiveness is greatest early in an encounter.

Procedural Justice

Studies consistently point to several elements as key to people's procedural-justice judgments.

- Being allowed to participate by explaining their situations.
- Seeing decisions made objectively based on facts.
- Being treated with dignity.
- Trusting the motives of decision makers.

NOTE: People have a strong desire to view the authorities as benevolent and caring. This view is tested during a personal encounter, and their views are shaped by whether they receive the behavior they expect from the police.

A Law-Abiding Society

The important role of legitimacy in shaping people's law-related behavior indicates the possibility of creating a law-abiding society in which citizens voluntarily obey the law and respect the decisions of authorities.

- This type of cooperation is based on people's feelings about appropriate social behavior and is not linked to the risks of apprehension and punishment.
- Procedural fairness leads to such voluntary compliance and cooperation.

Controlling Street-Level Police Discretion

Stephen D. Mastrofski, George Mason University

Background

Police leaders and other public officials have long been obsessed with exercising a substantial degree of influence over how policing is practiced at the street level. Currently, there is concern about

- how to eliminate racial bias,
- how to get officers to engage in more community policing and problem solving,
- how to get officers to make arrests when the law demands it, and
- how to better control the discretion of the police.

NOTE: The research fails to take into account relevant features of the policy and social environments in which officers operate. Things such as police unions, civil rights organizations, and the federal justice system.

Discretion Control

Building useful theories of discretion control can draw on a wide range of disciplines and from the literature on police reform.

- The process might begin by considering who attempts to influence police discretion and then inventorying the mechanisms of influence available.
- One cannot assume that there is a singular, hierarchically determined leadership that sets goals but that there may be many groups of players with influence.
- One must allow for the possibility of "organized anarchy," where the distribution of power is in flux or no dominant coalition emerges, creating ambiguity for street-level decision makers.
- Formal organizations establish structures, incentives and sanctions, supervision, and so on, to coordinate and control its members.
    - Police organizations find control of this sort highly problematic because the organizations are limited in their capacity to manipulate what employees really care about and the systems of control are cumbersome, conflicting, and loose.
    - Veterans tell rookies to forget what they learned in the academy.
    - The result is a system that tries to control undesirable behaviors rather than promote desired ones.
    - To promote desired behaviors, it has become popular to promote control through legitimacy rather than raw power in a transformational approach where the officer's compliance results from a personal transformation instead of compliance in exchange for something of value.

Police Culture

Another organizational element to consider is the police culture.

- Culture should be looked at as an independent variable over time and place to see its impact on officer discretion.

Environmental Influences

Efforts within the organization to exert control over police discretion do not occur in isolation from larger environmental influences such as the neighborhood, the city, the actions of local police officials, the appellate rulings, and so on. Researchers need to investigate things like the following:

- What sorts of control systems are most effective in a crisis, and how long are they effective after the critical event?
- How do appellate court rulings affect daily practices of patrol officers?

Generalization Problem

In technical terms, the extant research has a generalizability problem.

- We do not have a large and diverse storehouse of comparable studies so we can say with confidence how universal the findings are.
- The research on police discretion is biased regarding the types of agencies included—most studies are on relatively large forces.
- The research tends to occur at more progressive agencies that have less discomfort exposing themselves to scrutiny, and researchers look to work with those who are "the best" rather than those with problems.
- The measures of police discretion are, by and large, missing standards by which to judge.
- We need to ask, "What do we want police to do, and what explains variations in what they do?"

Police Arrest Research

Researchers know very little about the extent of enforcement "error," its patterns, and the things that influence those patterns.

- Measuring the patterns would be more useful than whether an arrest was made.
- Selectivity in leniency of whether an arrest is made is a part of racial profiling.
- Evaluations could be made based on expectations such as reducing the likelihood of future offending.

Hot-Spots Policing

One of the policing strategies identified as having strong evidence of effectiveness is hot-spots policing.

- There are two models:
    - The low-discretion model gives the responsibility to supervisors to decide which areas need hot-spots policing.
    - The high-discretion model puts the choice at the street level.
- It is both paramount and possible to measure aspects of police discretion that really matter to those who control it, but there are many parties with varied values and priorities for which to account.
- Police researchers can help facilitate a dialogue among representatives of the various groups.
- The product of the dialogue can provide a clear picture of differences and common ground in what should be measured in police discretion.

Conclusion

There is a lot to say about the importance of controlling police discretion and little to say about how to do it effectively or wisely.

- The highest priority is developing measures that matter to those who exercise it, oversee it, and experience it.
- Theories about discretion control and expanding the generalizability of findings are important.
- Those with the funds to shape the direction of policing research must establish this issue as high priority.

Environment and Organization: Reviving a Perspective on the Police

David A. Klinger, University of Missouri–St. Louis

Background

Both organizational and environmental forces exert effects on police behavior. The interplay between the two shape police practices.

- Police deal with a long list of transactions from directing traffic, to arresting suspects, to testifying in court, to dealing with reporters.
- Many of their dealings are often antagonistic, and police are not entirely in control of their interactions with others.
- As a consequence, police actions can be substantially influenced by the nature of the tasks, the features of the external entities with which they interact, and the broader social contexts in which these interactions occur.

NOTE: Researchers Reiss and Bordua noted that a thorough understanding of the organizational properties of police departments requires knowledge of how environmental forces penetrate and influence law enforcement agencies.

Research Difficulties

The vast differences in the tasks that police agencies undertake, the nature of the governmental entities to which they are attached, their size, and other features make it difficult for researchers to generalize about the American police.

- We lack comprehensive data about many aspects of police departments—the vast majority provide no information to any national data bank.
- Among the agencies that do provide data, the list of organizational properties they have reported on is a rather short one.
- The costs of research are so high that it limits the number of agencies that researchers can study, and the result is that some otherwise fruitful research designs have not included enough agencies to adequately examine the role that various structural features of police organizations and the environments in which they operate play in determining police practices.
- For researchers, it is difficult to generalize the results of a study across all the various types of police agencies and environments in the United States.
- Police agencies and the people within them are often unwilling to give access to outsiders into their inner workings.

NOTE: Even as some more progressive departments have allowed access, researchers have not shown much interest in organizational-environmental research. Rather, research has focused on micro-level questions about the role of situational factors such as how the race and gender of citizens affect police interactions.

Organizational Factors

Factors that affect the operations of organizations and the actions of their members include the following:

- Bureaucratization
- Task complexity
- Occupational differentiation
- Functional differentiation
- Nature of compliance regimes
- Span of control
- Technology

- Coupling
- Culture
- Professionalism
- Size

NOTE: Researchers and practitioners have suggested that many structural aspects of police organizations besides their size might well affect how officers carry out their duties. Unfortunately, the research to date is not sufficient to draw any firm conclusions.

Other Factors

There has been some research on other factors.

- There is research showing that rules and regulations can substantially affect how officers act on the streets.
- Research shows that shooting policies affect how officers use their firearms.
- How officers exercise their arrest powers has also been studied in relation to policies.

Environmental Factors

The notion that changes in criminal statutes can change how officers execute their duties when policing domestic violence highlights the fact that forces external to police agencies hold the potential to influence officers' actions.

- Research indicates the courts can influence police practices.
- The local political landscape can have an influence, but studies show departments have a substantial ability to resist efforts of elected leaders to change their practices.
- Aspects of communities such as socioeconomic status can affect police actions.

The Integrative Perspective

Work done by Klinger asserted that police agencies are loosely coupled organizations in which patrol officers are largely free from administrative constraints and that levels of crime and other sorts of deviance in the areas officers patrol are crucial determinants of how they carry out their duties.

- Klinger's key contention is that the social ecology of the communities officers' work drives how they will police. The theory does not take into account that community characteristics besides crime and deviance may also affect officers' actions, but it could certainly be expanded to do so.
- This theory also has room to incorporate external factors such as legal statutes.
- Differences of other sorts can also be incorporated by adding them to the list of macro variables; things such as city size, their degree of racial inequality, and their levels of violence.

Conclusion

Because police researchers have paid little attention to the organizational and environmental sources of police action, we have limited evidence about which aspects of police organizations and their environments actually affect police action and even less about the processes through which they exert their effects.

- The challenge is to develop more complete integrated models that precisely specify how macro-level organizational and environmental properties exert effects at the micro level of police interactions with citizens.

Science and Politics in Police Research

Samuel Walker, University of Nebraska, Omaha

Background

Police stand at the center of several issues that touch raw nerves in American politics such as race relations and the tangled relationship between race and crime. Public concern about these issues has greatly influenced police research.

- The relationship between police research and the external political environment is extremely complex.
  - Political factors have had a major impact in shaping the agenda of police research.
  - Research findings have shaped public discourse and policy.
  - The influence of politics has greatly enriched social science research on the police.
  - In the article, this involves the influence on research agenda setting rather than the suppression of truth.

Four Propositions

The author presents four propositions about the complex interplay between science and politics.

- Political factors have had a major impact in shaping the agenda of police research.
- Once a question or set of questions is introduced into police research, the process of normal science begins to operate.
  - Research findings raise unresolved issues.
  - The research on new issues is not externally influenced.
- The impact of external political influence on research has been beneficial and enriching.
  - External factors force researchers to address issues previously neglected.
- Police research has influenced the external political environment and played a significant role in shaping public policy.

Case Studies

Several case studies support the above four propositions.

- Racial profiling illustrates propositions 1, 2, and 3. It has forced on the research community enriched research on police. Scholars have been forced to direct attention to the neglected aspect of police-citizen interactions and have been forced to address different methodological issues related not just to the study of traffic enforcement but, more important, to the larger issue of racial and ethnic discrimination.
- The American Bar Foundation study of the police subculture in Gary, Indiana, illustrates proposition 4 regarding the impact of research on public policy. Evidence called into question the prevailing assumptions about the role of the police institution and set in motion thinking that led to reconceptualization of that role.
- Community policing also illustrates proposition 4 as the research influenced public policy and caused a complete reorientation of the role of the police.

NOTE: Larry Sherman argues that the best result would be a process in which researchers would address issues raised by police practitioners, and the practitioners would value and use the fruits of the research.

Conclusion

What observations can be made regarding the four propositions?

- External political influence in shaping the agenda of police research is not only pervasive but probably inevitable.
- There are two forms of politically driven agenda:
  - Racial profiling illustrates the form where an issue in the streets is thrust onto the national agenda.
  - The second form is where research is funded as a result of a policy initiative such as Clinton's funding of research to promote his community policing platform.

This does not necessarily mean that research is blatantly manipulated to make a political point.

- Despite the heavy influence of external politics on the research agenda, the case of community policing indicates that research can shape policy.

NOTE: There are important questions that merit further inquiry:

- Particularly important is whether the agenda of police research is more heavily influenced by external political considerations than is the agenda of other politically sensitive fields such as public education and social welfare.
- The impact of government policies, and war in particular, on research in the natural sciences.
- The relationship between the research and public policy and the larger political environment.

Research and Policing: The Infrastructure and Political Economy of Federal Funding

Lawrence W. Sherman, University of Pennsylvania

Police Practices

Of all the changes in police practices since 1980, one of the most dramatic was massive growth of knowledge about the causes and prevention of crime.

- Science learned more about crime since 1980 than in the preceding two centuries of criminology.
- Many indications show that police practices are more science based than ever.
- Unless the infrastructure of production and consumption of science for police work is substantially revised, we face a rapid decline in the growth of police science and an attendant loss of any continuing public benefits.
- The political economy of science policy has divorced scientific products from their intended users in ways that make usage less likely.

Research Comparisons

Understanding the record of other areas of science policy provides an appropriate context for reviewing evaluation policy for police practices.

- Agriculture and medicine had federal support to guide research policy and to ensure that research was closely connected to practice.
- Educators neither were partners with scientists nor took up the scientific method themselves. Research in education has had much less impact on teaching than it has had on agriculture and medicine.
  - The history of federal policy for education research resembles its counterpart in policing more than does "ag" or medicine.

- Reviewing all three disciplines shows that the political economy and infrastructure of federally funded research play a vital role in the sustained success and support for science.

Federal Science Policy

Since 1980, the primary responsibility for policing policy lay at the NIJ and was shaped by National Research Council reports published by the National Academy of Sciences.

- These reports focused mainly on research methods and strategies and did not address the infrastructure of evaluation research, especially the key issue of partnerships between scientists and service providers.
  - The new NIJ Crime Control Theory program solicited proposals for research on the effects of criminal sanctions and policing on crime. With some of the nation's leading criminologists on the peer-review panel, the program funded randomized experiments on the effects of police practices and was a major success.
  - NIJ reinforced the program with national conferences designed to brief police leaders on research results and this engaged professionals in the conduct of science more than ever before.
  - The Drug Markets Analysis Program (DMAP) was an example of success on two criteria.
    - A number of highly cited publications were produced, thus contributing to a body of scientific knowledge.
    - DMAP engaged police leadership in doing science.

This was the best example of how policing research could mimic what was done in "ag" and medicine, yet it was limited in scope and was replaced by a program that created partnerships in forty-one police agencies, the Locally Initiated Research Program (LIRP).

DMAP vs. LIRP

The differences between DMAP and LIRP that accounted for a lack of publications and involvement of police leaders were the following:

- All DMAP programs had peer review panels; LIPR grants did not.
- DMAP funding was much higher per site.
- DMAP projects supported substantial research time as well as police operational time; LIRP grants did not.
- LIRP projects did not attract the sustained attention of police chiefs.

NOTE: The LIRP was hampered by the lack of long-term funding for successful partnerships.

Applying Science to Practice

From 1971 on, a generation of police officers worked in the context of research as a major and highly valued activity of their agency. In the 1990s, a new generation of better-educated crime policy leaders increasingly turned to research for ideas and solutions to problems. The idea of the professionally informed and educated police chief emerged.

- The findings of major programs to test police practices became widely known among police executives and their top managers.
- So too did the results of basic research such as the hot spots of crime.
- New theories of police practice went from university to police agencies.
- Research as a career path in policing suffers from lack of long-term funding of the kind one sees in medicine. This needs to be addressed to get stability in funding and to promote the use of research as the standard of evidence for making policy.

Proposal: NIJ Centers for Crime Prevention

Programs like Kansas City's work in preventive patrol suggest what could happen with long-term commitment of research funding to large-city police departments.

- These departments could enter into long-term relationships with major universities and research organizations.
- Each U.S. city over 250,000 in population would have a crime center, coordinated and funded by the NIJ. Twenty states without a city this size would each have a center too.
- This would create a national network of eighty-seven research centers, which could encourage more rapid accumulation and synthesis of knowledge about preventing crime.
- Each center would be a resource for evidence about the local crime and justice issues.
- Local crime officials could get together for monthly reviews, and the NIJ would also have a key platform to engage leaders in research.
- These centers could participate in new national programs allowing for randomized trials using standard protocols and even random assignment of cities.

Creating the Infrastructure

The expiration of the statutory authority for the Department of Justice creates an opportunity for restructuring the political economy of police research, along with the rest of federal support for the social science of crime and its prevention.

- The plan for NIJ crime centers could be enacted with three key steps:
  - substantial funding levels;
  - allocation by research consumer institution—each center would be budgeted for fixed proportions of its funding to be dedicated to crime prevention, police, prosecution, urban courts, jails, prisons, and probation and parole; and
  - engagement of national organizations representing research consumer groups—to play a role in organizing conferences, hotlines, and help desks and disseminating research results.

Benefits

With online access to better info about policing, all citizens would be better informed about the issues.

- This could foster better deliberative democracy about the kind of police we all want and what it takes to achieve our goals.
- The dedication of resources for creating and disseminating knowledge could address issues of police misconduct and discrimination as well as issues of police effectiveness and efficiency.
- The wide range of research would be in collaboration with police agencies, and agencies would receive core funding.

NOTE: How the funding of basic research on crime would fare at a national level remains a concern.

- The pessimistic side says basic research funding would lose out.
- The optimists say that social science research has been cut so far back that this plan could only improve the prospects for basic research.
- In the end, if police leaders and practitioners become engaged as both consumers and producers of social science research, their demand for all kinds of research may grow accordingly.